SILICON

SILICON

From the Invention of the Microprocessor to the New Science of Consciousness

FEDERICO FAGGIN

Waterside Productions

Printed in the United States of America

First Printing, 2020

ISBN-13: 978-1-949003-41-3 print edition
ISBN-13: 978-1-949003-42-0 ebook edition

Waterside Productions
2055 Oxford Ave
Cardiff, CA 92007
www.waterside.com

The intuitive mind is a sacred gift and the rational mind is a faithful servant. We have created a society that honors the servant and has forgotten the gift.

—Albert Einstein

Being born is not enough.
We were born to be reborn.
Everyday.

—Pablo Neruda

To Elvia, Marzia, Marc, and Eric

TABLE OF CONTENTS

PREFACE

This book is the English version of *SILICIO*, my autobiography originally published in Italy on April 30, 2019 by Mondadori and followed by a second *Oscar Bestseller* edition in paperback published on June 2020. This English version is essentially the translation of the second edition incorporating minor changes throughout, except for the final chapter 7 that describes my ideas and considerations on the nature of consciousness and reality, which has been significantly changed from the Italian second edition. *SILICON* has also a brand-new Appendix 5 to augment the material covered in chapter 7.

The publication of this book in 2021 is occurring on the 50th anniversary of the invention of the microprocessor—a serendipitous coincidence. I am glad it worked out this way and I hope it will help spread to the English-speaking public my story and my perspective about one of the most important inventions of the 20th century. I also hope that my work in clarifying the nature of consciousness and the fundamental differences between human and artificial intelligence (AI), also described in this book, will help build trust and confidence that the emotional, intuitive, and spiritual nature of mankind cannot be challenged by our machines. I consider this subject to be particularly important and timely due to the rapid progress in AI and robotics combined with the many superficial and exaggerated claims fostered by the media.

The many people who helped me with the original Italian version of *SILICON* are recognized in the Acknowledgments at the end of this book. I would like here to express my gratitude to those who helped me with this edition, starting with my wife, Elvia, for her continuing and tireless support in reviewing and editing the manuscript. Kenneth Kales did the first pass of the final edit. Our son, Eric Faggin, and Prof. Brandon R. Brown have been extremely helpful in further editing and suggesting several improvements which have enriched this edition.

INTRODUCTION

I was born to a new life every time a mental structure made of prejudices, obsolete teachings, and uncritically accepted beliefs was shattered and I came out as if freed from prison. I was born to a new life every time my mind, observing from a new point of view, expanded to broader and different understandings. Above all, I was born to a new life when I stopped rationalizing and began listening to my intuition, opening myself to the mystery of my own consciousness.

I feel like I've already lived and completed three lives and I am now living my fourth. In the child enchanted by the flight of airplanes were already present seeds of the future maker of the microprocessor. And in the mind of the physicist who believed in the possibility of creating conscious computers was already stirring a faint awareness of the absurdity of such an idea. Much work was necessary to clear me from prejudices, dogmas, and preconceived ideas; above all, to free me from what appeared to be obvious.

My first life took place in Northern Italy where I was born, educated, and had my first work experiences. In early 1968, a few months after marrying Elvia Sardei, we moved from Milan to the San Francisco Bay Area and started a new life with a different language and culture. In the second life I achieved what I was most passionate about at that time: inventing and developing new technologies and products, starting with a novel method to make metal oxide semiconductor transistors (MOS Silicon Gate technology), with which I later designed the world's first microprocessors.

Then, surprising myself, I decided to start my first company, Zilog, Inc., which led to my third life, a line of work I never thought was in my genes: one of a serial entrepreneur in high tech business. In this new stage, I had to learn how to deal with situations far less understandable and controllable than those I had encountered in the domain of technology; for example, the unpredictability of markets, people and events. I also discovered how some of my hidden traits greatly influenced my behavior and that of others. This turn towards my inner life was even more unexpected than the decision to start my first company, and it led me to an extraordinary awakening described in chapter 5, which then deeply changed the rest of my life.

For many years I lived a double life, so to speak. By "day" I continued my business as an entrepreneur, by "night" I devoted time and energy to the development and understanding of my consciousness, allowing the transformations of thoughts and attitudes that spontaneously emerged to change my life. This gradual integration of inner and outer realities began about thirty years ago. The contrast between the two could not have been greater because the study of the outer world is based on science founded on the truth of shared experiments. The study of the inner world instead is subtle, since consciousness is personal and its contents are private.

I started my fourth life ten years ago when I decided to retire from business to focus exclusively on the scientific study of consciousness. This passion would later become the mission of the Federico and Elvia Faggin Foundation, a nonprofit organization created in 2011.

I was motivated to write this book to convey the essential messages I gathered in my four lives, telling not only the story of the inventions and enterprises in which I participated, but also sharing the most intimate account of my journey. Through direct experiences and profound reflections, I was led to a better comprehension of some crucial aspects of the nature of consciousness.

1
My First Life

Life can only be understood backward, but must be lived forward.
—Soren Kierkegaard

I was born in Vicenza, Italy, on December 1, 1941, the second of four children. My father was a well-known and esteemed teacher of history and philosophy at the *Liceo Classico* of Vicenza. Later he obtained his professorship and taught at the University of Padua as well. As a scholar, and prolific writer of academic books, he was particularly interested in mystics and idealist philosophers such as Meister Eckhart, Plotinus, and Arthur Schopenhauer. His last publication was the Italian translation from Ancient Greek of *The Enneads* of Plotinus, a work he completed one year before his death.

During my early years, my mother was a housewife who took care of her two sons: me and my brother Giorgio, who was two and a half years older. When I was five, I was awakened in the middle of the night by loud moans that seemed to be coming from my parents' room. I didn't know what was happening, yet somehow I understood that it was best to stay quiet. In the morning I had the surprise of meeting my new little sister, Anna Allegra. Five years later it would be the turn of my youngest brother, Franco.

The war and the years in Isola Vicentina

Men are at war with each other because every man is at war with himself

—Francis Meehan

On the day of my birth, World War II was already raging in Europe and a sense of precariousness and fear was widespread. It became worse just six days later, on December 7, 1941, when the Japanese raid on Pearl Harbor brought the United States into the conflict.

A couple of years after, in 1943, following the Allied Forces invasion of Sicily, my parents decided to move back to Isola Vicentina where both had been born and raised. Our family lived there until 1949 in the patriarchal complex of my paternal grandparents. It was a group of buildings constructed on three sides around a courtyard, bounded on the fourth side by a vegetable garden and an outhouse. There was also a pub, called *Osteria*, mostly run by the women of the house; a carpentry shop where quality furniture was built—grandfather Antonio's main activity; and a large shed where two big red threshers and all kinds of lumber were stored. The threshers were leased to farmers during the harvest season and represented a side business for my grandfather.

Isola Vicentina was the center of an agricultural area where corn, wheat, and hay were the primary crops. Many farmers did not have electricity in their homes or running water, radios, and indoor bathrooms. Most of them still used oxen-drawn plows, just like their ancestors had done for centuries before them, and remained mostly untouched by the industrial revolution that had already transformed many big cities around the world.

The Veneto region, roughly equivalent to the size of Vermont, had been part of the Venetian Republic for many centuries and the Venetian dialect had continued to be the main language of our region and the language spoken by my parents at home.

Fig. 1 – Federico's parents, Emma and Giuseppe, with Giorgio (left) and Federico, at Isola Vicentina (1944).

I still remember the *filò* during the freezing winters. It was a gathering after dinner of the women and children in the stable next to the house, a warm and cozy place permeated by the smell of cows and oxen. The women did needlework and made yarn with old spinning wheels, chatting and laughing, while the children played and then fell asleep, cradled in the moving shadows cast by the dancing light of oil lamps and candles.

Looking back, I realize that only very few people living today have fully experienced life in the three major modern historical periods that have characterized human progress: the agricultural, the industrial, and the information ages. For example, my granddaughter Isabella, with her iPad and internet, has no idea about how people lived in earlier times. She would not be able to reconstruct the rich sensory and emotional experience of the *filò* because many aspects of that tradition are completely missing in our lives today and can hardly even be imagined.

Vicenza, being an important railway junction, was heavily bombed by the Allied Forces towards the end of the war to disrupt Axis supply lines to the German soldiers stationed in Italy. During one of these raids, our apartment in downtown Vicenza where I was born, was bombed, proving the wisdom of my parents to have moved the family to Isola Vicentina.

But not even Isola Vicentina was completely spared from the war because one of the main roads leading to Austria and Germany ran right through the small town. During the German retreat in 1945, there were many incidents. For example, one day a German soldier entered our house, rifle in hand, demanding food. My frightened parents obliged, and fortunately he left after taking only our modest provisions and nothing more.

Despite being only three and a half years old at the time, I also vividly remember April of 1945, the month our liberation arrived. I have a clear recollection of being on the balcony of my maternal grandparents' house, facing the main square where tanks and other war equipment were assembled to celebrate the event. I was waving the Italian flag at an American soldier perched on the turret of a tank who was greeting me with a smile. I could never have imagined that one day I would call America my home!

A few months later, my father took me to Vicenza. I remember the bombed-out streets pitted with holes and the rubble of fallen buildings. Yet, I could not understand what had happened because "war" had no meaning to me.

Not long before I turned six, on my first day of school, I was surprised to hear the teacher speak Italian. It was a language I only partially understood because at home and around us in Isola Vicentina, everybody had spoken the Venetian dialect.

After completing the second grade, I moved back to Vicenza with my family to an apartment on *Via dello Stadio, a* street that ended at the municipal soccer stadium. Except for those Sundays when a match was being held, traffic was minimal.

During the summer, the embankment of the Bacchiglione River in front of our home teemed with crickets. And in the warm evenings, I joined the neighborhood children chasing the fireflies that were everywhere. There was also an empty field nearby where we played with wooden swords imitating the heroes of the black and white movies we had seen on Sundays in the parish hall.

Back then, the presence of the Catholic Church in everyday life was much more palpable than it is today. I remember the priests' blessings of the houses that took place every year during Easter time and the long processions winding along the streets of Vicenza, amidst the songs and prayers of the devotees.

The use of strict discipline, even corporal punishment, was the norm in the typical family education during the time Giorgio and I were children, and we both received a good dose of slaps.

In other respects, however, we were freer and less structured than today's kids. We played a lot, losing ourselves in the games that we invented, and the playful environment we created was in stark contrast to the more severe atmosphere existing at home.

Fig. 2 – Federico in first grade at Isola Vicentina (1947).

My first model plane

One day I was playing in the field near my friend's home when I noticed a young man holding a model airplane. Quickly turning the propeller with his finger, he "charged" the rubber-band engine and then let go. To my amazement, the plane flew off! I forgot my friends and our games and ran underneath the model, a Piper Cub, looking at it carefully, trying to understand how a toy could fly. I was only 11 then but that experience had a big impact on my life.

I decided that same day to build my model plane with makeshift materials that I found around the house. I thought I had succeeded, but when I returned to the same field to let it fly, the model refused to stay aloft. Later I would come to understand that I had grossly violated the laws of physics.

I was lucky because the same guy with the Piper Cub was riding down the street on his bicycle just then. He called to me, intrigued by my gadget. As he examined it, he started laughing and then explained what I had done wrong. He also told me where I could buy the right materials and suggested I buy *The Modern Modeler's Manual*. That was the first book I purchased with my savings.

I read the manual carefully, but could not understand everything, especially the parts that described how to build a transmitter and a receiver to make a radio-controlled model. Having more goodwill than money, I could not afford the kits that supplied all the parts and instructions on how to assemble them, which meant I had to do everything myself. I imagined the plane, that was the step I liked best, then designed a plan and procured the raw materials with which to build all the parts and assemble the model. Finally, with great expectations and enthusiasm, I could experience how well it would fly. I even made my own glue by melting pieces of celluloid in acetone—a recipe that I found in the manual—where the sources of the celluloid were my sister's and her friends' broken dolls. No wonder, I thought, my glue had that odd pinkish color. Finally, I assembled the model and tested it with great anticipation.

My second model was built better than the first, but it still did not fly. At long last, my third attempt was successful. I still remember the euphoria in seeing my plane soar lightly. It was the same kind of elation that many years later rewarded the major effort I had made in designing the world's first microprocessor that worked exactly as intended. In both cases I had *materialized* an idea into an object, thus showing the creative validity of my thoughts.

My passion for model planes was a crucial educational experience: it gave me a purpose and taught me how to manage a project *from beginning to end*. If the plane didn't fly, I had simply made some mistakes from which I could learn. This passion also led me to choose the high school I would attend a couple of years later. It was not the one my father had in mind for me.

Fig. 3 – Federico at 14 with a contest model plane that he designed and built (1956).

An impossible dream

My enthusiasm for airplanes would have naturally led me into a career as a pilot were it not for an unexpected turn of events. At the same age I started building model planes, I discovered that I could not properly see with my left eye. My parents immediately took me to an ophthalmologist who diagnosed a retinal detachment. Sadly there was no cure then, and any explanation for why it had happened remained just as elusive. We knew it had to be from some recent trauma, but I could not recall anything of that nature.

More than 40 years later the answer would emerge. I remembered then that when I was 10, I had spent a couple of weeks at my uncle's farm in Isola Vicentina during the summer holidays. I had tried to hand-crank start the old tractor that my cousin Policarpo drove. That was the way engines got going before the invention of the electric starter. The motor kicked back and the recoiling crank hit my face so violently that I almost fainted. Since I had been forbidden to touch the tractor, I did not tell anyone what happened and when my cousin asked me about the red stripe blotching my face, I answered: "Oh, nothing." Surprisingly, I had suppressed the memory of the incident until it resurfaced with clarity 42 years later, following a deep introspection.

Losing sight in one eye made it impossible for me to even dream of becoming a pilot. But I rolled with the punches. *If I cannot fly airplanes, I can at least build them*, I thought. So when it came time to decide on which high school to enroll, I chose a technical school, the Rossi Institute, where I could learn how to design and build *real* airplanes. My choice was influenced by the information I received from Giuseppe Bedeschi, a family friend who had gone to that school and earned a diploma in electrical engineering. Giuseppe held an important position in an electric motor company and became a role model for me. I admired him for what he had accomplished and for his lifestyle.

When I told my father that I wanted to attend the Rossi Institute and get a diploma in aeronautical engineering, he was visibly disappointed. Dad believed that technical institutes were "B" schools since they did not allow direct access to the university. But I stood my ground. In the end, he accepted my choice without too much resistance, perhaps because during middle school I had not been a particularly distinguished student. I was much more interested in making model planes than studying Latin.

The Rossi Institute was a demanding school. The coursework lasted five years, like all other Italian high schools, and required about forty hours a week of lessons and laboratories, plus a lot of homework. For the freshman year, only 30 percent of the students made it through cleanly. The rest had to repeat the year or leave the school. For the second year, only half of those students made it through. Only the best students graduated without having to repeat at least one year.

When I started the Institute, I had consciously determined to give it my best. Having chosen this school against the advice of my father, I wanted to prove that I had made a good choice. My resolve to be a good student was also prompted by an interesting experience I had that summer.

One day, walking on the trail atop the embankment in front of our house, I felt for the first time that I could "hold" a single thought in my mind, and deliberately examine it, "turning it around" as if it laid in my hands. I was excited by the emergence of a new mental power I had never experienced before, one that gave me a capacity for deeper concentration. For the first time, I felt the sense of being *responsible* for my thoughts, rather than being at their mercy.

In the middle of my first year at the Institute, I also discovered with great regret that the aeronautical engineering program was no longer available for new students, which forced me to choose a different course of study. The only other discipline that interested me was radio technology. *At least that will teach me to design radio-controlled model planes*, I thought, and that was enough motivation for my choice.

By the time I was 16, I had come of age and started exploring subjects beyond those strictly required at school. I read a lot of Russian and French literature, taking advantage of my father's vast library. I also began to read books on physics and mathematics written mainly in French because they were the only ones available in economical formats. And I studied Spanish on my own.

I had received a traditional Catholic education that filled me with dogmatic answers to questions I didn't yet have the maturity to ask. Exactly the opposite of the wise teachings of ancient philosophers like Plutarch, who said: "The mind is not a vessel to be filled, but a fire to be kindled."

As a teenager, I was overwhelmed with many doubts that I tried to solve by engaging myself in religious practices. I was taught that faith was a gift that must be cultivated with prayer and by going to Mass. I had also been taught that by believing in God there was all to gain and nothing to lose. So, I decided to zealously attend Mass every day.

I resolved to bet on the existence of God, all the more so because I felt sincerely attracted to the figure of Christ. Sometimes, during the meditation following the Communion service, I even perceived a deep connection with Jesus, even though I could not understand the meaning of "divine nature." Of course, self-suggestion cannot replace faith. And doubts did not disappear by burying them. Indeed, many doubts did come back later.

During my last year at the Rossi Institute, I became interested in computers and transistors, recent inventions that were not yet a part of the school program. I read everything about them that I could get my hands on. The radio technology I had been taught was still based on vacuum tubes, destined to disappear completely in less than ten years. Computers and transistors introduced me to digital microelectronics, a much vaster field than telecommunications. Finally, I had found something even more exciting than airplanes, and before graduating I had embraced another great passion! My grade point average was 85 out of 100 possible points, whereas the second-best student at the entire institute, out of about 200 graduates, got 75 out of 100. This excellent result went unnoticed by my father, given his preconceived ideas about my studies. Only with time did I realize how difficult it is to eradicate prejudices. As Albert Einstein said, "It is easier to break an atom than a prejudice."

The Olivetti experience

With my diploma in *perito radiotecnico,* at age 18, when the so-called Italian economic miracle was in full swing, job opportunities were abundant. After a few months of rest, in the fall of 1960 I accepted an offer as an assistant engineer at Olivetti to work in the new Electronics R&D Laboratory in Borgolombardo, near Milan, where Olivetti's early electronic computers were being developed and manufactured. My job interview had been conducted by Ing. Mario Tchou (Ing. stands for a graduate engineer), the stern director of the lab, who personally interviewed all technical personnel.

I rented a room in Milan on Vicenza Street—an amusing coincidence—and shared it with Alberto Santi, one of my schoolmates who had also landed a job at Olivetti. We rode the company bus to Borgolombardo every working day and left for Vicenza by train every Friday night to spend the weekend with our families, returning together again to Milan on Sunday night.

Our first task was to attend a training course of about two months that was held for all new technical hires. There we learned about transistors and computers, subjects that were not yet taught even at the university. At the end of the training, I was assigned to the Circuits Department and my first boss was Achille Castelli. He spent most of his time studying academic articles on circuit theory, full of complicated mathematics. My task was to carry on with the project of another *perito* who was taking a leave of absence to fulfill his 18 months of military duty, an obligation from which I was gladly exempted given my eyesight disability. As the Italian saying goes, "There is a silver lining to every cloud."

I could not have asked for a better project. It consisted of designing and building a small experimental transistorized electronic computer for which the basic architecture had been described in broad outline in an American electronics journal. Its purpose was to study the types of circuits needed to build a complete electronic programmable calculator.

The heart of the computer was an arithmetic unit that operated on numbers up to 10 digits with an accumulator consisting of 10 decimal counters. The accumulator is the register that contains the result of the last operation. To add two numbers, the first one was loaded on the accumulator by counting as many clock cycles as the digit to be loaded on each stage, with all 10 stages in parallel, of course. The digits of the second number were then added to the first ones by counting as many clock cycles as was the value of each digit. If a carry was produced going from "9" to "0," the carry was stored. The next operation was to propagate all the carries to complete the operation. For the same number of transistors, this strategy was considered faster than using conventional binary adders followed by a conversion from binary to decimal numbers.

The output of the accumulator was displayed by 11 *Nixie tubes* to show the 10 decimal digits plus special symbols. These tubes used gas discharge to illuminate one of 10 superposed cathodes shaped like the symbols to be displayed. By selecting the cathode with the shape of the intended symbol, the symbol would become visible by emitting red light. In our case, there were 10 identical tubes displaying the numbers from 0 to 9, plus an 11th tube showing special characters like the sign of the number, percentage, and so on. It was a cumbersome and costly technology that was replaced 10 years later by the first commercially available liquid crystal displays.

When I started working on this project, the circuitry that controlled the Nixie tubes had already been completed and was working properly. The arithmetic unit (AU) had been designed but its construction had just begun. My main role was to assist Ing. Castelli, the project leader, carry out the construction of the small computer with the help of two other technicians.

After completing the construction of the AU, my next responsibility was to design the interface necessary to integrate an already existing magnetic-core memory system to the computer. This memory was a discarded part of a previous experimental computer. It consisted of a random-access memory (RAM) that stored 4,096 binary numbers of 12 bits each.

The design of the main registers, the instruction set, and the control unit for the entire computer would come next, though this phase had not even been outlined in its barest form. At this most challenging part of the project, Ing. Castelli felt he was not qualified to direct it and decided to transfer it to Dr. Sibani, a physicist, who then became my new boss. However, soon afterward, Sibani was involved in a serious car accident and was convalescing on the Versilia coast of Tuscany. He asked me to visit him in a village near Cecina to discuss the next phase of the project.

During our meeting, he gave me a couple of books on computer architecture and asked me to read them carefully and to be ready to discuss the subject when he would return to work a few weeks later. After raising some questions, it was clear to me that Sibani was not an expert in computer architecture. Just like me, he would also have to study the topic to figure out how to take the next steps. I decided right then that the situation was an excellent opportunity for me.

Fig. 4 – Federico (first from left) with the two electronic "periti" who worked with him (1961).

Back in Borgolombardo, I studied the books with much interest. When Sibani returned about a month later, I had essentially designed the remaining part of the system. He checked the design without making any significant changes and told me to carry out the construction with two more technicians to assist me.

The CPU used approximately 1,000 logic gates made with germanium transistors that were fabricated in Italy by SGS, now known as STMicroelectronics. All the circuitry required about 200 small, printed circuit boards housed on a single equipment rack. Finally, the input-output electronics, based mainly on a teletype system, completed the project and we had the computer working before the end of 1961.

Admitted to the university

Near the end of the spring of 1961, I discovered that graduates of Italian technical institutes like the Rossi Institute could be admitted to the university after passing a simple qualifying test.

At Olivetti, I had noticed a "glass ceiling." Many *periti*, despite having distinguished themselves, could not go beyond a certain career level. It was as if they needed the imprimatur of a university degree to act as a guarantor for them. In other words, these employees were often assessed not so much on their merits, but on less relevant factors, like, for example, the school they attended.

For a *perito*, the best way to get to the top was to create his own company. And many of them did exactly that, especially in the Vicenza metropolitan area, greatly contributing to the economic development of the region and country.

That being the situation, my career prospects would improve significantly if I earned a graduate degree from the university. Nonetheless, my main reason for returning to school was to learn physics and mathematics more thoroughly. I was especially interested in quantum mechanics, the somewhat mysterious theory that explains how semiconductors like germanium and silicon behave. Even though the physics course had a reputation of being the most difficult one at the university, I decided to take the admission test and if I succeeded, to leave Olivetti. Among the other candidates who took the admission exam was Franco Bertotti. Our chance meeting marked the beginning of a lifelong friendship. He later married Elvia's sister and thus he became my brother-in-law.

When I passed the test and told my parents I wanted to quit my job and enroll in physics at the University of Padua, my father pointed out that I already had a good, well – paying job and I should think twice before leaving my post. I was expecting that he would be happy with my decision, so I thought his concern could be about my ability to succeed in such a demanding course of studies, where many of his best students failed. I assured him that I was confident I would make it.

But my assurances did not seem to convince him, so I thought maybe his concerns were tied to economics: We were a family of four siblings and Giorgio, the oldest one, was already attending university. Our mother, just before the birth of our youngest brother Franco, had also bravely completed her studies to become an elementary school teacher to help support the family.

I told my father that I had saved enough to take care of myself, and all I needed was a place to sleep and to eat when I was at home. At that point, he consented. And I kept my word because during those entire university years I never asked for money, not even the weekly allowance that my siblings received. It had become a source of pride for me to be completely self-sufficient.

Looking back, I'm sure I could not have designed the first microprocessor nine years later without that early work experience. Without the Rossi Institute, I could not have landed a job at Olivetti in 1960. And without the passion for model planes, unleashed from witnessing that Piper Cub's gentle flight, I could not have mustered the determination to choose that school against my father's will.

As Max Frisch wrote in *Homo Faber*: "That things were done this way was more than a coincidence, it was a chain." How many more stars had to line up so that I could carry out the purpose of my life?

The university years

The university is an investment in oneself. And together with the public school remains the last great social blender capable of mixing incomes, wealth, and geography.

—Beppe Severgnini

Since I had wanted to complete my project at Olivetti, I decided to work until Christmas without fully understanding the implications of that decision on my studies. My first day at the University of Padua was Monday, January 8, 1962. Throughout the lecture on Mathematical Analysis 1, I did not understand anything because I had missed two and a half months of previous instructions and was not familiar with the material already covered.

That fateful morning I realized that it was pointless to listen to incomprehensible lectures. I had to first catch up on the already covered material before I could usefully go back to classes. In the Italian university system, there was no obligation to attend classes, except for laboratories, and no homework was assigned. There was only the final exam consisting of a written test that covered all the material taught in the academic year, followed by an oral examination conditional on passing the written test. I decided therefore to attend only the mandatory Physics Laboratory 1 course that fortunately started after the Christmas holidays. I counted on recovering the lost time by studying on my own and taking the final exams.

Three exam sessions were offered per year: July, October, and February. I decided to divide the load by taking Mathematical Analysis 1 and Analytical Geometry 1 in July, Physics 1 and Laboratory 1 in October, and Chemistry in February.

To make matters worse, the textbook of Analysis was almost impenetrable. The author boasted that he had not used a single figure in the entire set of three volumes of about 1,500 pages "to develop rational thinking without the intuitive but distortive support provided by the figures." These almost verbatim words still ricochet in my mind.

I hated that textbook with its many demonstrations ending with the phrase: "The rest of the proof is elementary and is left to the student," adding insult to the pedagogical injury perpetrated toward novices like me who spent hours on a proof that the author had declared to be elementary. I was called incompetent by that author even when I could finally understand the lessons on my own, without the guidance he was supposed to have provided. I figured the author had written it not for his students, but to impress his distinguished mathematical colleagues with his grandiose visions of logic and brilliance. Pure elitism!

Even so, the pragmatic side of my nature gave me the upper hand. I bought a different textbook, the one used by the engineering students who were treated more sanely than those of us taking mathematics and physics. And I also bought a workbook with step-by-step approaches to some typical problems, and their answers, so that I could verify my understanding and progress. Even today I shudder thinking about the amount of time unnecessarily wasted trying to understand on my own what could have been taught so much better and faster with a few illustrations followed by clear explanations.

Analysis 1 was my first exam. I passed the written test very well, but stumbled a bit in the oral portion. The examiner wanted the same rigorous approach to proofs shown in the infamous textbook I despised, a skill I had not yet completely mastered. I ended up getting a decent grade. That score turned out to be the lowest of my entire university career, but I was happy to have left that obstacle behind me. A few weeks later I took the Analytical Geometry 1 exam and did well. The two most difficult exams of my first year were over. Having overcome the arduous freshman climb up, from that point on the road would be all downhill.

During that first year, I studied at the Biblioteca Bertoliana, the public library of Vicenza, because it was a quieter place than home. There was also much more room to spread out my textbooks and papers than on the small desk in the bedroom I shared with Giorgio.

I remember well the summer of 1962 during which I prepared for the Physics 1 exam, scheduled for October. I was alone at home because my family was on holiday at the seaside, and finally was enjoying some intellectual pleasure, instead of the frustration I felt with Mathematical Analysis 1 and the hard work of Analytical Geometry 1. I particularly appreciated thermodynamics, expertly and exquisitely explained in the textbook by Enrico Fermi, the Italian physicist and Nobel laureate who created the world's first nuclear reactor. His clarity and depth of thought were exactly the reasons why I undertook the study of physics in the first place. In October, I passed with flying colors the demanding Physics 1 exam, and in February of 1963 I passed Chemistry.

Finally, I was caught up and could attend almost all of the second-year classes, just as I had originally planned from the very beginning. Had I known of the problems I would cause myself by starting late, I would have certainly left Olivetti three months earlier. However, as a popular Italian proverb says: "Graves are full of hindsight."

From the second year of university onwards, I regularly went to Padua and attended all the courses. My grades were outstanding, and I was on a roll until graduation. I was especially interested in solid state physics, circuit theory, cybernetics, and mathematics, topics that I enjoyed learning in-depth, well beyond the curriculum requirements.

Meeting Elvia

My third year of university was particularly important because Elvia, my great love and future wife, came into my life. I had seen her a few times at my home because she was taking private philosophy lessons from my dad. I had noticed her for her beauty, but I didn't have the opportunity to approach her. A few years later, we coincidentally were at the train station in Padua at the same time, both of us waiting to board the next train to Vicenza.

Finally, I had the chance to talk with her! Building up some courage, I approached and introduced myself as the son of Professor Faggin. We started chatting and discovered we had many points in common. She was from a family of teachers just as I was: her father taught Italian and Latin at the Liceo Scientifico of Vicenza and her mother taught mathematics at the Magistrali High School (the school that trained elementary school teachers). She also belonged to a large family, the eldest of seven siblings, and she too felt suffocated in a provincial environment. From that first meeting, I felt that she could be the person to share my life with, even though I feared her choice to be enrolled in medical school meant that we would have to wait many years before marrying.

A few months later I went to her house to help her prepare for her physics exam and met her beautiful family. Then, for a while, we lost sight of each other. When I saw her again about nine months later, I was happy to learn that she had decided to quit medicine and enroll instead in the faculty of letters, a far less time-consuming course of studies. Yes, that was good news!

During my last year of university, Elvia and I were going steady and spent many Sunday afternoons together. We often took long walks in the hills surrounding Vicenza, which we reached with my faithful Vespa 150 scooter bought with my savings from working at Olivetti. We also often walked to the Palladio's Villa Rotonda along the Valle del Silenzio (Valley of Silence). We were happy together and full of enthusiasm!

Back on campus, I had finished in October all of my third-year exams and started the mandatory one-year-minimum internship necessary to complete the thesis work. I was assigned an office in the basement of the Institute of Physics and decided to prepare an experimental thesis on "flying-spot scanners," a type of equipment used for the automatic reading of spark chamber photographs. My thesis required I design and build an advanced optoelectronic feedback system to obtain the necessary precision in the automatic measurement system.

I wanted to graduate in the October session of the following year, eager to start my new career as soon as possible. And so I applied myself unsparingly to complete the remaining four exams, plus the proficiency exams in English and French, and the demanding work on the experimental thesis. The thesis alone required at least half of my time that year.

I happily graduated *summa cum laude* in 1965 in just under four years, having earned an outstanding and uncommon final score. That day Elvia came to my graduation ceremony. She sat next to me at the reception that followed, held at the famed and elegant *Caffè Pedrocchi* across the street from the main entrance to the university. I kept admiring her. I remember she was wearing a green dress that fit perfectly and I felt truly proud of her. *Now that I have graduated, I can seriously think about our marriage,* I thought to myself. *But first I must find a job.*

My new work experiences

Thankfully, I was immediately offered an assistant professorship position with pay at the University of Padua, an exceptional offer in those days. Usually, the best students who wanted to pursue an academic career had to accept an unpaid volunteer assistantship for at least a couple of years. My assignment was to teach the Electronics Laboratory course to third-year physics students while continuing my research on flying-spot scanners. But at the end of the academic year, in the summer of 1966, I decided to leave the university and join CERES, a startup in Milano, working with Dr. Sibani, my old boss at Olivetti, who had started his own company.

I made this decision for several reasons, the most compelling being economics; university pay was not enough to support a family—a non-negotiable condition for my future. Therefore I opted for a career in industry, although I regretted not having been able to further deepen my knowledge of physics and mathematics.

CERES was a small company with less than a dozen employees, dedicated to developing thin-film circuits. It was also the Italian representative of GMe, General Microelectronics, Inc., the world's first MOS integrated circuit company. GMe had been started in Silicon Valley a couple of years earlier by two engineers who had left Fairchild Semiconductor. Their first commercial product was a 20-bit dynamic shift register.

Immediately upon my hiring, I was sent to visit GMe's headquarters in Sunnyvale, California, to take a one-week course on MOS technology. That was a requirement for me to be able to properly explain the technology and the product line to our potential Italian customers. The trip to Silicon Valley was also my first flight in a commercial jet. My only previous flight experience had been a short hop around Vicenza in an old Beechcraft twin-engine airplane, a coveted prize I had won when attending the Rossi Institute. I found the San Francisco Bay Area immensely energizing. I had a glimpse of an open society, cosmopolitan, dynamic, and meritocratic in contrast to the narrow mindset I had experienced in Italy.

After I returned home, we received an order from the University of Rome for about 10 100-bit dynamic MOS shift registers, the most advanced product that GMe produced. Unfortunately, GMe never managed to deliver the devices, and a few months later the company was sold to RCA. We later learned that GMe had never mastered the manufacturing process to make reliable MOS integrated circuits. As a result, my stay at CERES came to an end since the most interesting part of my work had evaporated. Fortunately, that one-week course on MOS technology facilitated my recruitment at SGS-Fairchild in Agrate Brianza, near Milan, the only Italian semiconductor company that produced silicon transistors and integrated circuits. It was a licensee of the US company Fairchild Semiconductor's bipolar technology and was also 30 percent owned by them.

I joined the brand-new R&D department, reporting to Ing. Fabio Capocaccia, whom I had also met at the Olivetti Laboratory in Borgolombardo. Based on the brief MOS course I had taken in California, I was assigned to develop from scratch SGS's first MOS process technology. Since SGS had several technical reports from Fairchild Semiconductor describing the physical properties of the interface between silicon dioxide and monocrystalline silicon, I was able to finish the job in a short time without much difficulty. After developing the manufacturing process, I also designed SGS's first two commercial MOS integrated circuits (details on the MOS manufacturing process can be found in Appendix 1).

Our wedding and honeymoon

Meanwhile, my relationship with Elvia had grown to such an extent that I decided to ask her to marry me and she joyfully consented. Now I had to face her father with a formal request, an obligation that could not be evaded in those days, and one that caused me some anxiety. For a couple of weeks I worried about how Rodolfo, my future father-in-law, would react to my request.

Finally, the day of reckoning arrived. Elvia greeted me at the door with a warm smile of encouragement and took me to her father's study. Professor Rodolfo welcomed me cordially, but that was not enough to dispel my embarrassment. When he looked at me with his piercing blue eyes, my mind went blank until I awkwardly found the words I had rehearsed. At one point, Rodolfo came to my rescue and told me that if I loved Elvia, he was happy to give his consent. Hurray! I could have embraced him, such was the relief and happiness I felt. That evening I was even invited to stay for dinner and a few days later I returned to my future in-laws with my parents to celebrate our official engagement.

Fig. 5 – Elvia and Federico celebrate their official engagement (1966).

From that point on I could freely visit Elvia's house where I always felt welcome by my future in-laws and at ease with Elvia's brothers and sisters. One night I even slept at her house—I'll explain so not to be misunderstood. In those days it was not proper to sleep under the same roof as the fiancée, except in cases of absolute emergency. And this was precisely what happened on November 4, 1966: the Bacchiglione River kept true to its name. It derives from *bacaliare*, meaning to clatter, and the river bellowed over its banks while I was visiting Elvia's home.

We were all engaged in conversation and so did not notice the calamity until the water had invaded the garden. Alerted by Gianfranco, Elvia's oldest brother, we went outside in the pouring rain. Defying the water that had already reached our ankles, we rushed to the garage, which was a bit higher than the rest of the ground, to save my precious Vespa. It was a successful sortie, but we were completely soaked.

Maria, Elvia's mother, hurriedly brought a large basin of hot water to wash and warm my feet. Grateful, I immediately took off my shoes and socks and, with a sigh of relief, plunged my feet into the water, my eyes squinting with enjoyment from the warmth. When I opened them, Elvia's brothers and sisters had gathered in the kitchen and were looking at me curiously.

To avoid being the center of attention, I invited them to keep me company. Elvia and some of her sisters accepted and we started to play with our feet inside the water. Elvia's grandmother Anna, mindful of the times when girls were not allowed to even show an ankle, in seeing such promiscuity looked worried. "Feet have no sex!" I quickly said to reassure her amid our laughter. Despite our good humor, the flood of 1966 was terrible. Via Nazario Sauro, where Elvia lived, had turned into a rushing river of mud and became impossible to navigate. So, I stayed for dinner and then slept in a sofa bed in the professor's study, after wishing Elvia good-night with a kiss, obviously very chaste.

On September 2, 1967, our wedding was celebrated in the church of San Pietro by the parish priest, Don Adriano Masetto, whom we had known for many years. We spent our honeymoon in the Dolomites, my favorite mountain range since childhood, where I had vacationed several times. Elvia knew them only through the descriptions of the famous Italian writer Dino Buzzati, who in his stories often evoked "the triumphal high dolomitic valleys enclosed with white crags." She also knew Buzzati's famous painting where the Milan Cathedral was transfigured into a cathedral of dolomite rocks, with spires and pinnacles, and was quite happy when I proposed to spend our honeymoon there.

From the magical peaks, we finally had to go back to the valley, meaning, return to Agrate Brianza to live in the rented apartment we had just finished furnishing the week before our wedding.

Fig. 6 – The wedding day (1967).

Toward the end of 1967, SGS asked me if I was interested in going to California for six months as part of an exchange of engineers between SGS R&D and Fairchild R&D. For me, it was a great opportunity to return to Silicon Valley and Elvia could not wait to visit San Francisco, and California in general. Before leaving, we returned to our cherished Dolomites for a week of vacation during the Christmas holidays and skied the beautiful snowy slopes. Rested and full of expectations, we then embarked on our new adventure.

We landed first in Philadelphia, Pennsylvania, on February 9, 1968, where I participated with my boss Ing. Capocaccia in a semi-conductor technology conference organized by IEEE, the powerful Institute of Electrical and Electronics Engineers. Then, in a round-about way to San Francisco, we visited Washington, DC and New Orleans and even stopped for a few days in West Virginia to visit a friend.

2
My Second Life

Nothing great in the world has ever been accomplished without passion.

—Georg Wilhelm Friedrich Hegel

I t was love at first sight. Spring was in full bloom in the Bay Area's Santa Clara Valley. We were in the land of opportunity, the mythical place dreamed of by so many young people around the globe, and I was on assignment with Fairchild Semiconductor, the most advanced semiconductor company in the world.

About two weeks after arriving, we rented a small furnished apartment in Mountain View, not far from the Fairchild Semiconductor R&D Laboratory in Palo Alto where I started working in late February of 1968. On my first day, I was assigned a desk in Dick Aldrich's office, a process engineer expert in bipolar transistors who had been in that lab for a few years. Dick was a rather friendly, if somewhat taciturn type, and soon invited us for dinner at his home in Sunnyvale where he lived with his wife and two children. Elvia and I brought an excellent bottle of wine, according to Italian custom and mindful of Euripides's words: "Where there is no wine, there is no love, nor any other pleasure have mortals." To our surprise and a bit of embarrassment, only water, milk, and soft drinks were offered with dinner. I hadn't known that the Aldriches were opposed to drinking alcohol. We had made a false step even if meant with the best of intentions. Later I discovered that many

American restaurants served alcoholic cocktails before dinner, and that wine generally was not served during meals, a strange practice for Italians since wine is an integral part of lunch and dinner.

In those days I also met Danny Gentile who worked as a process technician at Fairchild. He was born in Fasano, in the Puglia region of Italy, and had been living in San Jose for many years with his Italian-American wife and their three children. Elvia and I were often invited to their house on Sundays, where we would enjoy barbecues and pleasant conversations until late.

Danny had a hobby of buying, restoring, and reselling exotic Italian cars like Ferraris and Alfa Romeos. He had become an expert mechanic and always had at least a couple of automobiles he was working on. When I needed a car, he found a used 1962 Chevrolet Impala for me, which I bought directly from its original owner. And when I found myself in financial trouble due to SGS being two months late in paying my salary, he lent me $500 so we could meet our basic expenses. Elvia and I felt grateful for his generosity and friendship.

Fig. 7 – Elvia and Federico in 1968 with their first car, a 1962 Chevrolet Impala.

The appreciation for good wine was a trait I shared with some of my other Fairchild friends like Chuck Steele, Sal Cagnina, and Tom Menzies. They too, like Robert Louis Stevenson, believed that "Wine is poetry bottled." They also agreed with Alexandre Dumas, that "Wine is the intellectual part of dinner." With Píndaro, who claimed that "Wine elevates the soul and the thoughts and anxieties move away from the heart of man." And with Galileo Galilei that "Wine is nothing but sunlight, mixed with the wetness of the vine." Together we enjoyed many blind tastings, which amply proved that when it comes to wine, the price is much less related to taste than people think. Elvia and I stayed in touch with them and we still occasionally see each other to this day. I must say that we found it much easier to socialize in Silicon Valley than in Agrate Brianza.

We rejoiced and soon it turned to tears.
—Dante Alighieri, *The Song of Ulysses*

On most weekends Elvia and I visited towns around the marvelous San Francisco Bay area, and the beaches, villages, and parks along the Pacific Coast, soaking up the beautiful weather that characterizes this extraordinary part of the world. Then in midspring, Elvia gave me wonderful news: we were expecting a baby!

Andrea Rodolfo was born on December 31,1968 six weeks ahead of schedule. He seemed perfect, so much so that the doctors did not realize his lungs had not yet fully developed, and thus they did not immediately put our son into an incubator. When the doctors finally noticed that something was wrong, it was too late. Our little one had drained all his resources trying hard to breathe on his own. In two days he passed, from coming to life at the end of '68, to leaving life at the beginning of '69.

It was a great pain. He was a beautiful child.

In life there are days full of wind and full of anger, there are days full of rain and full of pain, there are days full of tears; but then there are days full of love, which give you the courage to go on for all the other days.

—Romano Battaglia, *Infinite Night*

Fairchild Semiconductor, the Father of Silicon Valley

Fairchild Semiconductor was founded in 1957 by eight engineers who had left Shockley Semiconductor. They included Robert Noyce, Gordon Moore, Jean Hoerni, and Jay Last. Their original mission was to develop and manufacture bipolar junction transistors made of silicon to meet the high speed and stringent reliability requirements of the nascent US aerospace industry. The earlier germanium-based technology had reached the end of its course and the industry needed better semiconductor materials for higher performance. It is interesting to note that the total production of germanium transistors in the United States in 1957 was about 30 million units. Today, a single chip costing less than one dollar can easily contain more than 30 million transistors, and that chip also includes all their interconnections. This progress was unthinkable back then.

Within a few years of its founding, Fairchild became the leading company in the fledgling microelectronics industry thanks to the seminal invention of the planar process by one of its co-founders, Swiss engineer Jean Hoerni. Up until then, transistors were fabricated one at a time. With Hoerni's invention, it became possible to manufacture many of them simultaneously, side by side, on the surface of a thin slice of monocrystalline silicon cut from pure crystal. That slice was called a wafer (Fig. 8).

The planar process was based on an earlier discovery that silicon dioxide can act as a barrier to dopants. This property could be exploited by growing an oxide layer on the surface of a wafer and then opening windows in it wherever junctions were desired. This could be done by using a photolithographic process, followed by a chemical etching (Fig. 8), with a method like the one used for making printed circuit boards.

Ultraviolet Light

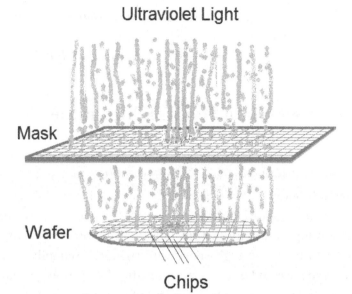

Mask

Wafer

Chips

Fig. 8 – The essence of the planar process, based on photolithography, is illustrated in this image. The wafer is covered by a thin photographic emulsion, called photoresist, sensitive to ultraviolet light. A beam of light passes through a mask that has transparent and opaque areas. The photoresist hardens in places where it is illuminated by the light. In a subsequent processing step, called chemical etching, a chemical attack removes the material that is not protected by the hardened photoresist. Illustration by F. Faggin.

After the oxide was removed, the junctions—the active part of the transistors— were created by thermal diffusion of the appropriate impurities (dopants) previously deposited into the silicon. Typical dopants were boron, phosphorus, and arsenic. At the end of the process, the wafer was cut into individual transistors which were then separately packaged.

Hoerni's process drastically reduced the size and cost of transistors, while greatly improving their performance. Above all, it made possible the *monolithic integrated circuit*: the true revolution of microelectronics. With the planar process, the transistors were lying next to each other, therefore they could be directly interconnected on the wafer itself. In other words, instead of individually packaging the transistors and then interconnecting them with other components on a printed circuit board, the same function performed by the printed circuit board could be done on the wafer itself.

What was missing though was a method for insulating each transistor within the wafer so that they would not interfere with each other. This insulation had not been required when the transistors were individually cut and packaged. Bob Noyce, the head of Fairchild Semiconductor, invented a process to solve this problem, making it possible for the first time to produce a monolithic integrated circuit (IC). It was 1961 and the first commercial IC, a simple resistor-transistor logic gate (RTL), was designed by Jay Last and went on the market in 1962.

Nine years later the microprocessor was born by combining the entire functionality of a programmable computer within a single integrated circuit. The microprocessor represented a fundamental qualitative leap because *the part became the whole* when the many integrated circuits with which a computer was built became a single chip. "Computing," then, became a property of a monolithic piece of silicon: a microchip.

The history of the integrated circuit is an example of how many fundamental inventions have their roots in previous inventions that generally go unacknowledged. Often the final inventor credits himself, or is credited, for the entire process without recognizing the prior essential contributors. The history of the integrated circuit is one such example because Jean Hoerni's earlier seminal invention is hardly ever mentioned in connection with the IC.

The history of the integrated circuit

The *concept* of an integrated circuit was presented for the first time at the United States Electronic Components Symposium on May 7, 1952, by Geoffrey Dummer, who stated: "Now it seems possible to imagine electronic components in a solid block without wires." This prediction was made at the time when the industry had just managed to successfully manufacture the first germanium bipolar junction transistors. However, Dummer was never able to turn his idea into a working device, even though he tried for many years.

Jack Kilby of Texas Instruments won the Nobel Prize in Physics in 2000 for his 1959 invention of what he called an integrated circuit. It was not a monolithic device because it required the placement of separate components within a small package, followed by *manual* wiring, a quite expensive and unscalable process. According to Kilby, the interconnection of separate components was meant to be performed in a single operation. However, this was easier said than done and was never accomplished because Hoerni's planar process, combined with Noyce's transistor isolation process, provided a far superior manufacturing method.

The planar process was the *seminal* invention that offered the only practical method for manufacturing *monolithic* integrated circuits. It was universally adopted by the global microelectronics industry and is still in use today. Transistors and integrated circuits made with the planar process were initially very expensive, so their applicability was limited primarily to the US missile and space program where small physical dimensions, low power dissipation, high performance, and high reliability were of paramount importance. However, the potential was enormous because over time the cost of a single transistor within an integrated circuit could decrease exponentially by increasing the wafer diameter and simultaneously reducing the physical dimensions of the transistors. Thus, an ever-increasing number of integrated circuits, each containing a growing number of transistors, could be fabricated on a single wafer whose diameter, initially less than 2 cm, reached 30 cm in the late 1990s, where it has remained to this day.

To achieve the essential goal of low cost, it was necessary to produce only a relatively small number of *standardized* parts since the unit cost of an integrated circuit decreases as the cumulative number of units produced increases. The designers of circuits with discrete components, however, were opposed to standardization, claiming that their circuits did operations that no standard integrated circuit (IC) could do. Their protests were motivated more by fear that the IC would eliminate their trade than by the reasons they were giving, ones rational only in appearance. This initial *ideological* opposition slowed down the adoption of the ICs until prices became sufficiently lower, at which point the resistance lost the battle, and true rationality prevailed over territorial disputes.

The adoption of standardized ICs rapidly increased the production volume with a corresponding further reduction in costs, thus establishing a virtuous circle that continues today. The final blow was given by the microprocessor because its programmability allowed customizing the same component by using software, albeit at the system level rather than at the circuit level, thus eliminating the original problem at its root. Henceforth the microprocessor gave back to the system designer the original freedom denied by the standardization.

Towards the second half of the 1960s, the price of ICs dropped to the point that many new industrial and commercial applications emerged, thus prompting rapid growth of the semiconductor industry. In 1965 Gordon Moore, then director of the R&D Laboratory of Fairchild Semiconductor, witnessed that the number of transistors in an IC had doubled every year since the beginning in 1962. He boldly predicted that this trend would continue for the following 10 years. Not only was he right, but his prediction has been immortalized as Moore's Law.

Of course, this is not a physical law valid anywhere and forever. Such exponential growth cannot increase indefinitely. It must slow down as the physical size of the transistor approaches the irreducible size of the atoms from which transistors are made. In fact, the doubling period for logic ICs has gradually increased from one year in 1965, to three years in 2013, with an average of two years for the period 1970 to 2013. Considering that the doubling time increases slowly, Moore's Law has provided the industry with an invaluable tool for planning and forecasting.

The MOS Silicon-Gate Technology

The same year the planar process was invented at Fairchild Semiconductor (1959), the seminal metal-oxide-semiconductor-field-effect-transistor (MOSFET) was invented by Dawon Kahng and John Atalla at Bell Labs. The MOSFET, or simply MOS, uses an operating principle that is different from bipolar transistors. In MOS transistors, the signal amplification is obtained by controlling the electrical conduction at the interface between the silicon and silicon dioxide (SiO_2). This control is easily achieved by changing the voltage applied to an electrode, called *gate*, that is placed over a thin insulating layer of oxide that bridges two junctions called *source* and *drain* (Fig. 9).

The MOS transistors were smaller and less expensive to manufacture than the bipolar ones but were also much slower and less reliable. Therefore, all the first integrated circuits used bipolar transistors for which the operating principle was identical to the first discrete diffusion transistors made with germanium. In 1968, MOS ICs accounted for less than five percent of the total IC production and their reliability was still inadequate. It took many years for the industry to learn how to make reliable MOS ICs.

When I joined the Fairchild R&D Lab, I was assigned to the MOS Process Development section then headed by Les Vadasz. That meant I had two bosses because I continued to report to Capocaccia at SGS-Fairchild, Italy, as well. The same day I set foot in the lab, Vadasz asked me to choose one of two projects to lead: (1) Design a special dynamic MOS shift register, or (2) Develop a self-aligned MOS technology using gates made with silicon instead of aluminum.

I chose to lead the latter because I had remembered Capocaccia mentioning the concept of self-alignment and I clearly understood its advantages in reducing the harmful effects of parasitic capacitances, especially the ones between the drain and the gate (Fig. 9). The parasitic capacitances are unwanted because they greatly reduce the performance of the MOS transistors. Especially detrimental is the overlap capacitance between the gate and the drain electrodes because its effect is multiplied by a factor much larger than one during the switching operation.

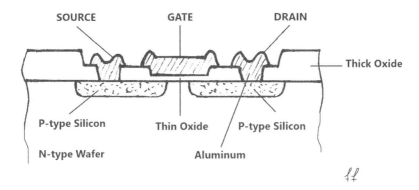

Fig. 9 – Cross-section of a P-channel MOS transistor with aluminum gate. By applying a negative voltage to the gate, a conduction channel is created at the interface between the thin oxide and the N-type silicon, allowing for current to flow between the P-type source and drain electrodes. Notice that the gate significantly overlaps the P-type silicon that form the source and the drain, thus creating "parasitic" capacitances that slow down the transistor switching speed. Illustration by F. Faggin.

The invention of the silicon-gate process

Do not give up. You would risk doing it an hour before the miracle
—Arabic proverb

The first engineers to use amorphous silicon to make silicon-gate transistors were J.C. Sarace and his collaborators at Bell Labs. However, no one had yet invented the process architecture needed to make integrated circuits with silicon gates. The Bell Labs method could only make discrete transistors, not ICs. Following that lead, Tom Klein, an engineer working for Vadasz, measured the difference in the threshold voltage that could be obtained by using heavily P-doped silicon instead of aluminum for the gate electrode of an MOS transistor. This could be easily done without building an actual silicon gate transistor.

Klein found that the MOS transistor threshold voltage could be reduced by 1.1 volts with important benefits in speed and power dissipation (see Appendix 1). Vadasz informed me of these experiments but did not tell me anything about the previous work done at Bell Labs, of which both he and Klein were well aware. I became aware of it only after having successfully completed the project.

My most important and urgent tasks for the project were to:

1. Invent the architecture of a new process to make isolated self-aligned silicon gate transistors.
2. Develop a method for the precision-etching of deposited silicon patterns.
3. Design in detail the new manufacturing process.
4. Design a test pattern suitable for measuring all the critical parameters of the new process.

After those tasks were completed, I had to design an integrated circuit with the silicon gate and prove its performance and reliability advantages over an equivalent production chip with the metal-gate process.

I struggled for days trying to figure out the right process architecture. I asked all the local experts for help, including Vadasz and Klein, but none of them knew how to do it either. After about a week, an idea came to me. If I started by etching a "tub" in the initial oxide where the entire MOS device was supposed to be located, I could then solve the problem (Fig. 10).

This was a new approach compared to the old method of creating metal-gate MOS transistors in which the first step was to define the source and the drain regions separately. This was the indispensable invention to making self-aligned gates, and just like many intuitive ideas, it became obvious only after having found it. The detailed description of the MOS technology with aluminum and with the silicon gate, and their comparison, are too technical to interest most readers. This material of historical importance is little known and rarely discussed even in specialized texts. It is included in Appendix 1 for the curious reader who has a technical background.

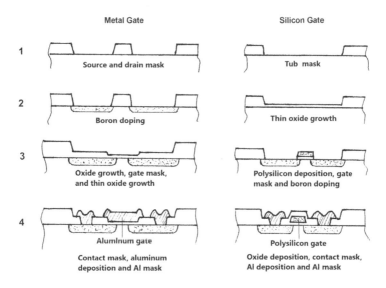

Fig. 10 – The figure shows four sections of a MOS transistor to illustrate the fundamental differences between the metal-gate transistor (on the left) and the silicon-gate transistor (on the right). The differences are obvious, especially in the early stages of the process. Notice that the gate capacitance of the silicon-gate technology (SGT) transistor, and especially the parasitic gate-to-drain capacitance, are much lower than the metal-gate version. Contrary to metal gate, with SGT this capacitance is also not susceptible to variations introduced from the misalignment of the gate to the first mask. Furthermore, the polysilicon gate is buried under oxide allowing the aluminum to cross over the gate, impossible to do with metal gate. Illustration by F. Faggin.

The next problem was how to connect the silicon gates to the junctions in the most efficient way. An aluminum strip could be used, but this would have required a lot of valuable area. So I came up with the creative idea of a *buried contact* (Appendix 1). With this contact, the amorphous silicon was connected directly to a junction without using aluminum. This method would require one additional masking operation, though in return it would greatly increase the circuit density since the metal lines could run over the buried contact. Having already acquired experience with the design and layout of integrated circuits at SGS-Fairchild, this idea seemed extremely useful to me, especially for logic circuits for which the density was mainly limited by the metal interconnections.

About ten days after my arrival, I described to Vadasz and Klein how I intended to fabricate MOS integrated circuits with silicon gates (Appendix 1). Although Vadasz approved my overall process architecture, he claimed that the buried contact would never work. When I respectfully disagreed with his assessment, he was adamant in forbidding me from even trying the idea.

My boss was an authoritarian type, therefore I decided not to confront him. I had been educated to defer to authority. However, a few weeks later when I started designing the test pattern, I decided to also include a couple of structures that would allow me to build and characterize the buried contact. It cost nothing extra and I wanted to find out if my idea worked. I was sure it would remove a major limitation of MOS technology.

The addition of the buried contacts to the self-aligned gates, also "buried" under the oxide, would achieve the same interconnection density possible with two layers of metal. Moreover, two layers of metal were not yet feasible at that time. This became a crucial advantage because it almost doubled the circuit density for MOS random-logic circuits. It was indeed indispensable to designing the microprocessor a couple of years later.

The next step was the development of a chemical solution to etch the silicon. Nobody knew how to do this. Then, after reading a paper on how to dissolve bulk silicon with a mixture of nitric and hydrofluoric acid, I decided to do my experiments by diluting different proportions of the two acids in deionized water. After many attempts, I found the best ratio to achieve the optimal differential etching rate between silicon and silicon dioxide while maintaining excellent dimensional control.

It took about 10 days and a new pair of shoes to reach that goal. The shoes were collateral damage from a spilled drop of the hellish solution. Fortunately the corrosion stopped at my socks just before reaching my skin. The wafer fab operators later called that solution "Freddy's etch," a variation on the nickname Fred they had given me.

The Fairchild 3708, the world's first commercial IC with SGT

To further characterize and optimize the new process, I designed a test pattern called XTPG (eXperimental Test Pattern for silicon Gate) that contained all types of structures suitable for measuring the critical parameters of the new technology, including the buried contact. The manufacturing process was described in a "run sheet" that accompanied each batch of wafers, called a *run*. The run sheet described, step-by-step, the sequence of all the operations to be performed, from beginning to completion, including the equipment to be used and their settings. By the end of April in 1968, I had already fabricated the first functioning MOS transistors with silicon gates by designing and fine-tuning the entire run sheet of the process.

Since the electrical characteristics of these early devices were promising, the time had come to design an entire integrated circuit with the new process technology and compare its performance to a similar device with an aluminum gate. Our manufacturing engineers had told us that the Fairchild 3705, an 8-port analog multiplexer with decoding logic, had stringent specifications and was the most difficult product for the company to produce. They said that if the silicon-gate technology (SGT) could improve on its manufacturing, there would be great value. We did indeed well prove it.

The Fairchild 3708 was the first commercial MOS product with self-aligned gates, replacing the Fairchild 3705 which used metal-gate technology (MGT). Furthermore, the 3708 would provide a convenient platform to further characterize the SGT and improve on its performance, if necessary.

The 3708 consisted of eight very large transistors (Fig. 11) that had to behave as much as possible like ideal switches, meaning that when one of the transistors was active, its resistance had to be very low; and when it was inactive, its leakage current had to be negligibly small. Furthermore, the switching speed had to be as high as possible, which was a difficult requirement due to the large input capacitance of those transistors. The chip also contained a decoder so that each transistor could be selected by simply using a 3-bit address. The most difficult parameter to control was the leakage current, caused mainly by the presence of impurities in the silicon and the large area of the junctions.

It took a couple of weeks with the help of a draftsman to complete the circuit design and the layout of the 3708. Then the laborious process of creating the masks began. The whole procedure lasted several weeks, and finally, in early July, the first wafers were completed. The 3708 worked immediately and its performance was far superior to the 3705. I was extremely happy and turned my sights to complete the characterization of the SGT.

This task required the preparation of some special runs where certain critical parameters were intentionally manipulated to simulate their maximum allowed variations in production. During this phase, I discovered with great disappointment that the amorphous silicon tended to break at the high oxide steps created by the tub mask. I should not have been surprised by this finding because the amorphous silicon was vacuum-evaporated using the same method employed for the aluminum deposition where similar problems already existed.

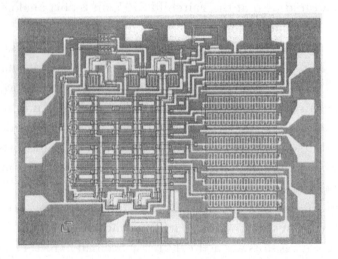

Fig. 11 – Picture of the Fairchild 3708, the world's first commercial circuit using SGT. First sold at the end of 1968, this device had superior characteristics compared with the metal-gate version called Fairchild 3705. The serpentine patterns at the right of the picture are the gates of the large transistors. Their ON-resistance was three times lower, and their OFF-resistance was more than 100 times higher than the 3705's.

Fortunately there was another way to create silicon films at Fairchild. That process used the chemical decomposition of silane (SiH_4) at low pressure and at temperatures between 650°C and 750°C. This method produced *polycrystalline* silicon instead of amorphous silicon, with grain sizes up to 10 nanometers, depending on the growing conditions. The problem could be elegantly solved because the silicon atoms were depositing like snow coming from all directions, thus properly covering the steps instead of rays of atoms coming only from one direction when using vacuum evaporation. This, together with the tub mask, was another crucial difference with the transistors with common source made by Bell Labs using amorphous silicon gates.

Sometime later I discovered that the bipolar group had developed a process to drastically reduce impurities in the wafers. This process consisted in the deposition of a protective layer of vapox (silicon dioxide obtained by chemical decomposition) followed by a heavy phosphorus doping on the back silicon of the wafer. The wafer was then subjected to temperatures ranging from 800°C to 900°C while the phosphorus diffusing in the silicon acted like a sponge, segregating the impurities that were naturally diffusing toward it given the high temperature. The silicon layer with a high concentration of impurities was then eliminated by chemical etching. This process was called *phosphorus gettering* and drastically reduced the leakage currents and other problems due to impurities, and as a result significantly improved the long-term reliability of MOS integrated circuits.

This same method could not be used with metal-gate MOS circuits because the aluminum would rapidly diffuse into the silicon at temperatures above 600°C. Since the polycrystalline silicon could withstand temperatures above 1200°C, the phosphorus gettering could be performed, reducing the leakage current of MOS ICs by more than a factor of 100, and eliminating the residual threshold voltage drift that occasionally afflicted the MOS devices with aluminum gates. Finally, the long-term reliability of MOS ICs had reached the same level enjoyed by bipolar ICs, overcoming another major obstacle to the unconditional adoption of MOS technology.

The low leakage current was also of fundamental importance in the development of dynamic random-access memories (DRAM), where a bit is represented by the electric charge stored in the gate of a MOS transistor. This method could not be used if the electrical charge dissipated too quickly due to excessive leakage current.

With the 3708, the comparison between the SGT and the MGT was simple because all the key parameters of the two chips could be directly compared. At the end of the various improvements and characterization, the results were truly remarkable. The 3708 in comparison to the 3705 was five times faster, had a leakage current of between 100 and 1,000 times lower, and the ON-resistance of the analog switches was three times lower.

After the 3708 chip's reliability was demonstrated by Fairchild's quality assurance engineers, the product was launched later in 1968. The 3708 continued to be produced with wafers that I supplied until the process was finally transferred to the production department of the MOS division located in nearby Mountain View.

Becoming a US resident

June of 1968 was a memorable month. First, the developments of the SGT and the 3708 were proceeding in earnest. Then, in mid-month, I was requested to present a paper on the SGT at the prestigious IEDM Conference (International Electron Device Meeting) that was to be held in Washington, D.C., in October. This was to be my first public speech at an international conference, and I was asked to give a dry run of my presentation to Gordon Moore, head of the R&D Lab. I was happy that my work had been chosen but I was also surprised by the decision to divulge this project before it was completed. I was 26 years old, still learning English and trying to understand the American culture, so I just thought that in America things were done this way.

Also during June, Fairchild Semiconductor, which was then directed by Bob Noyce, decided to sell its stake in SGS-Fairchild in a surprising move. Vadasz offered me a job to stay at Fairchild and I gladly accepted since I wanted to finish my project, and both Elvia and I had no desire to return to Italy. My official date of employment was set for July 1, 1968.

On July 1 the lab was abuzz with news that Gordon Moore and Bob Noyce had left Fairchild to start a new company, later to be called Intel. In short order, many other employees including Andy Grove and Les Vadasz left Fairchild to join the new company. I immediately suspected that Intel would use the SGT given the strong interest shown by Vadasz, Grove, and Moore in my project. My suspicion became near-certainty when Intel also hired the technician who made the vacuum evaporation of silicon for my experiments. Tom Klein assumed the position vacated by Vadasz and became my new boss. Klein, Vadasz, and Grove were Hungarians who had fled their country as young men during the 1956 uprising. They were socially connected, and Vadasz and Grove had become close friends.

Throughout the four and a half months Vadasz had been my US boss, he kept a matter-of-fact stance with me, never showing much appreciation for the work I was doing as a guest scientist-engineer. I was excited about the possibilities of the SGT and a bit puzzled about his apparent nonchalance. It was beyond the range of my imagination to think that all these people would start a company based on the technology I was developing.

In October of 1968, I presented the SGT technology at the IEDM Conference in Washington, D.C., (Fig. 12) [1], following Gordon Moore's decision to disclose that technology in June of that year, a few weeks before he left Fairchild to found Intel.

IEEE - 68C46 - ED

INTERNATIONAL ELECTRON DEVICES MEETING

OCTOBER 23, 24, and 25, 1968

3.4 INSULATED GATE FIELD EFFECT TRANSISTOR INTEGRATED CIRCUITS WITH SILICON GATES, F. Faggin, T. Klein and L. Vadasz, Fairchild Semiconductor Research and Development Laboratory, Palo Alto, Calif.

The Silicon Gate Technology is a new approach to fabricating insulated gate, field effect transistor circuits, in which the metal gate electrode is replaced by a doped, silicon electrode. The work function difference between the gate electrode and semiconductor bulk will now be determined by the doping of the gate electrode. This leads to normally off p-channel devices with threshold voltages typically between 1.1 v and 2.5 v on <111> material with 1000Å gate oxide. It is a self-aligned gate structure and has a buried-gate electrode which allows crossover of gate regions and closer spacing of source-drain contact. The fabrication needs 4 masking steps and was found to be compatible with existing planar technology.

Devices manufactured have shown excellent reliability features under very severe, accelerated aging conditions (—15 to —30 v reverse bias at 300°C). An integrated 8 channel MOS multiplexer with decoding logic was designed and fabricated to prove the suitability of this technology for integrated circuit manufacture.

Fig. 12 – This is a summary of the paper I presented in 1968 at the IEDM Conference in Washington, D.C. announcing the development of the SGT.

Soon after I became an employee of Fairchild, several colleagues were encouraging me to buy a home, claiming it would be a good investment that would also give many tax benefits. So in August of 1968, we decided to buy our first home with the intention of creating a more stable situation for our planned family. After scouring the area with a realtor, we finally chose a house in a new residential complex under development at the foothills of Cupertino. Elvia and I were still living in Mountain View in the same apartment we had rented shortly after our arrival in Silicon Valley.

The cost of the new home was higher than similar homes in the surrounding areas like Mountain View or Sunnyvale, but Cupertino was less crowded and closer to the hills. We also could choose the plot of land and the style of house from six different models with further customizable options. Our parents generously lent us a good portion of the money for the down payment and construction began towards the end of October. It felt like a dream to have our own home so soon after our wedding.

The residential development stood on land that a few months earlier had been a large walnut orchard. With rare foresight, not all of the trees had been cut down. On our property, we had three of them and they produced large quantities of excellent walnuts. Soon we learned how to preserve them properly so that they could be enjoyed throughout the year. We loved those generous trees which, in addition to the fruit, gave us fresh shaded areas, and shelter for the bluebirds—there were so many, it was a pleasure to watch them flutter around without fear. We planted azaleas, camellias, and rose bushes that grew wonderfully, and we maintained a perfect lawn.

Almost all of our neighbors came from other parts of the United States or other countries and worked for the various high-tech companies beginning to flourish in the area. Few of our neighbors could claim to have been born in California and this fact brought us all together and made us feel even closer to each other. We were all pioneers, even if we arrived in a Boeing instead of a horse-drawn wagon.

It is interesting to note that fifty years later, Silicon Valley has not yet lost the feel of a frontier because tens of thousands of new engineers and scientists still come every year from all over the world, bringing their vitality, skill, and spirit of adventure to the creation of an ever more connected world.

The NIH syndrome

Toward the end of 1968, after the success of the 3708, Fairchild's management decided to transfer the SGT process to the MOS production wafer fab located in Mountain View. My work on the SGT was essentially completed, even though I had to remain available to assist the production team in case any problems came up. I was also writing a voluminous document on SGT, part of the internal "Technical Publications Series" used to disseminate successful technologies and projects to other Fairchild departments.

I expected that our chip designers in the MOS division would be thrilled to have such superior new technology, but that is not what happened. Despite the commercial success of the 3708, they resisted adopting the SGT. My contact in the division had told me the circuit designers were complaining that the layout used more area than the metal-gate design, the opposite of what I had promised. This was my first encounter with what is commonly called the "NIH syndrome" which stands for "Not Invented Here" syndrome, because engineers often refuse to adopt what was not created within their division, even if the invention had been achieved in the same company.

This is typical in many big companies, a cultural problem that at Fairchild was worsened by animosity between the R&D and the operating divisions, with accusatory fingers pointing in both directions. Employees of the operating divisions complained about having to pay all the bills of the R&D scientists and engineers, and considered them haughty and interested only in their theories. R&D employees, on the other hand, criticized their colleagues in the operating divisions as being interested only in solving their immediate problems without thinking about the future.

That's when I began to understand why so many people leave their companies to start new businesses and why startups are essential for bringing new ideas into the world. I was also beginning to realize that if a company did not have a strong culture of innovation, it would likely resist new ideas because those would bring change. And the change would involve risk and require more effort, thus disturbing the status quo that many people want.

When I received negative feedback on the layout limitations of the SGT, I could not believe it. I immediately asked to see the test layouts made by the chip designers of the Fairchild's MOS division.

I was amazed to find that the engineers had automatically translated the same topology used with a metal gate into a silicon gate
without even rethinking the differences between the two technologies. No wonder they could not find any advantage! The layout with
the silicon gate required a different approach they had not figured
out although it was plain to me.

I had thought the designers would naturally understand how to
use the new technology, but I had assumed too much. I should have
given them clear examples to demonstrate how to apply it. I was so
close to my creation that the way to do the layout might have been
obvious only to me. So I prepared some examples that clearly showed
how to do the layout with the SGT, highlighting its advantages, especially when using the buried contacts (Fig. A4 in Appendix 1).

But after delivering my examples, there was a new objection. I
was told the SGT did not allow for making isolated capacitors. They
said the capacitors were indispensable to creating the *bootstrap loads*
they were using in almost all of their integrated circuits. The bootstrap load was a special type of circuit, described in Appendix 1,
that enabled achieving an output voltage equal to the supply voltage
in a dynamic logic gate, enhancing a very efficient and widely used
design technique called two-phase dynamic logic, also described
in Appendix 1. This technique was also named quasi-static logic
because it allowed for easily mixing static with dynamic logic circuits.

With their old metal gate, an isolated capacitor was trivial to
manufacture. With the new SGT, it was impossible because the
polysilicon prevented the formation of a junction under the gate
oxide. Undoubtedly, the new problem they raised was valid and its
implications were serious, although it could have easily been solved
with an additional mask. My opinion was that the benefits of the
SGT were large enough to warrant the cost of one additional masking step, but that was not the conclusion of the managers.

I understood precisely the importance of the bootstrap load for
logic circuits. But when everybody else had given up on the idea
of making isolated capacitors, I did not stop thinking about how
to get around this problem. It took about nine months before I

recognized that the metal electrode of the capacitor in a bootstrap load is always polarized in such a way that an inversion layer *would exist* in the underlying silicon, *even though there was no diffusion under the oxide.* In other words, the operating conditions of the bootstrap load were such that there would always be a "virtual diffusion" under the polysilicon, even in the absence of a real diffusion.

All I had to do was create a large area in the tub mask, corresponding to the drain of the bootstrap load transistor, and place a polysilicon region inside of it (Fig. A6 in Appendix 1). Such an insight produced in me the same exultation I felt when I had the equally simple and fundamental intuition about the tub mask, the missing idea in the work of the Bell Labs engineers. As usual, after I solved the problem, the solution appeared to be deceptively simple.

I then designed a test chip with different bootstrap load geometries to verify that the idea was sound. It was, and it worked perfectly. Finally, there was no longer any obstacle between me and the success of the SGT. My strong desire that this technology be second to none gave me the strength to persist until my work was 100 percent done, not 98 percent. I found out later that for most projects, what appears to be the last two percent takes far more time, passion, and commitment than one generally expects.

Shortly after Vadasz had left Fairchild to join Intel, I also fabricated the buried contact by using the XTPG test pattern (Figure A3 in Appendix 1). This was the invention he said would never work. As a matter of fact, it functioned perfectly on my first try and without any effort. I also made several test layouts to prove that with buried contacts the designs would be much more compact, especially for random-logic circuits.

With the addition of the bootstrap load and the buried contact, the SGT allowed for integrating into the same silicon area about twice the number of random-logic transistors than previously possible with the metal gate, and also for obtaining a speed about five times higher with the same power dissipation. These advantages were huge!

The SGT with my two additional inventions was the technology that enabled the microprocessor, DRAM memories and nonvolatile memories as early as 1970. Without these innovations, the world's first microprocessor, the Intel 4004, would not have been feasible in 1970 because it would have had to use static logic, making its cost and power dissipation prohibitive for commercial applications.

The only other practical method for making complex logic circuits was to use an entirely dynamic technique called four-phase logic. This was a complex solution that required computer-aided design and produced half the circuit density of the SGT and a quarter of its speed—still insufficient to create a microprocessor with adequate performance at a reasonable cost.

Patenting the SGT

Following the IEDM presentation of the SGT in October of 1968, its timely patenting was an important and urgent matter since Fairchild had a one-year grace period to apply after such disclosure. If they did not, the invention would become public domain and no longer be patentable. Klein was the person responsible for the protection of all the inventions made in his group, and he told me he was pursuing the patent. I knew next to nothing on matters of US patent law and trusted him. At that time, I was not even aware of the existence of the one-year grace period after public disclosure, and whenever I asked him how the application was proceeding, he reassured me that everything was going well.

In reality, he applied for a patent in October of 1970, two years after the public disclosure of the SGT, and six months after I had been hired away by Intel. The patent was finally granted on June 27, 1972, with inventors Thomas Klein and Federico Faggin under US Patent number 3.673.471. But it contained only a single claim: The use of polysilicon for the gate of the transistor obtained by thermal decomposition of silane in an atmosphere of hydrogen. This process had already existed at Fairchild and the idea of using it for the SGT was suggested by Klein, thus justifying that his name appear first in the patent.

However, the embodiment of the invention, which was the unique process architecture that I had invented, could no longer be patented because of the expiration of terms caused by the filing delay. Klein had told me more than once that he expected a job offer from Intel. But this never happened, and several months after I had left Fairchild Klein went to work for National Semiconductor and brought with him the SGT.

In mid-1969 I made another important invention at Fairchild. This one consisted of starting the silicon-gate process by growing a thin layer of silicon oxide followed by the deposition of a silicon nitride layer. The nitride was then removed chemically, except in the tub areas, by using the "negative" of the tub mask. Next, the initial oxide was thermally grown just as in the original procedure. Since the nitride layer doesn't let oxygen diffuse through it, the oxide grows everywhere except in the tubs, consuming the silicon in the wafer and thus moving the boundary of the oxide "inside" the original silicon surface for about half the total thickness of the oxide. In this manner the tub sits in the middle of the total thickness of the oxide, eliminating any possibility of breakage of the aluminum over the field-oxide steps.

My boss Klein decided not to patent this important invention, and some years later the same idea was invented independently by someone else. It became widely used in the industry under the name of LOCOS. Most disturbing though was that Klein did not patent my invention of the buried contact either. It was Vadasz who filed a patent application for the buried contact on December 28, 1970—in his name and without my knowledge—while I was already employed at Intel. His action was to protect the 1103 memory, the first 1024-bit dynamic MOS RAM, that used my invention to reduce the chip size.

When I learned approximately three years later what he'd done, I confronted him, reminding him that I had described the buried contact to him at the end of February in 1968, with Tom Klein present, and that he had been adamantly against the idea asserting that it would never work. He said he did not remember but admitted,

"The idea somehow got stuck in my mind." He proposed that we immediately talk with Andy Grove who then tried to convince me that things like this happen all the time in the industry and that it was not a big deal.

I didn't like at all the way this incident was handled. Yet, how could I have protected my interests? Sue my employer and then be blacklisted? This was one of the reasons that led me to start my first company, Zilog, Inc., about one year after this unpleasant occurrence. Afterward I found out from Tom Rowe, the MOS process development manager at Intel, that Vadasz had asked him to patent the buried contact. Tom told me that he refused, saying, "I'm not the inventor. You told me what to do." So I let him know that the buried contact was my invention at Fairchild.

In 1997 Robert W. Bower was inducted into the National Inventors Hall of Fame for the invention of the self-aligned gate MOS transistor, described in US patent No. 3.472.712. Bower understood early on the importance of making a self-aligned gate [2]. His invention used a process architecture similar to the one I had invented at Fairchild, but with aluminum rather than silicon. However, his process could not even function because it used aluminum and ion implantation rather than polysilicon and conventional thermal doping (Appendix 1 for details).

If Klein had patented my process architecture in 1968, my perfectly working invention would have prevailed over Bower's. However, since my architecture had not been patented, Bower became the official "inventor" of the MOS self-aligned gate technology even though his process was never used.

I learned at great expense that patents are important and that I should have been more careful in protecting and defending the paternity of my inventions.

The SGT becomes a milestone of the entire industry

While Fairchild had been reluctant to adopt the SGT, Intel immediately embraced it, making it the cornerstone of the company. When

Vadasz joined Intel, he had already seen the 3708 fully working and even had a copy of the SGT run sheet. This was a big advantage for them. Many years later, Gordon Moore attributed much of Intel's success to the invention of the SGT implying that the technology had been invented by his company. He also stated that it was difficult to make the SGT work, adding that this was the reason why it took a long time for the industry to copy it. But what Intel never acknowledged was that the SGT was first created at Fairchild and that the first commercial IC to use SGT was the Fairchild 3708. The main reason why Intel developed the technology relatively fast was their prior knowledge of Fairchild's work.

Intel further claimed that their 1101 (a 256-bit static RAM) was the first IC to use the SGT. They feigned the 3708 never even existed. On the other hand, the company's leaders believed in the SGT—and "believing" was the missing ingredient at Fairchild where I was the only one who understood its superiority and fought for its adoption with all my youthful passion. It was Fairchild's loss and Intel's gain. I was still at Fairchild when the 1101 was introduced, so I settled for the consolation prize of having both the SGT and the 3708 introduced in a cover story in the September, 1969 issue of the prestigious *Electronics* magazine (Fig. 13) [3].

Contrary to metal gate, the silicon gate was surrounded in its entirety by the highest quality insulator then known, silicon dioxide (quartz) thermally grown at 1200°C. This valuable property allowed for the creation of new device types that were not feasible with metal-gate technology. In early 1970, Dov Frohman joined Intel bringing with him the technology he had been experimenting with at Fairchild during 1969 and 1970. He was working on *floating* polysilicon gate devices, meaning MOS transistors with gates not connected to anything. Using quantum tunneling, it was possible to charge the floating gates with electrons, thus producing long-term nonvolatile memories. This was feasible because the floating silicon gates surrounded by quartz were perfectly insulated from the rest of the circuit.

At Intel in 1970, Frohman began designing the world's first electrically programmable ROM. Called EPROM (erasable programmable read-only memory), this memory could be erased by subjecting it to ultraviolet light and then be rewritten into. The EPROM was the forefather of a whole new class of nonvolatile memory devices, like the flash memories, for example, that have revolutionized mobile devices.

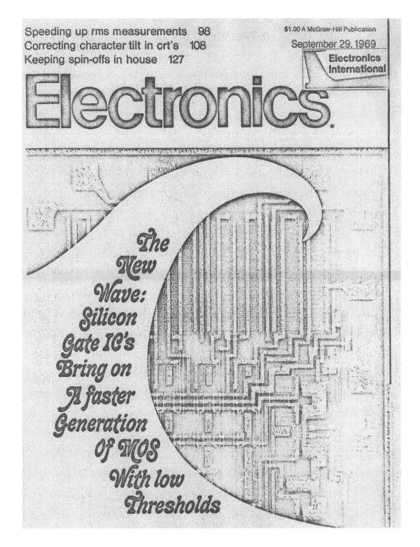

Fig. 13 – The first article published in a magazine about the SGT. This cover story described both the process technology and the first commercial IC to use self-aligned gate: The Fairchild 3708.

The SGT was also essential to realizing another important invention, the so-called charge-coupled device or CCD. Originally invented at Bell Labs in 1969 and intended to be a new type of serial memory, CCDs became the first solid-state image sensors. CCDs eventually revolutionized the entire field of cinematography, astronomy, and digital photography, greatly expanding the range of functions achievable with solid-state electronics. The first commercial CCDs were successfully produced using the SGT and marketed in 1973 by Fairchild. Without the SGT, it would have also been impossible to make fast and reliable DRAM in 1970 and the microprocessor a few months later, since the leakage current, circuit density, and speed of metal-gate MOS transistors were insufficient for these purposes.

The unconditional superiority of the SGT resulted in its universal adoption by the global semiconductor industry during the second half of the 1970s. Ten years later, the bipolar technology that had dominated the entire industry in 1968 had been completely replaced by the SGT, save for a few minor applications and legacy products destined to disappear.

Only recently did the architecture of MOS transistors have to be modified by using other gate materials to reduce their critical dimension below 45 nanometers (Fig. 14). This change occurred in 2007 and was predicated by the need to use insulators with a much higher dielectric constant than silicon dioxide. Between 1969 and 2007—a span of nearly forty years—the SGT was the workhorse for the entire semiconductor industry.

The SGT is still used today in the year 2020, in the most advanced flash memories that have reached the mind-boggling density of one terabyte (1,000 gigabytes) in a single chip, requiring the 3-D integration of more than one trillion transistors. The SGT remains one of the most influential technologies fueling the incredible progress of microelectronics, starting from the invention of the planar process.

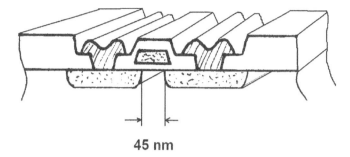

45 nm

Fig. 14 – The critical dimension of a MOS transistor is the length of the conduction channel controlled by the gate. Forty-five nanometers in the figure shown (45 nm = 45 billionths of a meter) was first achieved for production devices in 2007. In 1968 this dimension was 8,000 nm. In 2019, it had reached 7 nm, the dimension of a large protein. Illustration by F. Faggin.

3

The First Microprocessor

The microprocessor is a miracle.

—Bill Gates

By the end of 1969, Fairchild was rapidly losing its leadership, primarily due to the defection of executives and engineers who had moved to many other startups. I was quite disappointed by the slow adoption of the SGT by the MOS division. When Intel announced its first silicon gate product in the fall of 1969, I felt resentful towards both Fairchild and Intel for entirely different reasons. Intel had declared their intentions: They wanted to become the leading company in the emerging semiconductor memory market. Their main objective was to replace the magnetic core random-access memories (RAM), then universally used on mainframe computers and minicomputers, with solid-state components.

My frustration fueled my considerations to leave Fairchild. Contributing to these reflections was also my desire to become a chip designer of complex ICs using the SGT, the technology I was sure was going to speed up the progress towards large-scale integration (LSI).

I confess that a part of me also wanted to prove to Fairchild and to the world that the SGT was the best technology of all, despite objections from the Fairchild engineers and the so-called experts of almost all other semiconductor companies. I wanted to experience a liberating: "See, I told you so!" I also thought that chip design, rather than the development of manufacturing processes, would become the new frontier of microelectronics. The industry was on the verge of LSI, with the promise of building chips with more than 1,000 logic gates. This undertaking would require a lot of experience in the design of systems as well as circuits. I also wanted to return to my first interest: designing computer systems with a few chips instead of a cabinet full of printed circuit boards like I had done at Olivetti eight years before.

While I was mulling over what to do, I was contacted by National Semiconductor and interviewed by its executive vice president, Pierre Lamond. He wanted me to develop the SGT and backed up his offer with a big increase in my salary. However, I did not want to repeat the work I had already done, not to mention that it seemed unethical to transfer to National the SGT I had developed at Fairchild.

That offer, nevertheless, convinced me that it was time to leave Fairchild and gave me the incentive to contact Les Vadasz at Intel, asking if he had a challenging chip design project for me, and we set up an appointment.

Marzia

Every child that is born brings to the world the news that God is not yet tired of men.

—Rabindranath Tagore

The spring of 1970 was a period of great change: I had decided to leave Fairchild and our daughter was about to be born. We desired to have a child with all our hearts, and this time we wanted to make sure everything would turn out well, so, in her last months of pregnancy, Elvia's sister, Irene, had come from Italy to help. I felt much calmer at work now, knowing that the two sisters were keeping good company.

On the day of my preliminary interview at Intel, Elvia began to have labor pains. I immediately called Vadasz to move our appointment. He seemed annoyed by the postponement. On March 6, 1970, Marzia was born. This was the same day that Irene turned 19, and so we celebrated with a double birthday party!

Marzia had beautiful black eyes and a head covered with dark hair. To announce her arrival, we hung a large pink ribbon outside the door of our house, a purely Italian custom that aroused the curiosity of our neighbors.

Less than a month after the birth of our daughter, I was hired by Intel to be the leader of the "Busicom Project." I started working in the MOS design department headed by Vadasz, who reported to the director of operations Andy Grove. At that time Intel was still a startup with about 120 employees, of which 30 to 40 were technical and management personnel and the rest were manufacturing operators, mostly young women.

On my first day of work I met Stan Mazor, an engineer who worked for Ted Hoff, the head of the small application research group. Stan told me that the Japanese company Busicom had asked Intel to design twelve custom LSI chips based on Busicom's logic design. I later found out there were only seven chips, and they already implemented a programmable solution rather than being useful only for a single product as Mazor implied.

Stan said that Ted had come up with a set of four chips—a CPU, a ROM, a RAM, and an I/O—with which to build a general-purpose computer able to solve not only Busicom's immediate problem of making a printing desktop calculator, but also to produce more sophisticated programmable calculators with the same components. This work had been done together with Busicom's engineers over a few months during 1969.

Stan gave me the general specifications of the four chips and added with a nervous smile that Masatoshi Shima, Busicom's engineer in charge of the calculator design, would arrive in a couple of days to check on our progress. He expected to find the logic design of the

CPU completed and the other three chips already in the layout stage, as Intel had promised. The problem was that no work had been done since November of 1969 and Busicom had not been informed of that!

I was speechless when I saw the project schedule that had been committed. I had less than six months to design four chips, one of which, the CPU, was at the limit of what was then technologically possible. I had no one to share the workload with, plus Intel had never designed random-logic chips. Furthermore, Intel had neither adequate tools nor any design methodology to make a quick and error-free design. Vadasz, my boss also made it crystal clear that he had no time to help me because he was completely consumed with the development of the 1103, considered then to be the future of Intel. Lastly, he, and especially Andy Grove, thought my project to be opportunistic, unwanted, and a dangerous diversion from the strategic direction of the company. Andy later said in an interview: "I was running an assembly line designed to build memory chips. I saw the microprocessor as a bloody nuisance." But making custom circuits had been an idea imposed by Bob Noyce, Gordon Moore, and the vice president of marketing Bob Graham to get faster revenues while waiting for the memory business to mature.

The Intel 1103 was to be the first 1024-bit MOS DRAM, the product destined to break through the magic threshold of a penny-per-bit, a price that according to industry estimates would have made semiconductor memory competitive with magnetic core memory. Given the lukewarm market response to the Intel 1101, the slow and power – hungry 256-bit static RAM, the very survival of the company was tied to the future success of the 1103.

The only Intel product line with any market traction was a family of dynamic shift registers that were the second source to the shift register product family designed by National Semiconductor with metal-gate MOS technology. Thanks to the SGT, the Intel chips had better performance than those of National, allowing Intel to successfully compete at higher prices. I understood then why National was so anxious to get their hands on the SGT and had made me such a generous offer a few months earlier.

Leading the Busicom Project

Reflecting on the schedule of the Busicom Project, which had forecasted a layout time of seven weeks with two draftsmen for the CPU, only two weeks more than the time required to layout a simple memory, it was clear Vadasz had no understanding of the nature of the problem. A memory chip is much faster to layout than a random-logic chip because in a memory circuit all the cells are identical, whereas in a random-logic device almost every circuit is unique and must be individually cut to size. In the end, the layout took 14 weeks, working overtime with three draftsmen.

Fortunately I was young, eager to challenge myself, and understood computer systems as well. I knew how to do logic and circuit design and had experience in both MOS chip design and process development. Above all, I intimately knew the capabilities of the MOS SGT, a new technology that practically nobody else was familiar with at that time. This was an extremely rare combination because, even in those days, engineers were quite specialized. I felt that if I could not do it, nobody could. Indeed, I held an ace in the hole: My most recent invention, *the bootstrap load* with silicon gate that Intel did not yet know about and without which it would have been impossible to make the microprocessor.

The invention of the bootstrap load with silicon gate was indispensable to designing random-logic circuits of the complexity of the CPU with the speed, power dissipation, and cost necessary to be marketable. Moreover, given the absence of any random-logic design methodology at Intel, my deep knowledge of the SGT led me to develop a new approach for random-logic chips that could exploit the strengths of the SGT. This method was based on the use of the bootstrap load (replaced a few years later with depletion loads) and on the adoption of the buried contacts that allowed two layers of interconnections. It turned out to be highly successful and was used for all the early generations of microprocessors at Intel and Zilog, the company I founded at the end of 1974.

A couple of days after the start of my new job, I went with Stan to the San Francisco airport to meet Masatoshi Shima arriving from Tokyo. Shima was anxious to verify the progress that had been made since his last visit in October of 1969. In particular, he wanted to check the logic design of the CPU to make sure it would work in accordance with the agreed-upon specifications. As head of the project, I gave him the material Stan had handed me a couple of days before. He told me impatiently that he had already seen those documents many months before. When he discovered that this was all there was to check, he became furious with me. In his anger, he did not seem to understand that if no work had been done during the previous five to six months, it was not my fault given that I had just been hired.

It took almost a week for him to calm down and accept the situation. During that time, I resolved a couple of architectural problems I had found and started working on the missing design methodology. I also prepared a new schedule that would give Busicom the first samples of the four chips by the end of December, on condition that I could immediately hire an engineer and a couple of draftsmen to help.

My new plan was extremely demanding and required me to work seventy to eighty hours a week to keep the overall schedule, which was nearly impossible to achieve, yet had been promised by Vadasz. I told Shima that if he helped me there would be a chance of meeting the deadline since it would take time to hire the people I needed. The difficulties were resolved when Busicom accepted the new plan and Shima was given permission to stay for six months to assist me. Finally, I could start designing the "4000 family," the new name I had given the project.

My first impressions

My initial impression was mixed. I liked the idea of creating a CPU in a single chip, a possibility that had been talked about for some time. In fact, Lee Boysel, head of the MOS design group at Fairchild, was the first I know to advance this same idea in 1968, stating that with MOS technology it would be possible to realize a CPU in a few chips and eventually in a single chip. I also liked the idea of a family of chips working perfectly together as a system.

However, despite being enthusiastic about designing a CPU on a chip, I had several misgivings about the proposed architecture. I found it incomprehensible to use 16-pin packages for all the chips, especially for the CPU, because it forced the use of a single 4-bit bus to shuttle the 12-bit addresses and the 8-bit instructions four bits at a time, thus heavily sacrificing the hard-to-get speed. But utilizing only 16-pin packages was dogma at Intel in those days, even though the adoption of up to 40-pin packages was already widespread in the industry.

Furthermore, the way the CPU addressed RAM seemed to me rather baroque, to put it mildly, requiring a complicated sequence as if it were an I/O operation. I could not understand why addressing RAM had to be so convoluted and different from any other CPU. There had to be a better way of doing it. But the last thing I needed, given the enormous delays with the project, was to modify an architecture that had already been blessed by the customer. So I devoted myself solely to verifying that the architecture was free of errors and set my heart at peace for the long journey needed to make the 4000 family a reality.

Designing the 4000 Family

The credit belongs to the man who is actually in the arena.
—Theodore Roosevelt

Designing a production integrated circuit required many steps, starting with the formulation of the architecture and basic specifications of each chip, followed by the logic design, circuit design, layout, and so on. The first step was done by Ted Hoff, with the assistance of Stan Mazor, interacting with the Busicom team. The task of Hoff's "Application Research" group ended with the specifications of the chips. Everything else had to be done in the MOS design department, where the actual design and development of the chips took place.

I led the project in that department without any further contributions from Hoff and Mazor, neither of whom were chip designers. Indeed, Ted Hoff distanced himself from the project and never took an interest in its progress. Early on I had asked him to clarify some points of his architecture, but he answered dryly: "It's your project now, you need to figure it out yourself." I was taken aback and after that response there was no further communication between us for the entire length of the project.

After completion of the specifications, the design of each chip went through the following sequence:

1. Logic design
2. Circuit design
3. Composite layout
4. Rubylith cutting
5. Mask-making
6. Fabrication of first silicon
7. Test and debugging of the chip
8. Modification of the chip in case of problems
9. Chip characterization
10. Development of production test patterns
11. Transfer to production

Just the process of going from circuit design to fabrication of the first devices (called first silicon) required a minimum of six to nine months depending on the complexity of the chip. From first silicon to transfer to production, it took another three to eight months, conditioned by any difficulties encountered. Therefore, from start to finish, anywhere from nine to 17 months were needed. After the transfer to production, the responsibility for the product would rest with the production engineers.

Most other MOS semiconductor companies such as Fairchild Semiconductor, Texas Instruments, AMI, and General Instruments, had experience in custom circuit design. Their main business was in fact in custom chips, the primary application of MOS technology at that time. They had extensive libraries of circuits for which layouts and operations were already characterized and guaranteed. They also had sophisticated computer simulation programs for the design and verification of logic and circuits and for the generation of test programs. Not to mention the special equipment for the characterization and testing of logic circuits, and the presence of engineers experienced in the entire process who could guide new employees to design rapidly and flawlessly.

Intel had none of these resources and yet it was embarking on designing a CPU that no one had ever attempted before. What's more, the only technology that could do the job, the SGT, was a gamble because it had never been used for random-logic circuits and required a different layout style than the metal gate used by all the other companies.

Due to the lack of methodology, adequate infrastructure, and expert logic chip personnel, I was forced to perform many more tasks than those of a typical project leader in this field. I also had to make the logic design of the four chips, a task that was normally performed by the customer. Above all, it was necessary to invent the new design methodology with SGT, starting with the worst-case design of the logic circuits. I needed to establish the set of rules that would ensure that a logic gate would work under the worst combination of supply voltage, temperature, and manufacturing process variations. I also had to design and build a tester for the debugging and characterization of logic chips because Intel had similar equipment for only memory chips.

I had promised Busicom delivery of samples of all four chips by December of 1970—under duress, I might add—less than nine months away. And since the CPU alone would have required more than eight months, we had to work on all four chips simultaneously, staggering them so that critical resources could be used optimally. I decided to start the design in the sequence of 4001, 4003, 4002, and 4004 because it would allow me to incrementally develop the methodology and most of the circuits needed for the extremely challenging chip: the 4004. Besides, Intel could regain Busicom's confidence by showing that the simpler chips would work at first silicon.

The 4001, 4002, and 4003 chips

The 4001 was a 2048-bit read-only memory (ROM), state of the art at that time, with the addition of four metal-mask programmable I/O lines and relative control logic, which was more than twice the amount of random logic used in a standard ROM. A ROM is a type of memory that can only be read but not changed. The software code, called firmware, is generally developed by the customer and is indelibly "written" into the chip with a custom metal mask towards the end of the manufacturing process.

I did the combined logic and circuit design in a couple of weeks and gave it to Shima to check. He was a good logic designer and was also the engineer assigned to develop the firmware for the Busicom calculator—the first intended application of the 4000 family—however, he was not a chip designer and knew little about MOS circuit design and technology. But he made up for that inexperience by being interested in learning and extremely detail-oriented, important qualities given the lack of verification tools at Intel.

At the beginning of the design work, I told Vadasz that I had to use bootstrap loads for each chip, otherwise the job could not be done (See Appendix 1 for technical details). I assured him that I had already solved the problem at Fairchild and that I had verified its operation. Convinced like everyone else that bootstrap loads were impossible with the silicon-gate process, he either did not trust or didn't understand. So he asked me to explain it to Dov Frohman, a PhD in physics who had left Fairchild about a month before me.

When I first told Dov that I had finally figured out how to do the bootstrap loads, he scolded me: "You can't make isolated capacitors with silicon gates!" So I explained in detail how they worked and told him that I had already successfully built and tested them at Fairchild. He left without saying a word.

The next day I saw Bob Abbott, the engineer who reported to Vadasz on the 1103, drawing what looked like bootstrap capacitors on the 1103 layout. I asked him what he was doing. He replied, "Vadasz told me to put these capacitors here." I asked if he told him where the idea came from. Bob answered, "No. He didn't say anything about that." Vadasz had taken my solution without acknowledging that I was the one who had solved that tricky and long-standing problem and now championed bootstrap loads when everybody else had given up.

To avoid having to do computer simulations of the various circuits, except in extraordinary cases, I prepared a series of standardized MOS characteristics based on actual measurements of the worst-case transistors manufactured by Intel. Using these charts, I could quickly calculate the size of the transistors needed to achieve the required speed based on the expected capacitive load. It was a graphical calculation method like the one I had learned at the Rossi Institute to size vacuum tube circuits, well before computer simulations were possible.

Another of the early challenges was to invent a new type of flip-flop, a circuit that can only exist in one of two states, that when powered up would always come up in the same state instead of a random one. This was necessary because all 16 pins of the 4001 had been used and there were no other pins available for an external reset signal. This flip-flop was essential to guarantee that immediately after the power was turned on, the state of the external bus connecting all the chips would "float" to avoid any bus contention that could damage the chips. The circuit I invented for this purpose worked very well and it was later patented for Intel under my name [6].

The layout of the 4001 began the day my first draftsman, Rod Sayre, showed up for work. He came from Lockheed where he was a mechanical draftsman and didn't even know what a chip was. At that time layout draftsmen were harder to find than engineers, and all the ones working at Intel were busy with memory projects. This meant I had to train Rod from scratch. Over time he learned the trade, but at first I had to draw freehand all the circuits of the 4001 and Rod simply copied them in final form with a ruler, placing them where I showed him in the composite layout. It took a couple of months before he became proficient.

After the 4001 layout was completed, Rod laid out the 4003 in two to three weeks. The 4003 was the only simple chip of the family. It had a 10-stage static shift register with serial input, serial output, and 10 parallel outputs enabled by appropriate signals. The 4003s could be cascaded to create longer shift registers to scan keyboards, control printers, and work for many other applications.

I designed the 4003 in a couple of days by using a new static flip-flop that I had co-invented with Fabio Capocaccia when I was working at SGS-Fairchild. I had employed that circuit in a commercial 16-bit static shift register I designed in Italy in 1967 [7]. I utilized the same flip-flop extensively for the counters and several other functions in all the 4000 family members because it reduced the number of transistors compared to other known circuits.

Then came the turn for the 4002, the RAM memory for data. The 4002 was organized into four registers of 16 + 4 nibbles each (a nibble is equal to four bits) for a total of 320 bits. Each dynamic RAM cell used three transistors like the cell employed in the 1103, and the chip had a 4-bit addressable output port. The 4002 included a fair amount of additional logic over a standard DRAM to provide on-chip memory refresh, the decoding of some special instructions for the 4-bit output register, and all the internal timing.

Its layout was done by a new employee who came from Fairchild, Julie Hendricks, the same draftswoman who had laid out the Fairchild 3708 a few years earlier. Fortunately, Julie had good experience, though mainly with bipolar ICs, so my workload was not increased too much. When Rod finished the 4003 layout he joined Julie to speed up the layout of the 4002.

Extremely busy, I was mostly absent from my family life and could not give Elvia much support in taking care of our newborn daughter. Fortunately her sister Irene gave her a helping hand. But when Irene had to return home to Vicenza, about three months after our daughter's birth, Elvia decided to leave with her, seizing the opportunity to introduce Marzia to grandparents and uncles. I could now devote myself, body and soul, to my work without feeling too guilty about my absence.

Before leaving Elvia asked me to continue keeping her informed about the progress of my work as we had been doing, especially on weekends when we would typically go for a long walk in the hills. She would then ask me a lot of questions about my work environment, the people I was interacting with, and especially the projects I was working on. I was happy to explain her what I was doing, even though her background was in humanities. She was also reading the electronics magazines I was a subscriber of, especially Electronics and Electronic News. And all this interest turned out to be quite useful when, years later, she was offered the opportunity to become a technology writer for an Italian publisher of popular electronics magazines.

The 4004 microprocessor

Finally it was time to start the design of the most complex chip, the 4004, while simultaneously keeping the other three chips moving along, each in a different phase of development. I also had to design and build a tester for the debugging and chip characterization that had to be ready two months later when the first silicon of the 4001 was expected to be ready. Happily, Hal Feeney, an engineer who had previously worked for General Instrument on several custom MOS chips with random logic, and Paul Metrovich, an electronics technician, were assigned to help me with the design and construction of the tester. We started with a discarded memory system and built a programmable pattern generator by adding new electronics, a paper tape reader, and adjustable pin electronics for driving and measuring the signals going in and out of the chips. The instrument was completed only a few days before receiving the 4001 wafers.

After I had designed a good part of the logic of the 4004, Shima offered to complete it. The remaining work was the control section which required a lot of attention. With the knowledge he had acquired from assisting me, I felt comfortable that he could perform the task given that I had already created all of the 4004's fundamental logic and circuit building blocks.

I had also perfected the design methodology, specifically the technique of combining logic and circuit design in a single document that contained the notion of how the chip would be organized in the layout. This method avoided the potential translation errors in the conversion from the logic diagram to the circuit diagram, and from circuits to the layout (Fig. 15). Moreover, it was possible to make a reasonable estimate of the load capacitances that the various circuits had to drive from the same document so that the transistors could be suitably dimensioned without further ado.

Given the extremely tight deadline, I had to start the 4004 layout before the design was completed. Therefore, I coordinated with Shima so that I could keep the draftsmen busy and get an excellent layout density while the rest of the design was still in progress. It was like fast-tracking a building, i.e., starting the building before the construction plans were completed; and since the 4004 was at the limit of what could be produced economically, I could not afford to waste any precious silicon real estate.

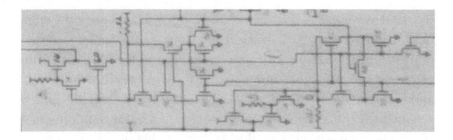

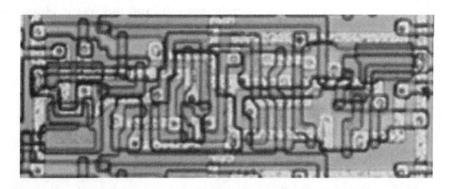

Fig. 15 –The figure shows the original circuit schematic and relative layout of a random logic circuit comprising 24 components (23 transistors and one capacitor for a bootstrap load on the lower left), which is part of the arithmetic unit of the 4004. Just for size, the entire chip contains about 2300 components.

Barbara Manness, an experienced memory layout draftswoman who had been at Intel from the beginning, joined Julie and Rod on the 4004 layout team. However, since none of them had ever done a layout with such a complex logic chip, I had to provide continuous supervision and coordination. Each draftsman had their drawing board and was working on a separate sheet of mylar. All these sheets then had to be merged seamlessly. I was the one who needed to maintain the overview and control of the final artwork to assure its integrity once the separate pieces would come together. And this was a real challenge, for no errors were allowed. The layout of the 4004 lasted about 14 weeks for a total of 42 man-weeks, compared to the five man-weeks required for the layout of the 4001.

After completing the layout of the 4004, I followed my urge to sign my work with my initials, F.F., in the metal layer of the layout itself, just like artists sign their creations. The silicon design was the essence of the first microprocessor and every line was necessary, functional, significant, and economical, while also contributing to the overall aesthetic effect. It was a work of art that established a new state of the art in microelectronics.

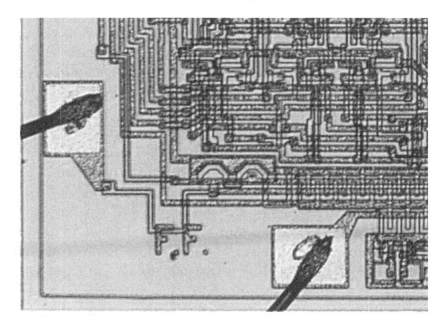

Fig. 16 – Magnification of the initials of Federico Faggin (F.F.) on the 4004.

This urge proved useful later when I left Intel to found Zilog and Intel tried to disavow my paternity of the 4004. My initials were like a "smoking gun," a proof of authorship reproduced millions of times and present in every chip produced—a claim that could not be erased.

Once the composite layout was completed, the long and error-prone process of creating the necessary masks for the chip fabrication began. First, it was necessary to generate a separate artwork for each mask, called rubylith or ruby, and then the rubies were delivered to an external service company that produced the masks by photoreduction of the rubies and by repeating the same chip pattern in an array that covered the entire surface of the mask. Appendix 2 describes this process in detail for the interested reader.

The ruby was a sheet of transparent mylar coated with a thin film of semitransparent red mylar that could be cut with a knife and peeled away from its backing layer. The ruby was placed on top of the composite layout on a precision cutting table so that the composite served as a guide for the process of cutting and peeling to expose the areas that would eventually be etched on the wafer. Checking the 4004's rubies took a few weeks of intense work and could only be done at the end of the process, while checking the composite could be carried out as it progressed. Shima and I bore most of the load for the ruby checking, although Hal Feeney and others also lent watchful eyes to catch any mistakes.

While the rubies of the 4004 were being checked, I received the first silicon of the 4001. I was nervous because this was the real test of my methodology: if the 4001 did not work properly, all the other chips would show the same problems. The construction of the tester had just ended, and I was happy when the oscilloscope showed the familiar waveforms that I had drawn so many times on paper. Now they were painted live on the display. I was almost stunned that the chip behaved exactly as it should have after so much work and so many passages prone to error: it was the miracle of technology and meticulous, patient attention! After a few days of checking and rechecking, I found that everything worked as designed, not only at room temperature but also at high temperatures and with excellent safety margins in both clock frequency and supply voltage. It was a great relief! My methodology had passed the litmus test and I no longer saw any obstacles for the remaining chips.

Fig. 17 – The Intel 4001. This chip was a 2048 bit ROM with metal mask, and was used to store the computer program. The chip also contained a section of programmable logic, also with metal mask, to give four lines of personalized input/output.

While the 4001 testing was proceeding, the ruby-checking of the 4004 had ended and Shima was about to return to Japan having already seen that the 4001 was working perfectly. On his way back home he took a detour to Egypt for a well-deserved vacation, while I continued to work 70 to 80 hours a week for many more months before I could take a break.

A few weeks later I was given the first 4003 silicon. That chip was also fully functional, which increased my confidence even further. At the end of November, the first silicon of the 4002 arrived. It also worked perfectly, except for a minor error that was quickly identified and resolved.

It works!

Finally the great day came when I received the first wafers of the 4004. The moment of truth had arrived. It was late in the afternoon a few days before New Year's Eve, 1970, and most employees had already left the laboratory. If the 4004 worked, I would meet the impossible schedule I had committed to Busicom almost nine months earlier. I was tense, but fortunately nobody else was around to witness me in that state. The hum of the instruments was the comforting background to the heavy beating of my heart that I could almost hear. With shaking hands, I put the first wafer on the prober, a special tool for making electrical contact on chips that are still integrated on the wafer. I lowered the probes on the first chip, waiting to see on the data bus the now-familiar activity just as the others in the family had shown … but … nothing happened. Without being discouraged, I said to myself, *it must be a bad chip*.

I lowered the probe onto another chip and then onto several more but kept getting the same result. *Maybe this is a bad wafer*, I thought. Then I tried another wafer, but the results were the same. At that point I was sweating profusely. For a moment I thought: *Nothing works! How could I have screwed up so badly?* Then I decided to look at the chips under the microscope, and sure enough the problem became obvious. During the manufacturing process, the buried contact mask was left out by a technician's oversight, so most of the transistors were not connected, hence no life. Now the schedule had been irreparably compromised by a trivial manufacturing mistake that was going to cost about a three-week delay. What a disappointment!

Weeks later I received a new run of 4004 chips. As usual, the wafers were delivered to me at the end of the day when the lab was almost deserted, and so I settled to spend most of the night testing the 4004. This time nothing had been overlooked and I made sure of that by checking a wafer under the microscope before loading it onto the prober. I breathed much easier after the familiar signals on the 4004 data bus appeared on the oscilloscope. From that point on everything proceeded beautifully. I kept on probing until about four a.m. and found that everything was working as expected.

Exhausted, I finally went home. As soon as she heard me enter, Elvia awoke from a light sleep that had overcome her as she anxiously waited: "How did it go?" Excited, I exclaimed: "It works!" We embraced, almost overwhelmed with feelings of euphoria and happiness, aware that something epochal had happened. On that cold January night of 1971, the world's first microprocessor was born!

I had just turned 29 and realized that nine years earlier I had finished building another computer by using thousands of germanium transistors and other discrete components. That computer had about the same characteristics as this new one, except the new one fit on a single printed circuit board instead of a few hundred, was 10 times faster, and consumed almost one thousand times less energy. Not to mention the cost. In those nine years, the progress in microelectronics had been truly miraculous.

During the following two weeks, I continued testing the 4004 and found two or three minor problems which I diagnosed and resolved quickly. Meanwhile, Busicom had built an entire simulator for the 4004 so that their calculator's firmware could be conveniently developed, verified, and modified if necessary. In the simulator, a RAM had taken the place of the 4001 ROMs. This was needed because the 4001 was programmed with a metal mask that took several weeks to fabricate and therefore was appropriate only when the firmware had been completely debugged.

Shortly after hearing the good news, Busicom sent me the four fully-verified ROM codes which contained the firmware of their first product, the Busicom 141-PF printing calculator. We could now manufacture the 4001 in parallel with the revision of the 4004 without affecting the calculator's production schedule. And in mid-March, when I received the first silicon of the revised 4004, we had also completed the 4001s.

Busicom could now test the operation of the entire calculator using an engineering prototype that was ready to receive all the missing components. When the calculator was turned on, it worked perfectly with all the 4000 family chips. A fantastic result! And a giant relief.

Intel immediately began selling components to Busicom in volume, avoiding the long design-in phase that normally follows the development of a standard product. The unique engineering prototype of the 141-PF calculator was later gifted to me personally by Yoshio Kojima, president of Busicom, in recognition of my successful leadership of the 4000 family. After keeping this historic heirloom in our home for 25 years, our family donated it to the Computer History Museum in Mountain View, California, in 1996 where it is displayed as the prototype of the world's first product to ever use a microprocessor.

Fig. 18 – The first CPU-on-a-chip in the world: The Intel 4004. This 4-bit microprocessor contained about 2300 random-logic transistors. The instruction cycle used eight clock periods of a two-phase clock at 750 kHz, lasting 10.7 microseconds. The typical power dissipation was 750 mW,

The Intel 8008 Microprocessor

In late 1969, Computer Terminal Corporation (CTC)—later renamed Datapoint Corporation—visited Intel with another custom circuit proposal. CTC was already purchasing Intel's MOS shift registers for its terminals, a typical application of shift registers at that time. They had plans to build a new intelligent terminal called Datapoint 2200, which had at its heart a simple CPU of its design to be implemented with bipolar TTL logic circuits, as was also commonly done at the time. TTL stands for transistor-transistor logic, a rich family of bipolar logic integrated circuits that had become the industry standard.

CTC had turned to Intel for the design of a custom bipolar RAM IC to perform the function of the stack pointer register of their CPU because their computer also was intended to use serial data memory made with shift registers. In those days, the stack pointer register was necessary to save the memory addresses of the main program to return to, following the execution of a jump-to-subroutine instruction. With only shift register read-write memory, it was too complicated to keep track of the return addresses in shift register memory. When they described to Stan Mazor the purpose of their custom chip, he boasted that Intel had the technology to make their entire CPU in a single MOS chip, not just the stack pointer, if they switched from serial memory to DRAM. That was indeed a bold statement to make given that Stan was not a chip designer. It occurred to me later that the CTC situation was a repeat of the one with Busicom.

CTC was eventually persuaded that Intel could integrate their 8-bit CPU into a single MOS chip and signed a contract for its development. The chip was internally called 1201 and Hal Feeney had been hired to head the project a few weeks before I had joined Intel. It was some weeks after joining Intel when I found out with great disappointment that there was another microprocessor in development. My displeasure was heightened by the fact that the CPU architected by CTC was more advanced and had a more general-purpose traditional architecture than the 4004.

I thought the CTC chip would be finished before the 4004 since Hal only had to design one chip, while I had four and my microprocessor was to be designed last. Nevertheless, I was so absorbed with the many challenges that I soon forgot about the 1201. As it turned out, Hal's project dragged on for a few months without much progress. It was then put on ice and Hal was moved to design a custom 512-bit static memory. In the summer of 1970, Vadasz then assigned Hal to help me design and build the characterization tester for the 4000 family.

Hal was primarily a logic designer. At General Instrument he had designed several custom chips by using their methodology and their many predefined and pre-characterized circuit blocks that Intel did not have. He was thus left to fend for himself at Intel without much help, just like me. And he had never designed a chip with silicon-gate technology. Contributing to the abandonment of the 1201 was CTC's decision in the summer of 1970 to proceed with the design of a TTL version of the CPU since the cost of TTL had recently collapsed, thereby making the price quoted for the 1201 no longer attractive.

Then, in late 1970, Bob Graham, Intel's vice president of marketing, found another company interested in the 1201. Japan's Seiko Electronics wanted to make a programmable desktop calculator to compete with the Hewlett-Packard HP 9100. Seiko's interest convinced Intel to negotiate with CTC for the right to use their architecture in exchange for forgiveness of their contractual obligation to pay for the 1201 chip development they no longer needed. This was a good deal for Intel since they had invested almost nothing in the 1201 chip design.

In January of 1971, as soon as the 4004 was successfully completed, Vadasz gave me the responsibility of directing the 1201 project by supervising Hal Feeney. My experience, combined with the now proven methodology and the existence of all necessary circuit building blocks, allowed Hal to do the detailed design of the 1201 by following the model of the 4004 thus bringing the project to its happy conclusion.

The 1201 required all of 1971 to complete. The CPU architected by CTC was as simple as the 4004 but more general-purpose and therefore more useful. It required more transistors only because the length of its word was 8-bit instead of four. The first silicon came out in December of 1971 and the product became commercially available in April of 1972 with the new name 8008 to indicate an 8-bit microprocessor. It was the world's first 8-bit microprocessor and became the "founding father" of the spectacularly successful x86 family of Intel microprocessors still powering most personal computers and workstations in use today.

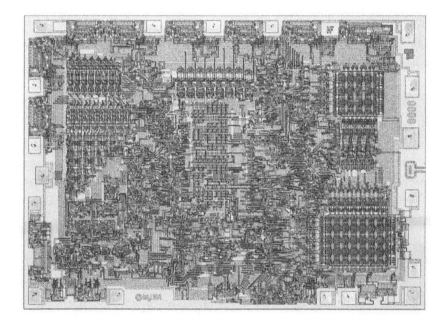

Fig. 19 – Intel 8008, the world's first 8-bit microprocessor. Note the similarity of the layout of the 8008 with that of the 4004. Introduced in April, 1972, the 8008 was packaged in an 18-pin package, could address 16 KB of memory and had an instruction cycle of twelve microseconds.

At the steering wheel of the winning car

An interesting and instructive development that came to light in April of 1971 provides an example of what often happens behind the scenes of the official stories. That month, Texas Instruments (TI) announced with much fanfare that it had successfully designed "the world's first CPU-on-a-chip." This announcement came more than a month after the 4004 had already been completed and sold to Busicom. In other words, TI claimed to have designed what they believed was the first microprocessor. Later we discovered that this development started as a custom project for CTC as a second source for the 1201 it had commissioned to Intel. The specifications that CTC had provided to TI were identical to those of the 1201. However, TI used the metal-gate technology, and therefore their chip area was twice that of the 1201 (8008), a size that Intel would have considered prohibitive to produce. This is a clear demonstration of the advantages of the silicon-gate technology with buried contacts and bootstrap loads compared to metal-gate technology.

Many years later, Vic Poor, CTC's engineering vice president and the person who negotiated the 1201 contract with both Intel and TI, told me that the TI chip never worked and was never used by his company. It was not introduced to the market either, not even after Intel's public announcement of the 4004 and 8008. It was only used for PR purposes. This shows that implementing the microprocessor at that time proved to be an impossible challenge even for TI, the top supplier of custom chips in the world, the company that had mastered the art of random-logic chips better than anyone else.

Even if the TI chip had worked, the credit for the microprocessor would still belong to Intel because the 4004 was first sold in March of 1971, one month before TI announced having prototypes of their chip. Execution was crucial, considering that the 4004 and the TI chip had started at about the same time.

In 1970 developing the microprocessor was an open competition among the best in the industry, and not a revolutionary idea. The microprocessor was inevitable, but its implementation required a sufficiently powerful technology. It was the SGT with bootstrap loads and buried contact that had the *right stuff* to reach the finish line first. The paternity of the microprocessor therefore belongs to the first one who invented the technology to successfully implement it and who also designed the chip, rather than to someone who conceived a specific architecture.

Many engineers by the end of the Sixties knew how to architect a simple CPU but not how to integrate all that circuitry into a single chip and make it work. The 4004 not only set a new standard for state-of-the-art technology, but also represented a work of great passion and dedication. I was indeed the driver at the steering wheel of the winning car.

The Blue Pheasant

Elvia and Bob Abbott's wife, Leslie, had become good friends. They often met at each other's homes to chat and let the girls, who were the same age, play together. One day the Abbotts invited us to spend the evening with them at a Cupertino restaurant-bar with a catchy name, The Blue Pheasant. They added, "It'll be a fun dinner with a big surprise." I had never eaten pheasant, but I knew it was considered a delicacy. What I did not know was another one of its features that had fascinated entire generations. I would discover that shortly thereafter.

The place was nice with sweeping views of an adjacent golf course, but the menu only listed traditional American cuisine. Was this the surprise? Fresh Pacific seafood instead of the tasty pheasant I was anticipating?

No way! The surprise came after dinner when the lights went dark, the music started, and the DJ announced that the dance competition was about to start and invited all those present to participate. Suddenly I understood why the place was called The Blue Pheasant! The pheasant is famous not only for its delicious meat but also for its enchanting dances, to the extent that Native Americans performed ritual dances in its honor.

I turned to Bob in embarrassment. I did not consider myself a good dancer, and even less someone who would participate in a dance competition. Bob, who was a skilled dancer, burst out laughing: "Come on, the important thing is to participate." He took Leslie by the hand and dashed with her to the dance floor. They looked to us as if they were already the winners.

Well, let's roll, then, Elvia and I exchanged a glance of understanding. We started dancing, determined only to have fun since we knew we had no chance. So we let ourselves go with the most animated steps, pirouetting through the room, inventing moves, under the amused gaze of our friends.

Then the music changed, the lights went dark blue and the slow dancing started. As I danced with Elvia in my arms, I felt a deep pervading emotion. God how I loved her! I could feel light coming out of my eyes and the same from her eyes. I felt like everything around us had disappeared, and that the two of us were soaring above the ground. The music ended, and still a bit emotional, hand in hand, we returned to our table.

At that point the DJ announced the winners. To our complete surprise, we heard the winners were … us! But even bigger than our surprise was that of Bob and Leslie, though they kindly congratulated us. The prize consisted of a small goblet-shaped silver cup. That improbable trophy made us laugh so much that we still smile to this day thinking about it.

From Exclusivity to the Worldwide Market

Early in the design of the 4000 family I discovered that Intel had stipulated an exclusivity clause with Busicom, making them the only beneficiary of that microprocessor family. I was disappointed because I anticipated a great market potential for it and wanted my work to have a far greater impact than just being a custom job for one customer. As the 4004 project neared completion, I started lobbying Intel's management to find a way out of the exclusivity agreement so that the microprocessor could be sold in the open market. Hoff and Mazor believed that the 4000 family would be primarily suitable for calculator-like applications and were sure that Busicom would never give up its rights. They also thought that the 8008 architecture was more suitable for general use than the 4000 family. Besides, they were concerned about how to market the microprocessor, a chip unlike any other.

But I was convinced there were many control applications in which the 4000 family would work well, despite its limitations, and decided to find out for myself. The opportunity came soon with a new project: The design and construction of a tester for the wafer-sorting of the 4004. For the tester control system, I decided to use the 4004 instead of a "state machine" made with TTL components as was commonly done then. I thought this would be the best way to find out if the 4004 was up to the task, and I also wanted to directly explore how other customers could use the 4000 family.

There were no programming tools for the 4004 and I did not have much time, therefore I wrote the program for the tester using mnemonic instructions and then translated them by hand into machine language, i.e., into the ones and zeros that reside in ROM. This was the essential task that had to be performed automatically by an assembler, thus making it the first customer tool needed. Since the 4001 (ROM memory) required a custom metal mask and made sense only when multiple copies of the same device were needed, I decided to use the product that Dov Frohman was then complet-ing: The 1702, the world's first electrically programmable and UV (ultraviolet light) erasable ROM (EPROM). The 1702 was intended to help develop, debug, and prototype the ROM codes then widely used in the industry for a variety of applications. Once the debug of the firmware had been completed in the field with EPROM, the code would be translated into conventional ROM chips with much lower production cost.

In my case, only one EPROM was needed for the development of a one-of-a – kind product in which a laborious TTL design was replaced with software much easier to develop and change. To do so, all I needed was to design an appropriate interface between the 4004 and the 1702, so that the 1702-plus-interface would behave like a 4001.

The tester design was successful and further convinced me that the 4004 would be effective for many control applications. I used this experience to continue lobbying Intel executives to widely market the 4000 family. I tried principally to convince Ed Gelbach, who seemed to be open to the idea. He was the new vice president of marketing, formerly the marketing manager at TI, who had recently replaced Bob Graham.

Finally, during a telephone conversation with Shima in the middle of 1971, I discovered that Busicom was in financial trouble. It could not effectively win against competitors that had calculators based on conventional custom designs, primarily because the price it was paying Intel for the chips was too high. He also told me that Bob Noyce and Ed Gelbach were to visit Busicom shortly. This was precious information. I mentioned my conversation with Shima to Bob Noyce, suggesting that he could get a release from exclusivity in exchange for lowering the price. Of course, I once again emphasized the fact that the 4004 had proved to be extremely valuable for control applications based on my direct experience with the tester project. Shortly after their visit to Busicom, I learned they indeed had obtained the release from exclusivity and that Intel had decided to introduce the 4000 family to the open market. I was delighted!

Announcing the microprocessor to the world

Ed Gelbach appointed Hank Smith, a promising engineer already employed at Intel, to direct the marketing of the emergent microprocessor business. Hal Feeney and I, along with Hoff and Mazor, helped the newly formed marketing organization prepare the technical documentation and market strategy for the launch. Hank coined a new name for the 4000 family: MCS-4, which stands for Micro Computer System-4 (bit) [8], [9].

The MCS-4 was followed by the introduction of the MCS-8, with the 8008 at its center, at the beginning of 1972. The rest of the MCS-8 family members were mainly standard Intel memories, which had been elegantly renamed with 8 – suffixes as if they had been expressly developed for the MCS-8 family. For example, the 2102 static memory was renamed 8102.

The birth of the microprocessor was officially declared to the world in November of 1971, eight months after the first sale to Busicom. A two-page advertisement published in the weekly *Electronic News* proclaimed: "Announcing a new era of integrated electronics," followed by a description of the key features of the MCS-4 family (Fig. 20). The impact of the microprocessor on our lives has been truly revolutionary, a statement that can only be applied to a few other inventions in the last century.

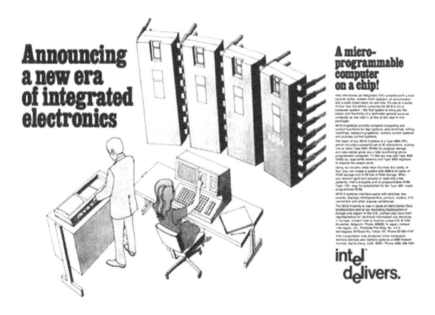

Fig. 20 – The first announcement of the microprocessor. This was truly a prophetic statement, a rare case in advertising where hyperbole is otherwise commonplace.

In the summer of 1971, a few months before this public announcement, I traveled to Europe with Hank Smith to visit potential clients. Under nondisclosure agreements, I described both the MCS-4 family, and the 8008 for which the layout was almost completed. The most interesting aspect of this visit was finding that, generally, computer companies were quite critical of our products, while companies with problems that our chips could help solve were very receptive. The most useful information about improving our products came from those companies that criticized us, such as Nixdorf Computer and ICL (International Computers Ltd.). Their feedback, even though given in somewhat disdainful tones, with the implication being: "What do you know about computers?" highlighted the shortcomings of our microprocessors compared to their computers. It is interesting to note that these companies, and many others, were wiped out in less than twenty years by refusing to embrace microprocessors.

I treasured some of this criticism, and by the end of 1971 had conceived of what would become the 8080, a much-improved second-generation 8-bit microprocessor that would solve all the major limitations of the 8008 while also adding many new features.

The 8008 used a pitiful 18-pin package that required about 30 additional TTL chips to interface with memory and I/O circuits, eliminating many of the advantages inherent in a microprocessor. All this was caused by Grove and Vadasz's unfounded and almost religious zeal, about packaging. Most of the additional components could have been eliminated by adopting a 40-pin package, but Vadasz didn't want to hear about it. Even worse, he didn't seem to care that the 8008 was two to three times slower than it could have been, due to the ridiculous packaging constraints.

The Intel 8080 microprocessor

I think all the great innovations are built on rejections received.
—Louis-Ferdinand Céline

At the beginning of 1972 I began urging Vadasz to start a new microprocessor project, the future 8080. I suggested that the 8080 would take full advantage of the new N-channel MOS process that Intel was developing for the 4K-bit DRAM memory, the next gateway to the promised land of the semiconductor memory market. I asserted that the 8080 would be about six times faster than the 8008 with a new bus architecture, a new interrupt structure, and many additional instructions to overcome all the major limitations of the 8008.

I tried everything to convince my boss that it was essential to use a 40-pin package to optimize the 8080 performance. But he resisted. Fortunately, at that same time, I was also designing a single-chip calculator that had to use a 40-pin package like the competitors' chips. For unfathomable reasons, Vadasz was comfortable using 40 pins for this ordinary chip, but not for the 8080 that could be sold for a much higher price. This was nonsensical. When I made this argument aloud, and with a lot of energy, he finally saw the light and asked me to write a memo to top management, with Ted Hoff as co-author, to make sure Ted agreed even though he had not contributed anything to my proposal. Vadasz clearly wanted to protect himself in case the project was rejected by top management. Therefore, in April of 1972 I wrote a proposal to Intel's top brass describing the 8080 project and requesting approval to proceed.

I architected the 8080 to be machine-code compatible with the 8008. It had many new instructions and additional features that could turn an 8008 into an excellent microprocessor. My goal was to get an instruction cycle time of two microseconds, six times faster than the 8008, and not far off from the speed of several contemporary minicomputers. Thus, many applications that were unreachable using first-generation microprocessors would become possible with the 8080.

Despite my impassioned proposal, it still took several months before I was given the green light to start. I hired Shima from Japan because he was a very good logic and firmware designer who had helped me well with the 4004 and had witnessed the entire chip design cycle. With what he had already learned, and with some additional training, I was convinced he could also become a good chip designer, even though he had never designed a chip before.

The project began in November of 1972, nine months after I had started pleading with management. After a few months of working closely with Shima, he became independent enough that a minimum of daily supervision was sufficient to keep the project under control.

The first silicon of the 8080 came out in December of 1973 and the chip worked completely, except for a few minor problems.

The 8080 was the world's first second – generation microprocessor. Announced and sold to the public in March of 1974 [10], [11], it was an immediate success. With the 8080 the microprocessor had come of age and the market began to expand rapidly, primarily because of the major speed improvements over first-generation chips that sparked the exponential growth that continues to this day.

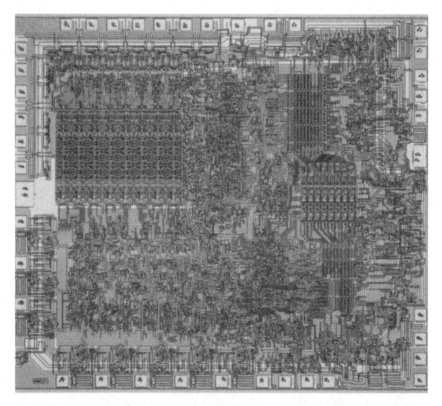

Fig. 21 – The Intel 8080, the world's first second-generation 8-bit microprocessor. The 8080 employed N-channel MOS with SGT with two power supplies: +12 and +5 volt, making TTL compatibility much easier than possible with P-channel MOS. The 8080 registers used static rather than dynamic memory, and the instruction cycle was reduced from 12 to 2 μsec!

Motorola became Intel's first significant competitor when it introduced its Motorola 6800, their first 8-bit, 40-pin microprocessor, six months later, using SGT. I have always been somewhat resentful about Intel's loss of nine months of market advantage due to the company having carelessly wasted the hard-won competitive advantage that had cost me so much effort. Fortunately, our 8080 managed to resist Motorola's 6800 incursion, even though our lead had been irreversibly shortened.

It took many years for Vadasz and Grove to embrace the microprocessor, for neither one had yet understood its revolutionary potential. In a special issue of *TIME* magazine dated March 31, 2003, Grove recalls: "So it was with amazement that we manufacturing types greeted the trade-paper ad that appeared on Nov. 15, 1971, 'Announcing a New Era of Integrated Electronics,' it trumpeted. Frankly, I was horrified. What was this new era? What was so special?" This quote captures the belittling attitude towards the work and vision I was so passionate about and was one of the main reasons why I decided to leave Intel in 1974 to start my own company.

The start of a new technology

Nobody can give you wiser advice than yourself.

—Cicero

Towards the end of 1973, Vadasz turned to me to work on a memory project. He needed my help because Intel was unable to deliver to Burroughs, a major customer, all the fast memories they needed. Burroughs had ordered a large amount of static 2102 RAM, but the yield at a 500-nanosecond access time was so low that Intel had accumulated a large inventory of unsold slow chips. Vadasz was under pressure because it was necessary to modify the manufacturing process and redesign the memory. I was surprised by his request since he had told me more than once that memory chips were much more difficult to design than microprocessors, as if designing memories were a far more refined art.

The 2102 was a 1024-bit static RAM using for the first time a single 5-volt power supply, the same used by bipolar logic chips.

Thanks to this choice, the MOS signals had become compatible with bipolar signals, solving once and for all a host of thorny problems that had beset MOS technology from the very beginning. However, operating at five volts was barely possible because, in the worst-case, the output voltage of a logic gate was slightly higher than the threshold voltage of the MOS transistors. Thus the manufacturing process variations would cause a wide distribution of memory access times.

Vadasz wanted me to reduce the gate oxide thickness, convinced that this change alone would solve the problem. After studying the situation, it became clear to me that his suggestion would have been just a Band-Aid. Instead, if we used *depletion-load* transistors, I calculated that all the production would be well under 500 nanoseconds (a detailed description of the depletion load is found in Appendix 1 for the interested reader). I pointed out to Vadasz that depletion-load transistors could also empower the design of fast logic circuits and microprocessors, making this technology very important for my group. However, it seemed that only memories were important to him.

Vadasz refused my proposal because it required one more masking step, even though there was no risk. After all, depletion-load transistors had already been used successfully. So I told him that his idea would not work and if he wanted to do things his way, he had to assign the project to someone else. In the end, he accepted my solution and left our meeting slamming the door angrily.

Six months later, the first chips were *five to eight times faster* than the previous version. Some chips even had 80-nanosecond access time, not much more than the bipolar RAMs that were quite expensive at the time. I told Vadasz that with some further refinements we could even go after the lucrative fast-bipolar RAM market that had seemed unreachable until then.

This was the beginning of the 5-volt, N-channel depletion-load process technology (Appendix 1) that would carry the industry forward for the next 15 years, essentially eliminating bipolar LSI technology from the market until it was in turn supplanted by complementary MOS (CMOS) technology, still using silicon gates. CMOS was a well-known, though expensive, technology used since the late 1960s for applications that required batteries. With the success of mobile phones, CMOS became mainstream and is today universally used.

The 2102A project that started as a stopgap ended up launching Intel into the highly profitable market of fast static RAM, successfully competing against bipolar memories, and gradually taking over one of the last bastions of bipolar resistance. By the late 1980s bipolar technology had essentially disappeared, except for some special applications. And the MOS technology with silicon gate had won not only the battle with the metal gate, but also the war with the incumbent bipolar technology, a result that the experts in 1968 would have considered unthinkable.

The History of the Microprocessor in Perspective

Some momentous inventions such as the car, the airplane, or the microprocessor offered solutions to many problems along a path that was generally and simultaneously recognized and pursued by many different inventors. In addition to the technical ingredients, there are other indispensable traits seldom mentioned, such as passion, courage, determination, and commitment, all necessary to make an invention work.

There are many "inventors" who devise an idea and patent it, but never develop it far enough to prove it functions well. Not to mention the crucial effort necessary to ensure that its realization takes roots in the world after it is embodied in a product. These so-called inventors wait for someone else to independently develop a similar concept, make it work, and create a market at great expense and effort, at which point they come out from the woodwork waving their patent, claiming the credit and the profits that belong to the hard work of others. I find this kind of widespread behavior reprehensible, even though it gives work to many lawyers. As fifteenth-century French writer François de La Rochefoucauld expressed, "The world will more often reward appearances of merit rather than true merit."

This is what happened with the microprocessor when Gilbert Hyatt emerged, *ten years* after the microprocessor had been created, and claimed to be its legitimate inventor, and demanded the glory and the dollars. Over the previous 10 years, Hyatt had fought with the US Patent and Trademark Office for a patent he kept updating based on hindsight rather than on foresight. His patent was finally invalidated in a case of patent interference fought by Texas Instruments. The case was especially profitable for the lawyers involved.

When Busicom had first visited Intel in April of 1969, contrary to the characterization given by Hoff and Mazor, the Japanese company had already developed a *programmable* solution to make a family of calculating machines that used the same chips. Busicom had turned to Intel following the recommendation of a consultant, Jim Imai, an expert on MOS technology and on the various companies that produced integrated circuits. In a surprising coincidence, Jim was also the engineer who taught the GMe course on MOS technology that I had attended in the summer of 1966 while working at CERES.

Jim told me many years later that, after having carefully assessed the logical design and speed requirements of the Busicom project, he knew those chips could not be done with the metal-gate technology. He felt it would require at a minimum the silicon-gate technology, though he was not sure it would be enough. He had therefore suggested to Busicom to turn to Intel as the only company that could potentially design their chips.

When Intel showed no interest in their original design and instead proposed a simplified architecture based on DRAM rather than shift register memory, Busicom had no alternative. And when Intel had delayed the start of the project by more than five months without saying anything, Busicom felt trapped and unable to go elsewhere, as any wise customer would have done under similar circumstances.

The Busicom design, however, was not just a "dozen custom chips to make a printing desktop calculator," as Stan Mazor had told me, but rather was comprised of seven chips, of which three constituted a special-purpose central processing unit (CPU). The fourth chip was a shift register for the data memory, the fifth was a ROM, and the last two were I/O chips to control the keyboard, printer, switches, lights, etc.

Thus, the original Japanese architecture already included a CPU, and their chip family was programmable, although it was specialized toward calculating machines and the CPU was too complicated to be built into a single chip. Their CPU used special macro-instructions to reduce the amount of ROM memory required to make calculators, but it addressed ROM memory like any other computer, while the serial data storage was addressed as if it were I/O. This is the origin of the "baroque" way in which the 4004 addressed the RAM of the 4000 family; it was a vestige of the Busicom design.

The official history of the microprocessor promoted by Intel was that Hoff and Mazor found a programmable solution to replace a set of custom chips—implying that these were not programmable—when in fact they were. However, even Busicom's solution was not as revolutionary as it may seem at first glance, without deepening the story.

The first company to introduce a successful programmable desktop calculator was Olivetti in 1965. It was called Programma 101 and was conceived and directed by Pier Giorgio Perotto. The Programma 101 was a programmable calculator realized with a small computer at its core, and it had a keyboard, printer, and magnetic card reader. It was a revolutionary idea that started a new market direction, a precursor for the personal computer, though it was specialized for numerical calculations.

The Programma 101 was made with discrete components packaged in compact three-dimensional modules. It also had a serial data memory made with four *magnetostrictive* wires (where the application of a magnetic field causes a change in density that propagates at the speed of sound along the wire). It achieved great market success with over 40,000 units sold, which was considered a large volume in those days. The great advantage was its programmability, and its success elicited a lot of competition for which Olivetti was unprepared. They sat on their laurels instead of immediately designing a more advanced model to overcome many of its limitations.

In 1968 Hewlett-Packard introduced the HP 9100, a programmable desktop calculator that was much more refined than the Programma 101, and became the new leader in the market pioneered by Olivetti. Busicom had simply followed the trail blazed by Olivetti and HP but added one important ingredient. They understood that if they could build a computer with a small set of chips, then they could reuse the same chips to make a family of different calculators. In other words, Busicom saw that with customized software and different amounts of memory and I/O, they could build different machines if its CPU was fast enough.

It was a very sensible approach because the high cost of chip development would be amortized by using the same chips on many different products, thus reducing their overall cost through the cumulative volume of their various applications. Furthermore, the development time and risk associated with any new product would be drastically reduced.

However, Busicom was unaware that Intel was already developing dynamic RAMs that would soon render obsolete the shift-register memories still dominating the scene for small computer systems. The success of the HP 9100, for example, was in large measure due to the use of a RAM made with miniaturized magnetic cores, a real *tour de force* by the HP engineers, rather than the primitive serial memory used by the Olivetti Programma 101.

The Japanese company had mischaracterized Intel to be like any other MOS firm that designed and manufactured custom circuits. It had not realized that Intel's corporate vision was to produce mainly standard products. Intel was only opportunistically interested in custom projects after realizing that it would take a long time before its customers would employ their memory chips for volume production. Custom chips would, therefore, help increase Intel's sales faster since the product development of the chips would proceed in parallel with the development of the customer's product.

When Ted Hoff saw the Busicom proposal, he immediately realized that the CPU was much more complicated than it needed to be given its reliance on shift register data memory. By using RAM, like all contemporary computers were already doing by then, Hoff could simplify the system architecture. At that time Intel was developing a dynamic RAM in which a bit used three transistors, instead of the six required for a bit of either a shift register or a static RAM. By replacing the shift register memory and the static RAMs used for the CPU registers and stack pointer with dynamic RAM, the total number of transistors could be nearly halved.

With the encouragement of Bob Noyce, Hoff simplified the Busicom design by using traditional computer architecture made possible by the elimination of the shift register and static memory. The result was the architecture of the 4000 family I described earlier [12]. That architecture, however, was no engineering feat, because any small general-purpose CPU would have resulted in a similar complexity, and many engineers knew well how to architect one, including me. The clearest proof that the CPU architecture was nothing out of the ordinary was the CTC architecture done the same year that resulted in the Intel 8008 microprocessor, as previously described.

Most of the MOS integrated circuits produced in 1970 were custom logic circuits with metal-gate technology and high-threshold voltage. These ICs also included ROM memories programmable with a metal mask to store the code owned by the customer. The only standard products to have a reasonable production volume were the serial memories made with shift registers. Almost all of the companies that produced MOS ICs, including Fairchild, were equipped to convert a logic design realized by the customer into one or more integrated circuits. This was done by interconnecting predesigned and characterized circuit blocks, followed by a computer simulation of the global system.

The initial lack of the bootstrap load and the topological layout differences of the SGT had created a strong barrier to its adoption by Fairchild. Furthermore, the use of the buried contact offered the opportunity to create much denser circuit layouts, though at the cost of further investment and changes in the existing stable of circuit blocks. Even when the 4004 was announced, no company had yet adopted the SGT for logic circuits, partly because of the costly modifications necessary to convert from metal gate infrastructure to silicon gate.

However, Intel was unique because it produced standardized memory ICs without the need for these high investments. The company's decision to produce some custom circuits as a secondary activity to increase short-term sales did not take into account the requirement to have a well-developed custom design methodology that would have required a substantial investment. Nobody at Intel had experience with custom circuits, especially Vadasz and Grove, both of whom had manufacturing process R&D backgrounds and no expertise in logic chips.

A microprocessor had to be designed from scratch because the existing custom – design infrastructure based on metal gate MOS was hopelessly inadequate to provide the necessary speed and density. The layout had to be "hand-packed" instead of assembled with predefined building blocks in Lego-like fashion which was adequate for less demanding custom chips. Most importantly, the SGT with bootstrap load and buried contacts was indispensable because even with hand-packed metal gate MOS layouts, the chip would have been too slow and too large to satisfy the requirements of a commercial-grade microprocessor. When I joined Intel, little of the necessary logic and circuit design infrastructure was available, so I had to develop all the missing ingredients, establishing a new state of the art with the 4004 chip design and layout.

The methodology I developed, combined with a rich library of circuits accumulated during the design of the 4001, 4002, and 4003, helped speed up the design of the 4004. Nevertheless, the 4004 still required a few additional circuits and more refined layout techniques due to the use of the buried contacts [13], [14]. *Without all these innovations, Hoff's architecture could not have been realized in 1970.*

Ralph Ungermann

In 1972, Vadasz abruptly told me he had hired someone to run Intel's custom chip business, which had been my job since the day I was hired. He explained that Intel wanted to seriously enter the custom chip business and that I had to concentrate on the microprocessor market. The name of the newcomer was Ralph Ungermann. Vadasz explained that he had worked for Western Digital where he ran a small design group developing custom MOS chips for telecommunications. Ralph had an electronic systems background rather than a semiconductor one like me, but Vadasz said his experience was important for the job Intel had envisioned.

From my point of view, Vadasz wanted to take away what I had built without the promise of a vigorous push in microprocessors, especially since I had not yet received the green light for the 8080 design, an idea I had been energetically urging for months. So I told him I did not like that move and I might leave Intel if he proceeded with his plan. A few days later, Vadasz retreated. Ralph went to work for me and I gladly transferred to him the responsibility for the custom projects with which I was involved. But it soon became clear that top management was not taking the custom circuit business seriously. They had no intention of making the necessary investments to turn that secondary activity into a meaningful business. Moreover, Intel was not cost-competitive with the best suppliers in that market.

Less than a year later, Ralph asked me for a leave of absence to help his wife Sue start a consulting firm in electronic systems testing, saying he would be interested in coming back to Intel if they had something better to offer him.

At the beginning of 1974, an important reorganization took place. Andy Grove became executive vice president, taking over marketing and sales in addition to his responsibilities for operations and R&D. As a result, Vadasz's responsibilities were much expanded with the addition of bipolar chip design, process development, and Ted Hoff's group in application research.

My responsibilities also greatly increased when I was assigned all of Vadasz's previous activities, except for dynamic memories which were Intel's main business line. I was previously head of the small machines group with about ten people reporting to me. In the reorganization, I was promoted to department manager with six groups comprising a total of about eighty engineers and technicians. So I asked Ralph to come back and take over the microprocessor group and lead almost all the projects that I had previously directed.

Unfortunately, 1974 was also a recession year for the US economy. This one was triggered by the 1973 oil embargo which caused gas shortages, high prices, and long queues at service stations. The semiconductor industry was not spared either, and Intel laid off about 10 percent of its workforce to adapt to the new market conditions. Despite my success, I was getting tired of having to fight for everything I felt was important. It was at this time that I decided to leave Intel.

In addition to the misappropriation of the work I had done at Fairchild, I was unwilling to bend to Andy Grove's harsh management style. Even if Intel had been perfect, I still yearned to run my own business as many entrepreneurs had done before me in Silicon Valley. Besides, I felt I was not receiving rewards commensurate with my contributions. *If I dedicated the same energy and initiative in my own company,* I thought, *I'll be soon economically self-sufficient.*

That summer of 1974 I decided it was time to leave. If Intel did not want to become a microprocessor company, I would create my own company completely dedicated to microprocessors. I asked Ralph if he was interested in joining me. Without hesitation he answered yes, even before knowing what I planned to do, and resigned from Intel shortly after. A couple of weeks later I told Vadasz that I wanted to resign to start my own company. He immediately asked me to talk to Grove. Andy was friendly and captivating at first, trying to convince me to stay. But when he saw that my decision was firm, our conversation took a turn for the worse. He told me that if I left Intel he would make sure that I would leave no legacy for my children and grandchildren. Furthermore, he said that if I did leave, I would never be successful. His words sounded like a mixture of a curse and blackmail, which only strengthened my resolve to leave. "Attila the Hun," the nickname Andy had earned because of his management style, flashed then through my mind. That name had never felt more appropriate.

Vadasz still found the nerve to ask me to delay my departure for a couple of months to find a replacement, telling me not to say anything to anyone about my decision to leave. I reluctantly agreed to "guard the fort," even though I later regretted having consented.

The last few weeks were very painful. I was fond of the many young and good engineers, several of whom I had personally hired and trained, and I was sorry to leave them. I felt like I was betraying them since I was forbidden to tell them that I was about to leave. The alternative of staying at Intel, however, had become intolerable. I realized only then, even if vaguely, that my decision would push me into a new direction, that of an entrepreneur. My second life, the life of a highly qualified physicist-engineer doing high tech work in a foreign country was about to end.

My last day was October 31, 1974, Halloween. That day also marked the beginning of a campaign aimed at erasing my name from the history of the development of the silicon-gate technology and the microprocessor. However, Intel's top management had not calculated a variable that would upset their plans.

Elvia's fight for the truth

Truth too often suffers, but it never dies.

—Tito Livio

After my last meeting with Andy Grove, I described the exchange to Elvia. I related, in a joking manner, what seemed to be Andy's incredible transformation from Dr. Jekyll to Mr. Hyde. I also tried to steadfastly reassure her that Grove would not carry out his threat. "Besides," I insisted with conviction, "he can't."

Seeing my deliberately playful attitude, Elvia smiled at first, but then immediately became serious in trying to reassure both of us that his menace was absurd and would not materialize. "They are just trying to intimidate you!" she started. "After all, how could it even be possible to erase your name when you are the first author on all the original documents of the MOS silicon-gate technology, the first microprocessor, and the 8080? The first microprocessor and the MOS silicon-gate technology are inextricably intertwined. The 4004 would never have existed without the new technology and the intimate knowledge you brought with you to Intel, especially the bootstrap load they did not even know about! You were the leader of both projects and the one directly responsible for their success!"

She continued: "How could a story that took place in such a linear way be changed? The architecture of the 4004 and its design took place independently in different organizations at successive times. How could the silicon design, never realized before and based on your new technology and methodology, be conflated with the block architecture of a CPU like many others of that time?

"How could it be possible to ignore the creativity, passion, and heroic dedication"—and here Elvia emphasized the word "dedication," implying hers and mine—"that was indispensable to implementing an idea that had languished for months before you took over leadership of the project? Thanks to you, Intel was thrust to the forefront of the microprocessor industry—a direction in which Vadasz and Grove didn't believe in!"

At that point Elvia caught her breath and fell silent, only to start again a moment later. "What about the architects, considering that Hoff distanced himself for fear that the 4004 could be a failure and never took an interest in its progress? Everyone at Intel knows about your contributions and your initiatives to introduce the microprocessor to the general market. In fact, before you left, they considered you the father of the microprocessor."

I was taken by her eloquence, forcefulness, and loyalty and I felt much gratitude for her support. Certain that the facts were too obvious to be ignored, we underestimated Intel's ability to manipulate the truth and the press. In 1975, almost immediately after I had left Intel, *Fortune* magazine came out with the first important article dedicated to the microprocessor. I had not been interviewed, and Elvia, who read it first, told me incredulously that I had not even been mentioned. I found out soon after that journalists and authors were being redirected elsewhere by the Intel PR machine. How ironic it was that the firm promoting an image of excellence, ignored the person who had contributed fundamentally to its technological excellence!

We both understood that Intel was motivated to not only minimize my contribution to all of its early microprocessors, but also to minimize my contribution to the silicon-gate technology that I had developed at Fairchild in 1968. Intel had copied that technology and used it in its memory chips. By eliminating the designer of the microprocessor, they could also strengthen their false claim on the SGT. For them, it was like killing two birds with one stone!

Elvia wanted me to react, but I told her that I did not want to entangle myself in legal quicksand against a powerful opponent with the press on its side. Instead, I wanted to keep contributing to the progress in technology, and to do that meant I didn't have any time or energy to waste. "My best revenge will be in my continuing achievements," I said.

It was then that Elvia, unable to tolerate such factual distortions, decided to take it upon herself to restore the truth. She had been fortunate in becoming head of the Palo Alto press office of Jackson Publishing Group in Milan, an important Italian publisher in the information technology field. She felt vested with professional authority and had numerous opportunities to make her voice heard. She participated in press conferences and technology events, talked to journalists and to anyone who would listen, and even met with Intel's top executives. She also started the website www.intel4004.com, thanks to the computer skills of our daughter Marzia, and continued to update it. The site includes a lot of documentation and information about my work at Fairchild Semiconductor and Intel. Whenever she finds misrepresentations, she writes the authors to have the errors rectified.

She also wrote many letters, several directly to Andy Grove, the main architect of the Intel revenge campaign. One Sunday she phoned him at home. He replied diplomatically and promised to correct the story a little bit at a time, explaining that it could not be done all at once. But that was only a deception to try to stop Elvia. There was no follow-through on his promises, and it was no surprise when I learned that my wife had been blacklisted by Intel and was no longer invited to their press events.

In her struggle, Elvia was sustained by the support of her family in Italy, particularly that from her mother and sisters with whom she spoke on the phone regularly to find comfort. Their words strengthened her conviction that the truth leaves too many traces to be completely suppressed, and that sooner or later it reemerges if you fight hard enough to recover it, even when facing a Goliath. Our children were also affected by this situation. What should have been a cause for joy and pride for our whole family had become a source of tension and uneasiness.

Intel continued its deviousness through attributing my work to others and leaving out or belittling my other creative and essential contributions, thus encouraging the beneficiaries of their distortions to become increasingly bolder. For example, both

Hoff and Mazor tried to take credit for the leadership of the 4004 and 8080 respectively, and still to this day, in all these fifty years, have never mentioned that I was the leader of *all* of the first Intel microprocessors.

In a 1988 interview, held in the prestigious Clarence E. Larson Collection, Hoff described his role in the creation of the microprocessor in the following way: "I am not a MOS designer... My role was primarily in doing the architecture and then later on doing support for the products. So, after the architecture was done, the instruction set defined, it was turned over to the MOS design team, they carried it there..."

The implication being that the real contribution was the architecture, while the design of the chip was nothing more than routine—exactly the opposite of the truth.

Even worse, on the few occasions when Hoff did mention my name, he attributed only the layout of the 4004 to me and failed to accurately describe my most important contributions, namely the design methodology based on the bootstrap load and the buried contact, the logic and circuit design, and my stewardship of the project up to its completely successful market introduction.

At the opening of the Intel Museum in 1992, Mazor was scheduled to be presented as the project leader of the 8080. But following our protests, Intel changed the presentation and correctly introduced me as its leader.

A staring contest

I am the invisible part of my gaze.

—Franco Arminio

The eyes can emanate light but also dark energies. Some looks caress. Some incinerate, or at least they try to. Andy Grove, CEO of Intel, tried that look once with Elvia. The occasion was the twenty-fifth birthday celebration of the microprocessor. The event was organized by Comdex at which I was honored for the Intel 4004 and 8080, and the Zilog Z80, among other microprocessors. During the ceremony, Andy and his wife Eva sat in the row in front of Elvia and me. At the end of the function we all got up, and while we were walking through the rows to exit, he circled back and extended his hand to congratulate us for the prize received. He then planted his eyes on Elvia's, staring as if he wanted to hypnotize her, while I was walking a few steps ahead of them.

Time passed and he kept staring, his eyes locked on hers, convinced that he could make her back down. But she never did. Not having succeeded, he walked away, then paused, and came back and repeated the same moves: a handshake and a stare – down with the same force as before. It was he who ended up looking away and set out for the exit while we followed at some distance. Andy did not notice and never knew that Elvia, shortly after, had reached out to me and was clinging to my arm because she felt her head spinning and was afraid of fainting. Having won the challenge, her energy was then renewed, and she felt even stronger. As Dostoevsky states: "Anyone who sincerely wants the truth is always frighteningly strong."

In 2014, Elvia and I also went to the opening of the National Inventors Hall of Fame Museum near Washington DC, in association with the United States Patent and Trademark Office. We were amazed to discover that Hoff was recognized in the following way: "Marcian 'Ted' Hoff, Jr. led the team that designed the first single-chip computer CPU." This was a false attribution because that was the exact role I had played, and thus he was credited with the chip design to which he did not contribute one iota. Stan Mazor, Hoff's assistant, also was falsely credited as the engineer "instrumental in refining the architecture and logic design of the single-chip CPU," when he had not contributed at all to the logic design.

Following our protest, the attribution was changed to the following: "Marcian 'Ted' Hoff, Jr. led the team at Intel that defined the architecture of the single-chip computer CPU, after which the CPU was designed in the MOS group under different leadership."

Mazor's attribution was changed to: "Stanley Mazor was instrumental in refining the architecture of the single-chip CPU."

Now in the National Inventors Hall of Fame Museum I am correctly recognized in the following way: "Federico Faggin joined the MOS group at Intel as principal designer and leader of the team that designed the first microprocessor after having developed the key methodology for random-logic design using silicon gate ..."

As Émile Zola wrote: "The truth is on the march and nothing will stop it." However, often it is necessary to fight hard for it. That is what Elvia did all those years. She has always been a formidable warrior with integrity, courage, values, and indomitability in the defense of justice and truth. Her example has helped me be truer and more just.

4

My Third Life

It always seems impossible until it's done.

—Nelson Mandela

The day after I left Intel, November 1, 1974, was my first day at my startup. Ralph and Sue had already rented 550 square feet of office space on State Street in downtown Los Altos. To save money, instead of creating a new corporation, Ralph had proposed that I purchase half ownership of Ungermann Associates (UA), the company that he and Sue had started two years earlier. I would be CEO, Ralph would be the executive VP and Sue would be the CFO. I agreed, considering that UA had practically no business, partly due to the economic recession, and thus we would not be encumbered in our future direction.

The next step was to decide what we wanted to do and then prepare a business plan for the venture capital (VC) community to get funding. That was the well-established path of any tech startup. To support the three of us until we got VC investments, Sue would continue to run UA helped by Ralph working part time, while I would concentrate exclusively on planning the new direction.

Not even a few days into my new life as an entrepreneur, I received a call from a journalist at the weekly magazine *Electronic News*. He had gotten wind of our defection and wanted to do a brief profile on us. His write-up appeared in the following week's issue, and a week after that I received another call. This one from Mr. Henderson of Exxon Enterprises (EE), inquiring if EE could be of assistance to us.

Mr. Henderson explained that EE was a venture capital organization funded by Exxon, the largest corporation in the world at that time, seeking to participate in the rapidly growing information sector. I told him that we were still planning our future direction, but that if he happened to be in town soon, we would be glad to meet with him. A few days later he called back. It turned out that he and his colleague Dan Matthias were going to be in the Bay Area that next week and wanted to make our acquaintance. *That was a quick comeback,* I thought.

I had been thinking about our first product since leaving Intel, mulling over the idea of a *single-chip computer* with a high-speed CPU optimized for I/O operations, with many programmable I/O ports, and sufficient internal ROM and RAM. Such a chip would solve many control problems that the 4004 was too slow to achieve and would be far more economical than the 8080. Texas Instruments had just introduced the TMS 1000 microcontroller, conceptually a similar product, but much slower and less flexible than what I had in mind. Therefore, after the second EE call, I went into high gear to prepare a preliminary business plan to discuss with them. Elvia, who had taken a typing class at Foothill College, came to the office to type the plan which she finished only minutes before our visitors arrived.

The meeting lasted more than two hours and went well. Mr. Henderson was an impeccably dressed financial expert and Dan Matthias was a high-energy, creative type who understood quite a bit about microprocessors and asked most of the questions, many of them rather pointed. We gave them a copy of our preliminary business plan and they left saying that in a few weeks they would let us know if they were interested.

Our plan showed that with half a million dollars we could reach the first milestone, which consisted of having a working chip and a development system with basic software, an absolute necessity for our customers to develop their custom firmware. Our proposed manufacturing plan was a novel idea in those days: we would contract the early wafer production to Synertek, the first company to offer wafer-foundry services, and later we would build our own factory when we reached enough production volume to warrant the investment.

The Super-80 CPU

After the meeting, however, I began to have second thoughts about our proposed product. My main concern had to do with the cost structure. I realized that unless we had our own wafer fab, we could not make any money because that chip would not give us enough margin to satisfy both us and the wafer foundry. On the other hand, if we decided to have our wafer fab from the start, we would have a costly factory to support for about two years with little revenue while we waited for our customers to design their products and go into high-volume production.

Having struggled with this problem for a couple of weeks, I finally came up with a solution. It was evening, Ralph was in the office working on UA business, and I was reflecting on what to do when the entire vision emerged in a flash of insight. I spontaneously let out, "Super-80!" I had figured that what we needed was a third-generation 8-bit microprocessor together with a truly integrated family of high-end system components—what the Intel 8080 and Motorola 6800 were not.

The CPU would use a 40-pin package with 5-volt supply along with the depletion – load technology I had used for the Intel 2102A. Its speed would be at least twice that of the 8080, comparable to most minicomputers, and the interrupt structure would be like the ones available in the best minicomputers of the day, which were all built with expensive bipolar technology.

In this way the chip family would have a much higher profit margin and allow us to use foundry services to seed the market before requiring our factory. Since the Super-80 would have a broad market appeal, we could initially support the company with the development system revenues while waiting for the volume chip business to materialize. Super-80! That name was chosen because the microprocessor I had envisioned needed to be machine-code compatible with the 8080, the new standard of the industry, and yet it would also include several new addressing modes and many other useful instructions and facilities.

But we still needed a viable *second source*, another independent supplier licensed by us, since very few customers would adopt our product and develop the costly software if they had to depend on the chip supply from an unproven company. A second source would have guaranteed an alternative supplier, significantly reducing the risk to our customers. Today, with the many capable wafer foundries available, a licensed second source would no longer be necessary. However, at the end of 1974 only the startup Synertek was offering foundry services with the depletion-load MOS silicon gate.

I felt good about this new strategy because all the key issues I had been struggling with would be resolved, at least on paper. But then I started stressing over another issue: My credibility with EE. Changing the business plan only a few weeks after I had enthusiastically presented it would not look good, I thought.

A few days later, Dan Matthias called saying that EE was interested in proceeding to the next step, but there were several issues they wanted to discuss. He proposed we meet just before Christmas. In preparation for that visit, I completed the overall system architecture, including a detailed block diagram of the CPU and its instruction set, and the concept design of the first four programmable peripheral components: a parallel I/O chip (PIO), a counter-timer controller (CTC), a serial communication interface controller (SIO), and a direct memory access controller (DMA).

Zilog, Inc.

We were also thinking about a name for our new company. I made a list of domain-specific words like electronics, semiconductor, circuit, logic, micro, integrated, computer, and so on, trying out new combinations that sounded good and were not already taken. Ralph and I would generally dedicate some time at the end of each day to come up with new combinations. Our criterion was if we remembered a potential name the next morning, we would consider it further. If it was not memorable for us, it wouldn't be for anyone else.

It took a while to get to "ilog," which I coined as the contraction of integrated logic. When Ralph heard ilog, he chimed "zzzzilog!" possibly influenced by the then-popular Datsun 240Z, a sports car that was highly prized in those days. I immediately replied, "Yeah! Zed, the last word in integrated logic!" We didn't think more about it as we left to go home. But the following morning, we both woke up thinking "Zilog." The name stuck and the rest is history, as they say.

Preparations for the EE meeting included updating the business plan with my new vision. I also revised the earlier idea by stating that the single-chip computer would be our second major product line to be introduced after we had built our wafer fab. After reframing the plan, my stress level appreciably decreased because it felt even more compelling and well-thought-through than the first one.

Our meeting went well, though Dan Matthias had some misgivings about the need for a second source. My impression was that he liked the current plan more than the previous one and my stressing over the changes had been unnecessary. Dan said that he would get back to us within a few weeks and we parted by exchanging well – wishes for the upcoming holiday season. My homework was to better articulate the need for a second source.

Dan had clearly identified a crucial element in the strategy, an issue that allowed only the choice of the lesser evil. Without an official second source, specifically a company to which we would give the rights to make and sell our product, Zilog could not succeed. Yet, if we picked an aggressive second source, most of the business could go to our competitor. It was, "damned if we do and damned if we don't."

The only way we could succeed was to stay ahead of the second source with new products while aiming to become the lowest-cost producer with our fab. Thus, our stable position would be a tug-of-war, a dynamic balance, rather than a winner-takes-all. The same dynamics were happening in the memory business where the sellers were forced to adopt a *standard pinout* and provide the same functionality so there would be a *de facto* second source, even if each supplier had to independently develop its own products. In other words, the need for multiple sources of supply was independent of the product and had to be solved one way or another.

Only a company with several independent factories could get away without a second source. Even in that case, however, a large customer would most likely want the right to make its own product if the supplier could not deliver. This requirement was finally largely alleviated decades later with the emergence of many independent wafer foundries, where customers now have the right to directly purchase products from them in case of supply problems.

For our situation, I identified only two companies that would be viable candidates for a second source, Mostek and Rockwell International, and that was as much as I was prepared to discuss with EE at our upcoming meeting.

Investment approved and new problems

At the next appointment Dan showed up with his boss, John Meier, and we reviewed the plan again and brought John up to speed. Ralph and I had good answers for all their key questions, including their concerns that Intel might sue us given that we were going to compete head-on. I said that we had left Intel only with our heads and we had completely avoided thinking about our own products while in their employ. Evidence of this was that it had taken us a while to put together our business plan. I added that Intel could not afford to sue us since they had misappropriated my buried contact invention created during my time at Fairchild and that I could prove this in court. My answers seemed to have been convincing enough to take that concern off the table.

John and Dan left saying that they would recommend the investment to their board, and if the deal were approved the next step would be to prepare an investment document. They also asked us if we had a lawyer. We answered yes because UA had occasionally used a lawyer for corporate and tax matters.

A couple of weeks after that meeting we received the good news that the EE board had approved the deal and that an investment document would be arriving in a few weeks. But the moment we received the contract and got our lawyer involved, all kinds of issues were raised, and the negotiation started to get bogged down. I did not know it then, but I later found that this is the way it always works.

It was now March of 1975 and I wanted to start the project because the market was not going to wait for the lawyers. Meanwhile, the UA business, despite Ralph's promises, could not support much more than the office rent. I had not received any salary since leaving Intel, and although I had some Intel shares, the stock market was quite depressed. On top of that, Shima, who had asked to join me the same day I told him I was leaving Intel, was putting on pressure to be hired. He wanted to leave Intel before starting a new assignment there, and that time was fast approaching. I was counting on him to do the detailed design of the Super-80 because I didn't know any other chip designer I could trust with such a critical project.

So I called Dan with whom I had developed a good relationship and asked for $10,000 a month to start the design while we completed the negotiation. I told him we risked losing momentum to the competition. He understood and we came to terms with a loan that would be forgiven if we could not reach agreement on the investment *and* if we went out of business. With those funds in the bank, we hired Shima to work on the Super-80 and Doug Broyles, a system engineer Ralph knew, to work with him on the development system.

Bringing in Shima proved to be more complicated than I had thought because at the last minute he requested to be reimbursed for the "lost gain" on his Intel stock option that he could exercise in the future if he stayed at Intel. That was a completely unreasonable request, but he was immovable and since we had no alternative we had to budge. We were talking about $30,000, a significant amount of money for us. Rather than involving EE, Ralph and I decided to foot the bill fifty-fifty. But since Ralph said he didn't have the money, I ended up loaning him $15,000, essentially depleting my entire savings. I now truly needed the salary scheduled to start a few weeks later in April when the EE loan would kick in, or else I would have had to sell some of my Intel stock.

Another monkey wrench in the negotiation was the valuation of the company and the firm demand that we have some "skin in the game." EE wanted more than 50 percent ownership and we had to put up 10 percent of the deal as collateral. That meant Ralph and I had to come up with $25,000 each. I convinced EE to use my Intel stock as skin in the game for both of us by signing a transfer agreement to EE in case we didn't meet our plan to have a fully-functional CPU by March 6, 1976, a propitious date coinciding with the sixth birthday of our daughter Marzia. If we achieved our goal, the collateral would be returned. If we didn't, it was theirs.

Part of the deal also called for assigning Ungermann Associates' intellectual property to Sue who could then continue to pursue that business on her own. She could not contribute to Zilog, and I did not want her as an employee. During the final negotiation there seemed to be no end to the difficulties and our lawyer began to resent EE's strong-arming to own 51 percent of Zilog, a controlling interest they were adamant about having. In the end, the skin in the game was all mine since Ralph didn't shell out a penny, and we received a $480,000 check ($500,000 minus the $20,000 repayment of the prior two-months loan) to fund Zilog for the next milestone.

Feeling the heat during those negotiations, I had also contacted Sutter Hill Ventures, a reputable venture capital (VC) organization.

They painted a dismal picture of the current VC landscape. The business had been badly affected by the collapse of the high-tech bubble, followed by an economic recession and downfall of the stock market. The VCs had gone into survival mode and were not interested in any new deals. Many were having trouble keeping their existing investments from failing. I found out much later that Zilog was one of only a handful of VC-funded companies in 1975. We had been lucky to find an investor in EE, but that luck claimed a heavy price years later.

The Z80-CPU

Those first seven months had been like a roller-coaster ride. I had to handle all kinds of unfamiliar issues under the stressful conditions of no income. I was pushed beyond my worst-case scenarios to bet all of my financial resources on the company, except my home which I considered untouchable. Now, finally, I could go back to doing what I knew best: managing a demanding engineering project.

We had seven additional employees staged to join us to complete the first phase of the plan, for a total of 11 of us. We did not want to hire any more people until the proof of the pudding—a working CPU—was in hand. Among the 11 was Dean Brown, who was responsible for the software of the development system, and Charlie Bass, who helped Dean. Shima had joined Zilog in April and the two of us worked on completing the CPU architecture and detailed development plan. Then Shima concentrated on the logic and circuit design of the CPU, and I concentrated on updating the design methodology with the new N-Channel MOS process with depletion loads that had not been used before for random logic, an area that was my specialty.

I developed a set of layout design rules that were relaxed enough so that the chip could be fabricated by any state-of-the-art factory. The reason was simple, I did not want Zilog to be dependent on

Synertek's design rules since we were not sure they could deliver. In those days, the manual layout and mask-making process accounted for about two-thirds of the chip development cycle. My decision proved to be wise when Synertek later turned out to be an unreliable supplier.

Toward the end of May, the design work had progressed to the point where the layout could be started. We had hired two draftsmen, a senior one who had briefly worked at Intel and then moved to another company, and a promising junior one. By mid-June, it was clear that the layout had to run at a much faster pace than the two draftsmen were able to maintain. So, I decided to step in and take over responsibility for it, otherwise Shima would have been overwhelmed and the entire project hopelessly late.

I worked eighty-hour weeks until the end of October when the layout was finally completed on time. In addition to managing the two draftsmen, I drafted with my own hands about two-thirds of the chip, working faster than the two draftsmen combined. I followed a strict schedule: From 8:30 am to 11:00 pm, Monday to Friday with a 30 – minute lunch break; and from 9:00 am to 7:30 pm on Saturday. I took Sundays off to get some rest and spend time with the family, except when I fell behind on the schedule.

During the layout phase, Ralph and Doug assembled a CPU simulator that used low-power TTL logic and wire-wrap boards. The logic was designed by Shima, who had translated the Super-80 logic design into the available TTL building blocks. The primary purpose of the simulator was to enable the parallel design of the hardware and software of the development system alongside the chip. Secondarily, it also allowed for checking the logic design, even though that was not strictly necessary. Toward the end of the chip layout, Ralph and Doug had completed its construction, which was then debugged by Shima. He found only one minor but subtle logic error that was immediately corrected on the Super-80 layout.

The simulator also included a 40-pin plug fitting into the Super-80 socket in the CPU board of the development system and behaved exactly as the future chip would. The debugging of the development system hardware and software then proceeded in earnest.

Meanwhile, Dean Brown and Charlie Bass coded the system software consisting of a bare-bones operating system, word processor, and assembler, plus a debugger for the customer software that worked in conjunction with specialized hardware to keep track of the Super-80's activity. Around the same time, we also decided on names for the five chips that made up the product family. The family name was Z80 and its first five members were: Z80-CPU, Z80-PIO, Z80-CTC, Z80-SIO, and Z80-DMA. This is also the order in which the chips were intended to be introduced to the market.

A scary time

Toward the end of the layout when there were only about 30 transistors left to draw, I became alarmed realizing that I would not be able to fit everything in. It was my worst fear coming true! The chip had to be a rectangle, therefore two fundamental dimensions, length and width, had to be established. The first dimension was fixed at the beginning of the layout, the second toward the end. Once the second dimension had been decided, all the circuits needed to fit within the rectangle so defined. If the last estimate were wrong, part of the work would have to be erased and started over! With contemporary electronic design automation (EDA) this is no longer a major issue, but we are talking about chips that were designed by hand many years before such tools became available.

When I realized that I had to erase a big chunk of the work already done, it felt like I was cutting off one of my limbs. But the problem could not be wished away. I had to cut and so I did. Still, I could not be sure I had rubbed off enough to fit all the missing transistors until I was near the end of the layout. For the 10 days it took to finish, I was in agony, unsure if there would be enough room. It was nerve-racking. When it was completed, the Z80-CPU layout was my masterpiece! To this day I'm very proud of it and still have never seen a random-logic handmade layout denser than the Z80.

Fig. 22 – The layout of the Z80-CPU. Hand-drawn by Federico (by two-thirds), the Z80 contained about 10,000 transistors and had an instruction cycle of 1 microsecond.

Right after finishing the layout I started writing the product manual. It was at this point when I realized we were potentially walking into a trap. If we used the same instruction mnemonics (the abbreviated names of the instructions) as the 8080, Intel almost certainly would have sued us claiming copyright infringement. But if we changed them the 8080 users would have to learn a new set of mnemonics even though the 8080 software would also run on the Z80-CPU. I had never liked the haphazard mnemonics of the 8008, originally decided by CTC, which also conditioned those of the 8080, so I decided it was a good opportunity to improve on them.

By a stroke of luck, a Swiss engineer had visited Zilog a couple of months earlier and described to Ralph his graduate thesis. He had come up with a rational naming convention for the instructions of a generic computer. His method made sense to me and I used some of those rules to name the Z80 instructions, thus changing all the 8080 mnemonics that were part of the Z80 instruction repertoire.

This new naming was more consistent and gave more information about the operation of each instruction, helping the many future microprocessor adopters who hadn't yet learned the 8080's mnemonics. We also dodged a potential bullet.

At that time I also negotiated a supply contract with Synertek, and everything was ready to roll by mid-December when we received the Z80 masks. In mid-January we received the first silicon and Shima got to work on finding out if we had any major problems. When drawing by hand nearly 10,000 transistors, full success at first silicon meant being able to completely check the chip by uncovering all the bugs and problems so that the next iteration would work perfectly. Nobody expected the chip to be perfect at first silicon. Indeed, it was already clear during the first few hours of systematic testing that there were some problems, but it took about one more week to check the entire chip for a final verdict. At the end of the process Shima had discovered only a few bugs, which were all easy to fix. The correction of the layout and masks then immediately started, followed by a new wafer run. I knew at that point the Z80 was a reality and we finally had a company!

Our new home

The hills surrounding the Santa Clara Valley had always reminded Elvia and me of those around Vicenza, and they offered spectacular views of the San Francisco Bay. So we engaged a real estate agent to help make our dream come true with a home in the hills.

After the usual touring around, we opted for a home at the northern end of Los Altos Hills, near Stanford University and the town of Palo Alto. It was a newly built house, never lived in, with a perfect location, and a beautiful view. It was exactly what we wanted, so much so that we bought it without hesitation and moved there in March of 1976 when Marzia was already attending the first grade. Fortunately, there was a school bus stop a short walking distance from our home.

All around us evergreen oaks stood out against the burnt gold of the grass in the summer and the lush green during the rainy season which typically lasts until April. It was also very private. We could see only two or three houses on the hill across from us but we never saw their owners, only their horses. We were immersed in nature and at the same time only a few minutes from Interstate 280 at the panoramic foothills of the mountains separating the bay from the Pacific Ocean. At that time, the last stretch of the freeway leading to San Francisco was still under construction.

On our walks in the neighborhood we would encounter many deer, rabbits, quails, wild turkeys, and raccoons. We also saw lynx, red foxes, and coyotes. The gardener even found a rattlesnakes' nest hidden among the weeds. Those kinds of reptiles did not bother us, in contrast with other snakes in coats and ties.

We are still fond of this wonderful place where we live to this day, with the various transformations and renovations that have occurred over time.

The Z80 works!

Back at the office, we received the first silicon of the revised Z80 masks on March 6, the exact date specified in the plan given to EE about one year earlier. When the wafers arrived, the development system hardware was already working, though most of the software was still in development. Shima put a wafer onto the prober that had a 40-pin plug prepared to fit into the CPU socket in the main board of the development system.

I typed "Control-C" on the teletype that was the human interface to the development system. The machine immediately echoed my input on paper. That simple operation required the chip to execute a rather complicated program. The Z80 worked! I happily ran to the local store and bought a bottle of expensive champagne and some glasses to celebrate with the team. We had met a stringent schedule *on time* and *on budget.*

We had also spent $400,000, exactly as planned. I even did some consulting for the Xerox Corporation in El Segundo, California to bring in an additional $20,000 to meet our budget. I wanted to impress EE and gain more of their trust by proving we were standing behind our promises. The next day I triumphantly called Dan to relay the news. He was impressed. Now I could also get my Intel stock back, the collateral "skin" of the founders—all of it my skin in this case.

The final thorough check by Shima took another ten days to verify that everything worked. The functionality, speed, power dissipation, and voltage margins over the entire temperature range were all found to exceed the specifications.

Next, we started several worst-case runs to build about 200 units. The tests were designed to perform a thorough characterization of the devices over the full temperature range and over the allowed manufacturing process variations, including the basic reliability tests, to make sure nothing was amiss. All went well, and so we started production runs of units for customer sampling.

Fig. 23 – The first Zilog ad appeared in the weekly Electronics News in May, 1976. It shows a comparison between the Z80-CPU and the Intel 8080.

The Battle of the '80s

Zilog was suddenly propelled into a period of hyperactivity to prepare for the product launch in May of 1976 and the first deliveries of the development system slated for June. We immediately needed more funds to hire a dozen new employees to help get us to the next milestone. Exxon came through with a convertible note of about $500,000 to be later turned into stock when we had completed a new business plan that included building our wafer fab. This time it only took a few phone calls to get the same amount of money that had taken seven months the first time around.

With new funding, we also hired a marketing agency for the unveiling of our first product. The announcement had to be bold and catchy, so we finally settled on "The Battle of the '80s," which included an ad appearing first in *Electronic News* and later running in other technical journals. The two-page spread compared our Z80-CPU with Intel's 8080.

It was like our product caught fire right out of the gate and news quickly spread around the world [15]. Soon after, German magazine *Markt +Technik* published the cartoon below showing our siege on Intel's 8080A castle. In the background are Exxon's oil refineries, Zilog's main investor.

Fig. 24 – Illustration in *Markt+Technik* of Zilog's siege on Intel's 8080A castle (1976)

Just one day after our announcement, we had customers walking into our office on State Street in Los Altos wanting to buy a sample for $200. The first was Cromemco, Inc., a startup that used the Z80 to develop a highly successful microcomputer business to replace minicomputers in low-end industrial applications. Their product was introduced at 4 MHz when they found that all of our chips worked at 4 MHz, though we had prudently introduced the product at 2.5 MHz to be on the safe side because we didn't yet know the speed distribution and didn't want to scrap any good Z80s that were too slow.

Copycats

Our second customer was Japanese-owned NEC, one of the top semiconductor companies in the world. I had already expected they would be among several companies that would try to copy the Z80, so I had already prepared some surprises for any copycats by instructing Shima to strategically place traps in the layout. Only Shima and I knew their locations, and we kept that information secure at our respective homes.

When I had been thinking about copycats six months earlier, I came up with the basic idea of how to make traps impossible to spot optically. These invisible defenses were enabled by the new depletion-load process (the process I first developed for Intel's 2102A) that allowed for two special types of MOS transistors: enhancement-mode and depletion-mode.

This made it impossible to distinguish the transistor type by optical inspection under a microscope since the transistor type was determined by a mask that left no optically visible trace. Proper load transistors were all depletion mode, and proper switching transistors were all enhancement mode. However, if a switching transistor was improperly made depletion mode, it behaved like a low-value resistor, and if a load transistor was improperly made enhancement mode, it would behave like an open circuit. This unusual feature made it possible to construct circuits that optically appeared to perform a legitimate function while they were instead sabotaging the operation of the chip.

Our seven traps in the layout had various impacts ranging from catastrophic to very subtle, thus making our defense increasingly harder to spot. The most devastating trap would cut off any communication between the internal and external bus while appearing to perform an auxiliary function of little relevance. The most malicious trap reproduced the obscure logic bug that Shima had found with the simulator, involving a conditional jump that failed if it was preceded by a hard-to-figure instruction sequence. I felt this strategy would create at least an additional six months of delay beyond what copycats would need to reverse engineer our product. In fact it took almost two years for NEC to introduce a Z80 clone, though I do not know how much of the delay was caused by our traps.

What I do know for sure is that National Semiconductor fell into them. Many years later, after I had already left Zilog, I was taking a summer MBA course at Stanford University when I bumped into an engineering manager who used to work for National. We knew each other and he said half-jokingly, "Damn you, Faggin!"

I asked, "What's your problem?"

"When I tried to copy the Z80-CPU to make a CMOS version for National, I lost nine months because of all your traps!"

I teased him back, "I thought a good engineer would have only lost six months."

With the Z80 now working, I started second-source negotiations with Mostek and Rockwell International and hired Len Perham from AMD to become our VP of semiconductor manufacturing. Len and I made plans for our first building that would also house our wafer fab. We commissioned Carl Berg, a successful Silicon Valley contractor, to design and build a 25,000-square foot facility.

In the meantime, we rented some additional office space in Los Altos on the same floor where we had originally started. We also leased a building in neighboring Sunnyvale to serve as the manufacturing plant for the development systems. With Ralph responsible for systems operations, we hired Dick Belanger to head up system manufacturing. Dick had also been the manufacturing manager for Intel's memory systems division.

In that first wave of hiring triggered by the fully-functional Z80, I also brought in Bob Sumbs from Microma, the world's first electronic watch company that Intel had acquired in 1972 and had gotten into serious trouble with in 1974. Microma was one of several ill-fated initiatives involving semiconductor companies lured by the illusion that technology alone was enough to conquer unfamiliar consumer markets. The result was a costly diversion that affected many, including Intel, TI, and National Semiconductor. Before Microma, Bob had been the VP of marketing for the Intel memory systems division until Intel sent him to Microma to be VP of marketing and sales to save a company that could not be rescued. Bob was a high-energy salesman, perfect for the start-up phase where determination, resourcefulness, and some level of improvisation were assets.

Thank you Elvia!

> *"One word, worn, but that shines like an old coin: Thanks!"*
> —Pablo Neruda

By the summer of 1976, Zilog had so many moving parts it was hard to keep track of them all. The stress, coupled with irregular eating, led me to serious health problems. One evening I was sitting at the dinner table with my family, as usual, nothing out of the ordinary, when I felt jolted by a painful twinge in my stomach. The pain became so unbearable that I asked Elvia to take me to the emergency room at nearby Stanford Hospital.

The doctors examined me, they even took X-rays, but could not find anything wrong. They apologized for not being able to give me any sedatives since my pain was the only information they had to guide them to a diagnosis. I was in agony for about three hours and then a fever started to mount, indicating that an internal infection was advancing. I remember feeling a strong impulse to beat my head against the wall to lose consciousness. Fortunately, that was the first and last time I felt such brutal pain.

As my fever was increasing, the doctor decided to urgently operate with a tentative diagnosis of a perforated ulcer. When they gave us some consent papers to sign for a vagotomy and a possible stomach resection, Elvia refused to sign at first, telling the doctor in no uncertain terms not to perform the vagotomy and resection even though they were routinely done for such a diagnosis. She finally signed only when she felt confident that the doctors would respect her request unless the procedures became necessary.

I remember my sense of powerlessness just before losing consciousness from the anesthesia. I had fought the pain as much as I could, but now needed to trust the doctor who was going to do the surgery. I let go and felt deep down that everything would work out. This was the first time in my life that I had experienced being completely and vitally dependent on a stranger.

When I woke up a few hours later in the recovery room, I learned that I indeed had a small perforation at the pyloric valve. The doctor had cleaned up the mess and stitched close the opening. In following Elvia's directions, he did not perform the other procedures that medical science would find out many years later to be damaging and completely unnecessary.

This was a big warning for me to pay more attention to the telltale signs and take better care of myself. Alas, the lesson was already forgotten the following day when people from the office started coming to my hospital room to discuss business issues.

Four days later I was back to work, and a few months later in October of 1976, only six months after Len and I had our first meeting with Carl Berg, we moved into our new building where the clean area of our future wafer fab was almost ready to be filled with new equipment.

Fig. 25 – Federico in front of the first Zilog building on Bubb Road in Cupertino (1977).

The importance of being self-sufficient!

Our goal was to be able to build our first Z80 chip by that upcoming January. And that's exactly what happened when one of our first test runs succeeded in producing just a single functioning Z80 on one of the five test wafers. Herb, the man in charge of the engineering assembly line, proudly pointed out the good die to me. I responded, "Package it right away!"

We had already improvised a little celebration for having achieved this crucial milestone, when Herb came back to me in great distress saying that the wafer had accidentally been dropped, breaking our single good die into pieces. It was like the end of the world for Herb. I reassured him, "Don't worry about it, in the next few days we'll have more chips than we need." We were finally self-sufficient!

Self-sufficiency had become vital because earlier in June, in one of my regular meetings with Synertek's CEO and their VP of marketing, when they realized they were building the Z80 microprocessor for us they demanded we give them the second source for our product. I was stunned. Here was a company providing foundry services while also trying to commit highway robbery. Adding insult to injury, the last few lots they had delivered to us had *zero* yield. I told them immediately that our relationship was over and that I was not going to pay for their zero-yield wafers.

This incident caused us to accelerate our wafer fab schedule since we now had lost our only source of supply. Fortunately, the second-source negotiations with Mostek were proceeding well and we agreed that they would deliver a large quantity of product to us at no cost before they could sell the Z80. That contractual provision allowed us to have about a one-year advantage over them. Happily, we never ran out of chips before our wafer fab kicked in.

During that period, we continued to exchange dinner invitations with Hal Feeney, the engineer who did the detailed design of the 8008 and was still working at Intel. Like us, he and his wife Mary Jo also lived in Los Altos Hills. Their home was well-furnished, warm, and welcoming. In their kitchen, the place of honor was occupied by a massive butcher's block that Hal had inherited from his father. As for Mary Jo, she had the soul of a *nouvelle cuisine* chef. I remember her wonderful salads enriched with all kinds of ingredients: walnuts, apple slices, celery, bean sprouts, corn kernels, etc., and each time in different combinations. She also knew how to present her dishes in such a way as to leave us speechless. They both loved the wild nature of the hills around their home and even recognized each animal that roamed in their backyard, individually naming some of them and studying their habits.

Those times with the Feeney's were always pleasant. Hal knew how to entertain his guests amiably. His conversation ranged from one topic to another and I was enthralled by his stories. However one evening, perhaps because of the abundant meal and libations, but most certainly because of my lack of sleep due to the fast-paced work at Zilog, I felt my eyelids irresistibly lowering. And no matter how hard I tried, I could not keep awake. As Banana Yoshimoto writes, *"when the tides of sleep progress, opposing them is impossible."* In short, Morpheus had played a trick on me. After a time I returned to myself to find Hal still talking. To my great relief, he did not seem to have noticed that I had temporarily nodded off.

The evening ended with hugs and the promise to meet again soon. That opportunity came about a month later. But, when we reached the door of their house, we noticed an unusual thing: a poster with a large picture, like the kind of banner used to report missing persons or the FBI's Most Wanted. Intrigued, I approached and saw that the person depicted was me. Hal indeed had noticed and had photographed me while I was sleeping with my head tilted, and I, in my blessed unconsciousness, had not known until then that I'd been caught!

The perfect storm

"He who seeds wind shall harvest storms."

—Italian proverb

The Z80-CPU was the last engineering project I managed, crowning the end of my technical career, my second life, and inaugurating my third life as an entrepreneur. That chip became wildly successful, powering many of the early personal computers and thousands of other applications in many fields. Surprisingly, the Z80 is still produced today in large volumes, almost exclusively as part of a system-on-a-chip. During its long life, many billions of units have been sold.

It turned out to have been a smart move to set aside my original product idea in favor of the Z80-CPU, though soon after its market introduction it was time for us to go back and develop my first idea. A couple of years later that product would become the Z8 microcontroller. Introduced in 1978, the Z8 became one of the best-selling microcontrollers in the market, and it too is still in volume production today.

Zilog was booming. On March 6, 1976, the day the Z80 was fully functional, we had 11 employees and 2,000 square feet of office space. In March of 1979 we had over 1,100 employees in several countries, two wafer fabs—the second one near Boise, Idaho—a system manufacturing plant in Sunnyvale, California, and a large chip assembly plant in Manila, Philippines. We had also spread into four additional existing buildings along Bubb Road in Cupertino close to where our first building was located.

However, success often brings out the worst in people, and it took a great toll on many of us, including me.

Over the years my relationship with Ralph had started to sour. There were some unpleasant episodes that I deliberately ignored, preferring to disregard them rather than face them directly. But they weighed on my heart and created a lot of inner tension. After he had become our chief operating officer, I noticed that he started to turn people against me, and it was clear he wanted my job. My life became miserable, and I could no longer suffer in silence; that intolerable condition had to end. I went directly to the board and explained the situation saying that one of us had to go. The board chose me to stay and Ralph to go. I won, but in truth, we all lost, including the company. This incident left me with deep feelings of bitterness and disappointment in myself, as well as with several unresolved questions.

The board also decided I needed someone to replace Ralph and said they had the right person, Manny Fernandez, the former CEO of another Exxon Enterprises startup that had been shut down. EE had hired Manny to fix that company, but when he took it over, he found nothing worth saving and suggested instead to unwind it. Therefore, he worked himself out of a job, thus gaining the respect of Ben Sykes, one of the managing directors of EE, who was also the *de facto* chairman of Zilog's board. When I objected, explaining that before making other changes I needed to reunify the company by having all the VPs report to me for some time to regain their trust, Sykes said no, forced his hand, and gave me no choice. Sure enough, when Manny came in, the VPs who had been reporting to Ralph were angry at me thinking that it had been my idea to bring a new chief operating officer on board right away. This happened in early 1979, and from that point on Zilog began to lose momentum. A series of events converged into a perfect storm.

Interlude

Between Los Altos and Cupertino is a vast nature reserve called Rancho San Antonio. The Rancho is open to the public and offers trails of varying difficulty leading to the foothills of the Santa Cruz Mountains. It is a place of great beauty where wild animals live in their natural habitat. For example, on one of our walks we saw more than a hundred wild turkeys, black and slender with their red wattles against the backdrop of a golden hill: it was such an amazing sight I had never seen before. For a long time, Elvia had walked every day with her friend Anna to the Rancho. They always met at the entrance where the path is flat. Soon after, the trail becomes steep and uphill all the way, but they were in good physical condition to tackle the climb. A few portions of the trail are shaded by oaks and redwoods and bordered by a cool stream gurgling over the rocks until the path becomes sunny again.

On one of their walks, they decided to follow a long path that led to the crest of the hill. They were immersed in nature, excited by the incredible beauty, when suddenly 15 yards away a huge mountain lion emerged from the hillside and crossed their path towards the steep valley below. Stunned, they exchanged a quick, fearful look. Fortunately for them, they were either against the wind, or perhaps the lion had already had a full breakfast, because it only momentarily turned his head in their direction before disappearing into the valley. With adrenaline in full force, they turned around and ran back to safety.

When Elvia told me what happened, she was still a bit shaken. They had taken a big risk because occasionally the newspapers would report that a mountain lion had killed a passerby or a cyclist. Elvia felt she was saved because her mission in life had not yet been fully accomplished. I like instead to think that the lion understood instantly of what metal Elvia is made of and ran for his life.

The Z8000

Among the first wave of new employees in March of 1976 was Bernard Peuto, a PhD in computer science and a computer architect, who worked for Amdahl, the company founded by Gene Amdahl, one of the key architects of IBM mainframe computers. I gave Bernard the job of architecting our next high-end microprocessor to be called Z8000. I had already determined that it should be a 16/32-bit CPU with 24-bit of address space, thus capable of addressing up to 32 MB of memory. In early 1976 that much memory appeared to be nearly infinite, since the newly introduced state of the art DRAM chips only stored 2 KB each.

It was also clear that the Z8000 could not be machine-code-compatible with the Z80 because the architecture and op-code assigned to the 8008, 8080, and Z80 instructions had been made without any forethought as to future expandability. Furthermore, the Z8000 architecture had to be regular and extensible to a future 32/64-bit architecture, making the Z80 the end of the line. I had reserved the Z800 designation for a future extension of the Z80 with memory space up to 16 MB, increased execution speed, and enhanced functionality.

Bernard was quite knowledgeable about computer architecture, with the scholarly erudition of a historian, but his imagination was limited, and his knowledge of computer applications was confined to mainframes, hardly the future of microprocessors. The main problem, again, was created by the number of pins available in a standard package, which exemplified a typical case of the "tail wagging the dog."

With 48 pins, we could have 16 pins for data and 16 pins for address, one pin per bit, with the rest of the pins dedicated to auxiliary functions, like in the Z80. To have the full 24-bit address in a single chip we needed a 56-pin package that did not exist. There was a 64-pin package that used a large area and was very costly, but I did not think it would work anyway. The best choice was 48 pins, which was only 20 percent larger than the 40-pin used by the Z80; but then we could only address 128 KB of memory (64K, 16-bit words). The idea of developing a nonstandard package on our own was out of the question, even for much larger companies than ours.

The solution Bernard proposed was memory segmentation, an approach originally used by the Burroughs B5000 computer. With memory segmentation, the memory was addressed as the number of the segment plus the address within that segment. Segmentation had many useful features, provided one did not need to cross the segment boundaries too often. This was indeed the case for most known applications at that time.

What neither Bernard nor I had imagined was the emergence of graphical user interfaces (GUI), like those used in the Xerox Alto computer and the Apple Macintosh (eight years later) that required linear addressing of large blocks of data the size of the display, generally much larger than 128 KB.

I had a hunch that something was missing with segmentation, but I could not put my finger on it. And every time I voiced my concerns to Bernard, he would emphasize its many advantages like the economy of memory (since most addresses would only be 16-bit rather than 24-bit), memory protection with user and supervisory modes, relocatable programs, and so on.

The other problem with segmentation was the need to have a second chip, a memory management unit (MMU), to perform the address translation when the overall memory was larger than 128 KB. True, one day we could integrate the two chips into one, but until that time a two-chip solution was something I could not stomach. However, Bernard knew how to be convincing. Rationally he appeared to be right since he was logically dispelling each of my specific objections, yet I still felt uncomfortable about possible negative consequences I could not clearly articulate. My instinct was sending a danger signal, but in the end, I gave in to logic. I should have trusted my gut feeling more and tried harder to find an example of a problem for which segmentation would have been disastrous.

Intel, faced with the same difficulty, also chose segmentation for its 8086. Their solution, however, could initially address four times more memory than we could with the Z8001, the single-chip Z8000 without MMU. Ultimately, the Intel solution won for political reasons more than for merit, because the Z8000 was far superior to the Intel 8086. Yet IBM picked the 8086 for their PC because Zilog was essentially owned by EE, a sworn competitor.

Had we chosen linear addressing, we could have likely won the Apple Macintosh socket that propelled Motorola's 68000 to fortune, though not as great as the one that befell Intel. We ended up being third excluded, caught in the middle of a political and a technical decision.

Captain Zilog

Bernard took a long time to complete the architecture of the CPU and the MMU, in part due to Shima's hostility toward him. The two were supposed to work closely together, but Shima was even more opinionated than Bernard and every time they met, they seemed to clash. Eventually, the specification was finished and Shima took over the chip design that lasted about two years. The Z8001 was introduced in 1979, six months after our direct competitor Intel's 8086.

Part of the Z8000's advertising campaign was the creation of a new character, "Captain Zilog." The captain was the hero of a technological story inspired by the famous writer-cartoonists Lou Brooks and Joe Kubert. Captain Zilog immediately gained a strong following among young microprocessor users, and the Z8001 was soon adopted by Olivetti for their personal computer. We were off to a good start.

Fig. 26 – Captain Zilog was the hero of a tech-novel, a marketing stunt that was part of the introduction of the Zilog Z8000 microprocessor in 1979.

Exxon Enterprises

During the negotiation with EE, Ralph and I had made no secret about our desire to turn Zilog into a public company, and in fact, I directly asked Ben Sykes if going public was also EE's goal. He said it was fine, omitting to tell us that their long-term objective was to create a fully owned division in the information industry to diversify the parent company. They had correctly identified this fast-growing market as the next major driver of the emerging global economy. Consequently, EE had already invested in some strategic segments of information technology.

When we first met, they had a minority interest in Qume, a company with a proprietary high-quality, fast printer, a majority ownership in Vydec, a word processor manufacturer, and similar ownership in Qwip, a fax manufacturer. After they had funded Zilog, they also invested in a liquid crystal display company, a solid-state laser outfit, and several other ventures. One of those others was Qyx, an electronic typewriter company that intended to compete with IBM Selectric typewriters by adding word processing to their typewriter. I was surprised when I found out that the Qyx's CEO was Dan Matthias and that his company had begun directly as a division of EE rather than as an independent startup. This gave a clear preview of the coming attractions.

The turning point

In 1976, when it was time for our second round of investment, the VC situation had improved a lot. I wanted to bring some outside investors to our company to diversify our financial base and to add some members to our board of directors with experience in the industry. The Zilog board at that time had five members: three from EE—Dan, John, and Ben—Ralph, and me. That combination was almost equivalent to having two members since Dan reported to John, John reported to Ben, and Ralph and I were always in agreement, at least at the board meetings. So, whenever it was time for a vote, Dan would look at John, John would look at Ben and when Ben decided, the other two seconded Ben's decisions. I felt we could do better than that.

Before this second round of financing, we had also been approached by Heinz Nixdorf himself, owner of Germany-based Nixdorf Computers. He was interested in investing in us, as was Bill Draper, a legend in the VC community. But when I told Ben that we wanted to have some outside investors, he replied that EE did not need any other backers. He stressed that they had been good to us and that they would continue to take good care of us.

It was clear that EE did not want anybody else in the deal. Now I understood why it was so important for them to have control of the company from the outset. Our only chance to include outside investors was to put up a fight, which could have ended with Ralph and me getting fired unless they felt we were indispensable to Zilog's success. The latter seemed like a remote possibility since, with the Z80 working, from their point of view it was just a question of management, and they believed that good managers like them could manage anything.

That was the turning point in determining Zilog's future. I had a feeling that if we accepted the EE conditions, we would never become the public company we had dreamed of. We would instead become an affiliate, or perhaps a division of EE, captured by Exxon's gravitational field, and permanently lose the already slim chance of gaining enough escape velocity to be free again. Unfortunately, my instincts proved to be correct.

By 1978 Exxon had created a large organization called Exxon Office Systems, comprised of three divisions: Vydec, Qwip, and Qyx, headed up by an ex-IBM executive. Zilog was not yet part of that organization, but the writing was on the wall. Exxon had declared war on IBM and I soon began spending more and more time at Exxon's headquarters on the Avenue of the Americas, New York City, than with our customers. With my falling out with Ralph and the EE takeover, I felt I had lost my edge. The final curtain came toward the end of 1980. With their man Manny Fernadez already installed as COO, Exxon wanted to consolidate Zilog with the rest of Office Systems.

Fig. 27 – This cover story featured Zilog and Exxon Enterprises. The article was already giving a clear indication about the future of Zilog in December of 1977.

An elegant way out

It was time for me to go. I suggested to EE a way out that would not create too many negative repercussions. I proposed that I be promoted to an open executive position within EE and move to New York. Manny would become the CEO of Zilog, I would become chairman of the board and help with the consolidation. If at the end of a six-month trial period I didn't like my position, I would resign, EE would purchase my Zilog stock, and I would leave to pursue other interests, as well as sign a noncompete clause. My plan was accepted, and I had to say goodbye to my first venture. Just before Christmas in 1980, we had a farewell dinner with all of our Cupertino employees. I received many presents and left with a warm send-off but a heavy heart.

I started my new job in New York in January of 1981, working at EE headquarters and returning on Fridays to the Bay Area to spend weekends with my family. In mid-May of 1981, I communicated to EE that I was not going to stay, the expected outcome on both sides. After getting a fat check from EE, I left New York for good and returned to Silicon Valley.

A few months later, in August, after I had already left EE, Zilog would be excluded from what would become one of the most important developments in computer history. IBM introduced their PC with the Intel 8088 (an 8-bit-bus version of their 8086 16-bit microprocessor). This product was a huge surprise because industry experts and pundits did not expect IBM, a company that had promoted large computers to be shared among many users, to endorse a personal computer, much less a PC that was an open system. IBM, then considered the diamond tip of American business, irreversibly changed the information industry. But it crippled itself way beyond what anyone would have ever expected by the avalanche of events caused by its own decisions.

The PC shaped the democratization of the information revolution for the next thirty years until the introduction of the Apple iPhone, which changed once more the market dynamics by pushing the revolution even deeper into society. It is ironic that Apple, the company that led the early personal computer revolution and single-handedly created the iPhone, today (as of October 22, 2020) has a market capitalization fourteen times that of ExxonMobil.

After four generations of microprocessors…

> *It isn't only for what we do that we are held responsible, but also for what we do not do.*
>
> —Moliére

During this tumultuous time, our family had been blessed with the birth of two boys, one after another: Marc was born in November of 1979 and Eric arrived in the same month of the following year. All our children were much desired and loved with all the love that I was able to give them. This love was like the kind I had received as a child, though only much later did I notice its limitations. Like my father, I also put my work and study first, convinced that my primary duty was to be a good provider. I did not realize then that the children needed above all my attention and care. When I finally understood this, they had already grown up.

In America, children typically leave the family at age 18. Our children left home much earlier: Eric, at age eight, spent a school year in Milan at the home of Uncle Franco and Aunt Viviana, and then returned for another year when he was 13. Marc spent his three middle school years with them at the International School of Milan, years that were precious not only for him but also for his uncle and aunt who had no children.

Marzia also spent several years in Italy, first in Vicenza attending the third year of primary school taught by my mother, and then the fourth year of Liceo Classico. She also graduated from the European Institute of Design in Milan to go on to enjoy success as an artist.

Now, after so many years of personal self-reflection, I realize that only by acquiring a new consciousness can a person interrupt from passing from generation to generation the chain of conditioning that perpetuates emotional wounds. As Jung wrote, "What we do not make conscious returns later as destiny."

When I left Zilog, I had spent about 10 years of my life creating and bringing into the world the first four generations of microprocessors. The microprocessor was like a child to me, a kid who had come a long way in the world and could now take care of itself [16]. It was time for me to do something else.

The experience with EE had reinforced my belief that only a startup company could catalyze the extraordinary passion, energy, and focus needed to innovate. It was a good bet that I would soon try my hand again at another startup.

Before embarking on a new venture, I first needed a long, restorative vacation with the entire family, something I had never been able to do before. During those last 15 years I had worked almost without interruption, taking not even half of my accrued vacation time. We waited for Marzia to finish school and then we all left to spend a couple of months in Italy with relatives and friends. It was time to stop and unplug. The sale of my Zilog stock had given me ample resources to comfortably support the family for the rest of my days without having to work again.

Unplugging, however, was not as easy as it might have seemed. Although I was physically a continent and an ocean away from Zilog, my mind was still there. Even on vacation, I kept thinking about what had happened and wondering how things would have turned out if I had made different decisions. Ever since Ralph had left the company, I was troubled by the thought that I also had my share of the blame for what happened. Given his provocative behavior, it was easy for me to attribute all wrongdoing to him. However, we know that it takes two to tango, so I also must have done something wrong. But what?

It took a while before I realized that I had contributed to the situation not so much with what I did, but with what I *did not* do. Instead of confronting Ralph the first time he hurt me with his behavior, I preferred to let go and endure in silence. I realized that this was my normal *modus operandi*, a behavior I had naturally adopted or been conditioned to by my education without being aware of it. When something hit me personally, I chose to let the offense slide by to avoid confronting the unpleasant. And then, only if circumstances turned unbearable, would I react strongly and unpredictably.

By not asserting myself at the first provocation, I had tacitly given Ralph permission to do more of the same, up to the breaking point of the final showdown. Although I was quite responsible in fulfilling my commitments to others, I had been *irresponsible* to myself. I kept thinking, *what prevented me from stopping him? Why was I pretending that nothing happened? Why was I protecting those who hurt me?*

Pandora's box

> *Be the hero of your life, not the victim.*
>
> —Nora Ephron

I also wondered: *What was to be gained from suffering in silence? What motivated me to be a victim?* Digging deeper, other questions surfaced: *Was this a hidden form of competition? Did I want to be superior to Ralph by suffering in silence for his aggressions? Was I also engaged in a power struggle, mine veiled and his brash?*

In his essay "Vittimismo," Massimo Recalcati, a prominent Italian psychoanalyst, writes: "Choosing to occupy the position of the victim ensures a nobility of soul and the right to unlimited compensation." Had I read these words ten years earlier, I would not have understood them because I was wearing a thick armor to valiantly defend the belief that my behavior was "noble." For the first time in my life, I saw the intricacies of human psychology that I had neglected in my urgency to follow my great passion. It took me many more years to understand that when I am irresponsible toward myself, I am also irresponsible towards others by allowing aggressive behavior to intensify and spread.

Starting with those questions, I began the first fundamental step of a spiritual journey that can only begin when one takes *full responsibility* for what happens in their life, for better or for worse.

I had opened Pandora's box and am still to this day confronting the deep psycho – spiritual issues raised by those questions. Over many years, I have discovered that to give honest answers, I had to detect and uncover the overlapping masks I had constructed to hide the truth from myself. Then, once a mask was unveiled, I had to understand what had motivated its creation. And to do this I had to openly face my fears.

It took me much more time to fully recognize that the events that made me suffer the most were those that eventually revealed my strongest resistance to acknowledging the truth about myself. As Hermann Hesse states, "I also began to understand that sorrows, disappointments and melancholy are not made to make us unhappy and take away value and dignity, but to mature."

5
My Third Life Continues

Success is not final; failure is not fatal: It is the courage to continue that counts.

—Winston S. Churchill

When I returned from our extended vacation, I realized I was free from the necessity of work. But free to do what? This question was disquieting. I felt a part of me pushing to do something, anything, while another part pulled to better understand what I wanted before embarking on a new adventure. For the first time in my life I realized that I had a compulsion to work, an urge to lose myself in activity. Was that my way to avoid looking inside myself? Was that the hidden purpose of my addiction to work? Despite these nagging questions, I was also watching with surprise and fascination the rapid changes taking place in the industry.

Toward the end of 1981, the extraordinary success of the IBM PC was becoming evident. That success was achieved by the company's choice to make their PC an open system. Their PC was even more open than the Apple II because its operating system had been purchased from Microsoft in a nonexclusive agreement. Therefore, all the key ingredients to create PC clones were available to third parties, which encouraged a market race to make the best PC. That excessive competition must have been either dismissed as inconsequential or not predicted at all by IBM when they decided to make their PC an open system.

Before the introduction of the PC, IBM was the quintessential business-to-business firm, selling large computers intended to be shared among many users. Apple instead sold computers for individual use to private customers. Hence, IBM endorsed computers for personal use within the business community where Apple had previously no chance of succeeding. This positioning encouraged many companies to create specialized hardware and software add-on products for every type of business and application, thus extending the utility of the PC far beyond what a single company could have ever achieved alone, even a powerful and productive corporation like IBM.

The IBM PC was indeed revolutionary—socially even more than technologically—because the company had sanctioned the idea of a *personal computer* for each worker. The emergence of many companies making PC clones allowed the market to benefit from a rapid exploration of all desirable features in all possible market niches. This condition created a gigantic testing ground for new ideas. At the peak of this collective madness, about a hundred different companies were making PC clones. Only a few survived, and some even prospered much beyond what IBM must have considered its worst-case projections.

IBM not only moved in the opposite direction of its traditional behavior, but it went too far for its own good in outsourcing its critical PC hardware and software components. Therefore, IBM created the conditions for Intel, Microsoft, Compaq, and many other companies to handsomely profit from its miscalculation, and to ultimately endanger its very existence. Simply put, they had played with fire and gotten burned.

It is interesting to look at the situation today compared with 1982, the year after the introduction of the IBM PC. The market capitalization of Apple in 1982 was about $940 million, exceptional even then for a recent startup, compared with IBM's $35 billion, the best of the lot. As of Oct. 20, 2020, Apple stood at $2,020 billion and IBM at $120 billion. Over the 38-year span, Apple grew over 2000 times while IBM grew 3.4 times, underscoring the different alignment of the two companies to the technological and market changes. Yet IBM survived while most other mainframe and mini-computer companies of that era did not outlast the tsunami created by the democratization of computing and communication that fueled the last four decades of the information revolution.

Cygnet Technologies, Inc.

All this ferment of ideas and innovations affected me as well, and so I joined the bandwagon by developing a special voice and data intelligent telephone that, once connected to a PC, would create an ideal tool for managers whose main activity was centered more on communication than on computing. This type of functionality had been proposed in the abstract for some time by several futurists who promoted the "office of the future" or the "paperless society," speculating on the many new possibilities offered by rapid transformation in the workplace caused by the upwelling information era.

As a first step toward that vision, I came up with the idea of combining a separate intelligent voice and data telephone with a PC to create an environment that seamlessly integrated voice and data communications with personal productivity tools. To that end I started Cygnet Technologies in early 1982, with Lauren Yazolino as VP of engineering, and Jerry Klein as VP of marketing and sales. Our initial capital was provided by Merrill Lynch Venture Capital and Bay Partners, who were later joined by Venrock and the Sprout Group, all VCs of great standing.

We called our product Communication Cosystem (Fig. 28). It was defined as "the other half of the PC," the half dedicated to voice and data communications to improve the productivity of small workgroups. In addition to automating communications, the Cosystem included a powerful email system that didn't require a central computer. It could automatically send electronic mail to multiple users and alert each one when a new email had arrived by turning a light on in their Cosystems. The Cosystem also enabled the PC to act as a data terminal, manage automatic and errorless file transfers, and perform many communication management functions for record-keeping and time-billing. It also offered several productivity tools such as contact lists and calendar management. For example, it allowed calling a telephone number written in an email or in a calendar by simply pushing a button on the telephone when the cursor was over the name or phone number.

Fig. 28 – The Communication Cosystem, "the other half of the PC," which managed the user's voice and data communications, along with many personal productivity tools (1984).

Bear in mind that this functionality was available before the existence of multi-tasking operating systems, and before the graphical user interfaces in the Apple Macintosh and in Microsoft Windows. It was also the time when the highest affordable data communication speed was 1200 baud, i.e., 150 characters per second (a character is a letter of the alphabet plus a small set of other basic symbols). This meant that a typical page of text took about 25 seconds to be transmitted. At that time, AT&T considered 9600 baud (bits per second) to be the maximum possible speed achievable with the standard two-wire phone connection. Thanks to the end of the US telecommunications monopoly, newly competitive and innovative market forces led to the internet revolution offering tens of millions of bits per second over the same phone lines.

The Communication Cosystem was formally introduced at the PC-Fair in San Francisco in early 1984 where it received a lot of attention from media and consumers alike, winning the prize for the most innovative product of the show. Unfortunately, its introduction could not have happened at a worse time in the telecommunications business. The breakup of the Bell Operating Companies in January of 1984 had caused a wait-and-see attitude in the market, dramatically slowing down the purchase of all new telecommunication gear, especially within medium and large sized companies, our target market. Those types of purchases required the blessing of their chief information officer (CIO) and/or the head of their telecommunication services. Those guardians of corporate order, given the market uncertainty, feared making wrong decisions, thus making it near impossible for us to gain critical mass.

Our business plan called for first-year sales of 15,000 units. That level would have allowed us to reach profitability and finance the development of the successor product to stay ahead of the game and fend off competitors certain to follow. Instead, we sold 5,000 units. Not terrible, but not enough to take off, thus discouraging investors and employees alike. The competition also showed up as expected. Major names like Compaq and ROLM offered integrated solutions that superficially appeared more convenient than ours, but in fact were more rigid and costly. They fared even worse than us, despite their greater resources and higher staying power. All of them eventually exited the business, just like we did.

In the final act, Cygnet Technologies was purchased in 1986 by Everex, an up – and-coming PC clone company more interested in our cumulative losses to reduce their tax bill than in our products. Everex did not want to take over responsibility for servicing the installed base of Cosystem users and so let a few exiting Cygnet employees take care of that obligation. Those ex-employees made a good living well into the nineties providing service to our user groups, many of which were in the military, until the internet tsunami put an end to it. That decade-long operational stretch is a testament to the usefulness of our product.

I remember casually meeting Steve Jobs soon after the Cosystem had reached the market in 1984. He congratulated us and then added dismissively, "but it occupies too much real estate." Surprisingly, the iPhone, first introduced in 2007, was the only product by then to achieve the type of voice and data integration combined with personal productivity tools that the PC-Cosystem combination had provided in 1984. Several Cygnet patents have also been cited to establish prior art in many patent litigation cases involving voice and data integration.

Over time, I realized that high tech startup companies generate enormous intellectual wealth even when they fail to produce economic wealth. They create the humus that fertilizes future innovations, provide the unique experiential ground for their managers and employees' personal and professional growth, and facilitate the success of future ventures.

The search for cognitive computers

In late 1985, Kevin Kinsella of Avalon Ventures, a seed venture capital firm in San Diego, had gotten wind that artificial neural networks might be a promising technology. These structures mimic the biological neural networks in our brain and can learn from examples. Kevin had met with Professor Gary Lynch of UC Irvine, who had some insights into the neuroanatomy of the olfactory cortex and had formulated some hypotheses about the learning process in rodents' brains. So Kevin brought together Gary Lynch and Lauren Yazolino, who had just left our Cygnet Technologies as VP of engineering, to explore starting a new venture. Lauren, knowing about my strong interest in machine-learning and desire to understand how the brain works, asked for my opinion on the opportunity. He arranged a meeting in early 1986 with Gary Lynch at the UC Irvine campus to discuss the state of the art in biological neural networks.

The lack of progress in artificial intelligence (AI) since the boastful promises of the early 1960s, had been disappointing. I had already concluded that the brain must process information by using quite different principles than computers. Therefore, I was curious to understand how the brain so effortlessly solves problems like handwriting and speech recognition that AI had such difficulty cracking. I offered my free consultation with the option of becoming a co-founder if I could find a reasonable business strategy to pursue.

After Gary's presentation, I was intrigued by the possibilities, though the science was still rather vague. He had no idea about how to convert the knowledge into a technology, much less into a product that could make a startup company successful. Back home I programmed a PC to simulate the type of networks that Gary had described and found them promising for handwriting recognition. Therefore, I became a co-founder and consulted on developing the business strategy, while intending to start working with them full-time after the sale of Cygnet Technologies, which was then being negotiated. Lauren was the CEO and Gary was a consultant together with Michel Baudry, a post-doc working for him. My initial work focused on understanding the neural network architecture of the rat's olfactory cortex described by Gary, and then figuring out the best way in which that architecture could be implemented using semiconductor technology, my specialty.

A short time later I came up with the idea of using floating-gate transistors to store analog values which emulated the synaptic weight, i.e. the effect of the output of a neuron on the input of another neuron. This was a new idea, since floating-gate transistors had only been used to store binary information. Adding the variable currents produced by analog synapses made with floating gates would allow us to perform tens of thousands of multiplications and additions in parallel, using only two transistors per multiply-add calculation, including the nonvolatile storage of the synaptic weight. This approach was many orders of magnitudes denser than what was achievable with digital technology in 1986, and potentially enabled the cost-effective use of artificial neural networks for real time pattern-recognition applications.

Synaptics, Inc.

The name of the company given by Kinsella, the chairman of the board, was Meno Corporation. Meno was the title of one of Plato's earliest dialogs about virtues, hardly relevant to our business, and *meno* in Italian means minus or less; not an auspicious name. I thought we could do better and proposed naming it Synaptics, a portmanteau of synapse and electronics, given that the core technology was going to be solid-state synapses. Everybody liked the name (Kinsella abstained) and it was adopted after checking its availability.

The initial vision I proposed was for the development of artificial neural networks capable of learning by using MOS floating-gate transistors. The first patent for Synaptics, issued under Faggin and Lynch, involved such structures [17].

I joined Synaptics full-time as CTO in the second half of 1986, after Cygnet Technologies' acquisition was completed. By early 1987, it was clear that it would take at least four or five years before we could have any useful technology with which to create some novel products. By that time, Gary Lynch was no longer providing consulting and there was no need for Lauren to be a full-time CEO for the foreseeable future. Furthermore, Kevin was pushing for a product right away, refusing to accept my conclusion that there was not even a technology with which to make a product, never mind a successful one.

I had also discovered that professor Carver Mead, one of the pioneers in computer aided design (CAD) technology at the famous California Institute of Technology in Pasadena, California, had been working for a few years on neuromorphic sensory systems made with analog technology. I had known Carver since 1969 when he was a consultant to Gordon Moore at Fairchild, and later at

Intel. After I explained what we were trying to do, he was interested enough to dedicate one full day a week to Synaptics.

I suggested to our two investors and board members—Jim Bochnowski of TVI and Keith Geeslin of the Sprout Group—that the best way forward would be to spend several years with a small team of young engineers and scientists developing the basic technology for learning systems, before deciding on which product to make. I said that to build a viable business would take many years, though we didn't need to spend a lot of money. I also proposed to take over as CEO and nominated Carver Mead to serve as chairman of the board, although my real job would be to develop the basic technology and vision for the company. They agreed, and we restructured the company in March of 1987.

By 1988 the vision had evolved to include general-purpose building blocks for making sensory systems based on neuromorphic ICs. That meant defining a family of chips for solving generic pattern recognition problems based on learning rather than on programming. The key was to address this class of problems with the same small family of mostly analog chips. The general idea was to combine various numbers of four or five different types of chips to build a variety of pattern recognizers, just like we do today with memory for which the amount and organization depend on the complexity of the program and type of data needed. The operation of the entire system would then be orchestrated by a general-purpose microprocessor or microcontroller. This goal, however, was easier said than done because we needed an overall architecture for neural networks that did not yet exist.

To develop the technology, we concentrated first on solving several difficult pattern recognition problems for potential customers, while in parallel developing the basic VLSI technology for neural networks capable of continuous learning, along with imaging technology for vision systems [18], [19].

One of the early custom projects was the design of a character recognition chip for Verifone to optically read the magnetic ink character set at the bottom of bank checks, and thus achieve higher accuracy than was possible with a magnetic reading for which those characters had been explicitly designed. This chip was called I-1000.

Verifone was the world leader in payment systems and had built an experimental point-of-sale check reader which consisted of a microcontroller and an I-1000. Extensive field tests had shown better results than those with a magnetic reader, and without requiring the motorized transport of checks necessary with the latter. The I-1000 was a highly sophisticated chip containing: (1) an optical imager; (2) two neural networks, the first for locating each character in the string and the second for recognizing it; (3) several analog-to-digital converters for the output data and; (4) the control logic to interface with a conventional microcontroller. The combination of the Synaptics I-1000 with a properly programmed microcontroller realized the entire electronics of the check reader.

Our product was announced at a joint Synaptics-Verifone press conference in June of 1992. Verifone later decided not to enter that business, despite having paid for the development of the chip. Their decision was a disappointment, even though the project taught us many useful lessons about the design of neural networks.

Fig. 29 – An experimental neural network chip designed at Synaptics (1989).

Is it possible to make a conscious computer?

Once I started working at Synaptics, I began studying biology and neuroscience on my own, subjects I had not studied at the university level. All of the neuroscience books I read described brain operation by reducing it to pure electrochemical activity with the hidden assumption, never explicitly stated, that this activity was identical to sentient perception. It seemed to me that there had to be both unconscious and conscious recognitions, the latter occurring through the feelings and sensations that are quite different from pure electrochemical activity. So, I asked Gary Lynch to explain how electrical activity in the brain could manifest itself in the form of sensations and feelings since the two could not possibly be the same thing.

As a psychologist turned neuroscientist, he replied, "Are you talking about consciousness?"

I didn't know then that "consciousness" was the proper word for what I was trying to express, but it sounded right. "Yes, how does consciousness work and why is this word never mentioned?"

"Oh, don't worry about it. It's something that happens in the brain and one day we'll understand it," he replied.

And that was the end of our conversation. I had never before thought about the nature of consciousness. Gary's position was entirely consistent with the materialist assumption that all that exists must be produced by the interactions of elementary particles. Over the years I had converted to the physicalist view of the world which holds that consciousness must somehow emerge from the operation of the brain. But how? It was not enough to say that it emerges "somehow." I needed an explanation.

I thought that if it arises from the brain, which is a complex information processing system like a machine, then a computer could be conscious as well, at least in principle. Taken by great curiosity, I began to think how I could make a conscious computer. This led me to reflect deeply on the characteristics of consciousness, and I soon encountered the great obstacle: the complete lack of understanding we have about the nature of sensations and feelings.

For example, let's consider how a rose is recognized by its smell. A rose emits specific molecules with unique three-dimensional structures. These can fit as "keys" in the "locks" of certain receptor molecules embedded in the olfactory cell membranes located in the nasal epithelium. When this happens, the cells containing the now-activated receptors produce electrical signals. These electrical signals generated by the specific mix of molecules emitted by the rose constitute the input signals to the neural networks of the olfactory cortex, and their output signals correspond to the name of the identified object: a rose.

A machine can certainly recognize a rose by its "emissions" through emulating the natural process I just described. However, a machine does not feel anything, while we feel the aroma or scent as well as recognize the rose as the source of that feeling. In other words, where the name of the recognized object is another symbol, the scent of the rose is not a symbol, it is something else. It is a sentient experience that connects us with our emotions and knowledge.

The scent is something completely different from the electrical signals generated by the neural networks. It is related to them, of course, but it is not identical, nor can it be produced directly from them since it has a completely different quality than electrical or mechanical activity. The scent of a rose, just like the taste of chocolate or the sound of a violin, is not another symbol. It is an *experience*, a feeling that makes symbolic data conscious. We know the scent exists because we feel it in our awareness. Consciousness is then the capacity to know the meaning of certain symbols.

A computer that identifies a rose by its aroma only mechanically captures the pattern of electrical signals produced by appropriate sensors of the rose's aromatic molecules (the chemical symbols). The computer is not aware of the scent of the rose, even though it may respond in various ways to the rose symbol. Thus, the computer blindly responds to a rose the way it has been programmed to, or in the way it has automatically learned. The computer can neither be aware, nor consciously know anything. Thus, the *comprehension* brought by consciousness is not accessible to a computer. Herein lies the fundamental limitation of artificial intelligence.

Feelings, sensations, and sentiments are not symbols like electrical or chemical signals. They represent instead the meaning of symbols in the "space" of our consciousness. Consciousness is *the inner space* where the translation of signals coming from the world are processed by the brain and take place in the form of feelings, sensations, and the meanings behind them that we perceive within. The nature of feelings is completely different from that of physical phenomena. A physical phenomenon is what takes place in the material world and is accessible from the outside through our senses and instruments. It is what gives rise to a so-called third-person experience common to all observers. A feeling, on the other hand, is a first-person experience accessible only from within by the owner of the consciousness.

This conversion of a rose symbol to its scent is an example of the so-called "hard problem of consciousness," as philosopher David Chalmers called it in 1995 [20]. It can be expressed as follows: What is the physical phenomenon responsible for the feeling associated with the scent of a rose? What something "feels like," a sensation or a feeling, is called quale (plural: qualia), and therefore the hard problem of consciousness can be stated as: "How do qualia emerge from matter?"

The hard problem of consciousness

Science cannot explain this phenomenon, and nobody seems to have the faintest idea about how this miracle happens. It is surprising that most researchers believe there is no miracle. We are so used to being aware that we generally do not recognize that consciousness cannot possibly emerge from unconscious matter. Only those who have begun to think seriously about this problem realize that consciousness is a fundamentally unsolved problem.

For years I tried to understand how consciousness could arise from electrical or biochemical signals. Invariably, electrical signals

can only produce other electrical signals or other physical consequences such as force or movement, but never sensations and feelings that are qualitatively different. Feelings are internal subjective
properties or states correlated to external properties of matter that
we consider objective. They represent a class of phenomena completely different from material phenomena.

It seems to me that just like electricity is a fundamental physical property that cannot spontaneously arise from elementary particles devoid of some essential electrical quality, the same could be
true for consciousness. Electricity and magnetism exist in macroscopic bodies because some elementary particles contain electrical
charge and magnetic spin. Likewise, consciousness may already be
contained in some essential form in the very elementary particles
of which everything is made. No one has been able to explain
how consciousness could arise from matter that does not already
contain some form of consciousness. Consciousness is where the
conversion from outer material symbolic reality into inner semantic reality takes place, and qualia are the bearers of meaning. But
couldn't consciousness also be the space in which the inverse conversion from meaning to symbols takes place?

If yes, this would imply that inner reality could have a direct
impact on outer reality as well, though classical physics denies this
possibility by postulating that only outer reality exists and inner
reality has no causal power. This is equivalent to saying that either
the inner world is illusory or that inner reality can only be influenced by outer reality though not vice versa. But then how can
interiority emerge solely from outer reality when the physical laws
control only the transformation of outer phenomena into other
outer phenomena? The logical conclusion of materialism is that
inner reality is illusory and meaning does not exist.

Yet the outer world is brought inside us through the sensory-
brain system and becomes an inner experience. If consciousness
did not exist, we should have no experience at all, inner or outer,
and therefore wouldn't know anything. Consciousness is needed
to know even the most trivial of things. Furthermore, if there is a

fundamental influence from outside to inside, shouldn't there be also an influence from the inside out?

It was then when I realized that consciousness can only be studied through first-person experiences, because no third-person experiment could ever reveal the subjective feelings I'm living through. Therefore, I decided to study consciousness using the only example I knew, myself.

Today I know that I am conscious within myself, but I cannot prove it. And if I cannot even prove that I am conscious, how can I prove if anyone else is conscious? The existence of consciousness cannot be objectively determined with any outer measurement. It is private and cannot be observed from the outside. Therefore, I can only know the true feelings of another person if that person discloses them to me, but my knowledge cannot be certain because that person could be mistaken or lying. Any external measurement can only reveal physical correlates of consciousness, but not what the person truly feels. Qualia, the bearers of meaning, are not visible in any way from the outside. This intense investigation was the ground from which some amazing surprises arose.

Awakening

Spiritual awakening is the most essential thing in human life, it is the only purpose of existence.

—Khalil Gibran

Despite having received a generous indoctrination during my adolescence, or maybe because of it, I progressively abandoned my religious beliefs as I grew older. By thirty, the only trace of religion left in me was the idea that there must somehow be a God. I imagined God to be like a creative principle for the simple reason that the universe could not have created itself, unless "universe" was another name for God.

By forty, I had fully accepted the materialist worldview and concluded that when we die it is game over, because consciousness must be a property of matter, given that only matter exists. Therefore, when the body dies, consciousness must do the same. *Reality is just like that. It is simple. No big deal. No point fussing over it.* Without being aware of it, I had been hypnotized by the materialist ideas about reality. I had accepted them the same way I had accepted the religious dogmas in my younger years.

I felt that even if God existed, He had to be too distant and too disinterested in human affairs to have any impact on our individual lives. And given my ephemeral life, and God's presumed disinterest in me, I had no reason to be interested in Him.

Midway in our life's journey

Midway in our life's journey, I found myself within a dark forest…
—Dante Alighieri

By the late 1980s, I had been successful in technology and business. I was wealthy enough that I did not need to work one more day of my life. And most importantly, I had a splendid family. I had indeed been fortunate and achieved everything the world said would make me happy. What more could I wish for? It was then that a crisis hit me. Just when I was at the height of my success, I got in touch with a deep dissatisfaction brooding inside me. I realized that I was very unhappy but pretended not to be, because I was preventing myself from experiencing my despair. I lived hiding in an artificial cocoon that I had constructed to shield myself from feeling my deepest and most genuine feelings. I only imitated being happy. Yet, I could not understand how I could be so unhappy when I had achieved everything that common wisdom says is necessary to be happy. *What is wrong with this picture?* I wondered.

Two more questions were insistently resurfacing, despite my attempts to suppress them and my preoccupation with my commitments: *what is the meaning of my life and what do I want from my life?*

Growing up, religion had given me answers full of hope before I had the maturity to ask the right questions. Now I could no longer renounce my rationality and my right to think with my own head. To have blind faith was too much to ask. On the other hand, my interpretation of materialism had taken away even the hope that hope existed, because it described a dystopian, soulless, and mechanical world. Once I had accepted the materialist vision, I could no longer content myself with fragments of wisdom gathered here and there, which praised virtue, beauty, commitment, altruism, and knowledge. These were all high-sounding but empty virtues since they were pure human constructs, illusions that would vanish with our certain death.

I had reached a stage of quiet desperation and almost felt dead inside; wondering, *what do I live for?* And at the same time I felt compelled to maintain a facade, given my responsibilities as a husband, father, and head of a promising company involving the wellbeing of many people. My spiritual suffering had bottomed-out and so I asked for help. I prayed, not verbally and not even consciously, searching for answers to my fundamental questions: "What is the meaning of my life? Is death the end of everything?"

Every time I fell into that desperate place where my life seemed utterly meaningless, I perceived at the very depth of my consciousness a weak but persistent *point of light* against a dark background. I found enough hope in that faint light to want to live.

A sudden illumination

> *... the love that moves the sun and the other stars.*
> —Dante Alighieri, *The Divine Comedy*
> *Paradiso Canto XXXIII, verse 145*

In December of 1990, while I was with my family at Lake Tahoe during the Christmas holidays, I woke up around midnight to drink a glass of water. I poured iced water from the kitchen refrigerator and moved to the adjacent living room to lazily look at the now dark and mysterious lake while sipping the refreshing water. When I went back to bed and tried to fall asleep again, I felt a powerful rush of energy emerge from my chest like nothing I had ever felt before and could not even imagine possible. The feeling was love, but a love so intense and so incredibly fulfilling that it surpassed any other notions I had about love. Even more unbelievable was the fact that I knew I was the source of this love. I experienced it as a broad beam of shimmering white light, alive and beatific, gushing from my heart with incredible strength.

Then suddenly that light exploded. It filled the room and expanded to embrace the entire universe with the same white brilliance. I *knew* then, without a shadow of a doubt, that this was the substance from which all that exists is made. This was what created the universe out of itself. Then, with immense surprise, I *knew* that *I was that light!*

The entire experience lasted perhaps one minute, and it changed me forever. My relationship with the world had always been as a separate observer perceiving the universe as outside myself and disconnected from me. What made this event astonishing was its impossible perspective because I was *both* the experiencer *and* the experience. I was simultaneously the observer of the world and the world. I was the world observing itself! I was concurrently *knowing* that the world is made of a substance that feels like love, and that I *am* that substance!

In other words, the essence of reality was revealed to be a substance that knows itself in its self-reflection, and its self-knowing feels like an irrepressible and dynamic love.

This experience contained an unprecedented force of truth because it felt true at all the levels of my being. At the physical level, my body was alive and vibrant like I had never felt before. At the emotional level, I experienced myself as an impossibly powerful source of love, and at the mental level I knew with certainty that all is "made of" love.

That experience also manifested the existence of another level of reality never previously lived: a spiritual level where I felt one with the world. This was *direct knowing*, stronger than the certainty that human logic provides; a knowing from the inside rather than from the outside involving for the first time the concurrence and resonance of all of my conscious aspects: the physical, emotional, mental, and spiritual.

I like to think that I experienced my nature both as a particle and as a wave, to use an analogy with quantum physics otherwise impossible to comprehend with the ordinary logical mind. The particle aspect was the ability to maintain my unique identity despite also being the world, which was the wave aspect. And yet, even my identity was part of the world, not me, because I experienced myself as the world rather than "my" point of view. Thus, I now see my identity as that unique point of view with which One—All that is, the totality of what exists—observes and knows itself. I am a point of view of One, a portion of One indivisible from it.

My experience has maintained its original intensity and clarity over the years and has changed my life from the inside out. It also continues to have a powerful impact to this day.

The difficulty in telling it

> And those who were seen dancing were thought to be insane by those who could not hear the music.
>
> —Friedrich Nietzsche

Before my awakening, if someone had described to me a similar experience, I would have dismissed it as their vivid imagination, as a daydream with no reality. Thus, I am sympathetic to the skeptic. Yet, that vivid experience occurred while I was awake and alert. It revealed a reality *more real* than the physical world I had previously thought was the only reality.

My situation is analogous to a sea creature that lives in the deep and has never seen either the seabed, sea surface, or sunlight, and is convinced that the sea in which it lives is everything that exists. Imagine its surprise if it were taken out of the water where it could experience the blinding light and warmth of the sun, to realize that the sea ends with a wavy surface. To see the sky with *clouds* moving about and birds flying, not to mention an island in the distance with trees springing up from the solid ground.

But once back in its home environment, this creature would find it impossible to convince its companions that the sea is not the only reality; that the sea actually ends and beyond it there is another world made of... At this point the poor creature would realize that there are no words to describe what it had experienced so vividly and clearly. Being misunderstood, it would never speak of its experience again, though it would keep it forever in its heart, sure of its reality, even though it could not properly describe it.

I know with certainty that the reality I experienced is even "more real" than the physical reality I previously thought was the *only* reality, even though I cannot explain what "more real" means. This awakening experience revealed that "reality" is a relative rather than an absolute concept. And in the years since, I have had a great variety of other spontaneous and extraordinary experiences that have gradually changed many of my ideas about the nature of reality. As Blaise Pascal puts it, "The last step of reason is to recognize that there are so many things that surpass it."

During those years I lived a kind of double life, the first dedicated to the inner exploration of my consciousness, and the second oriented toward the outer world as CEO of Synaptics until 1999, and then as its chairman until the middle of 2009. But the two lives have slowly integrated, helping their mutual understanding, and the process continues to this day. I have also kept a journal that has become an intimate and indispensable connective, aiding their integration.

6

LIVING A DOUBLE LIFE

Learn how to see. Realize that everything connects to everything else.

—Leonardo da Vinci

The Xerox Alto was the first computer to use a graphical user interface (GUI) with icons and a mouse as the pointing device to "navigate" the virtual desktop represented on the computer screen. Both the GUI and mouse were invented by Douglas Engelbart at SRI International and were later perfected at Xerox PARC (Palo Alto Research Center) where the Alto computer was developed in 1973 and used internally for many years, though never commercialized. It was 1981 when Xerox introduced the Xerox Star, the first commercial computer with a GUI and mouse. That system was as innovative as it was expensive, limiting sales to only 25,000 units.

Inspired by the Xerox innovations, Apple introduced the Macintosh personal computer in 1984, popularizing the new interface and creating a large market for the mouse. Microsoft followed suit at the end of 1985 with Windows, a GUI software layer sitting on top of the PC-DOS operating system used by the IBM PC. The introduction of Windows instantly created a large aftermarket for the mouse to serve the installed base of PCs, and in time, the mouse became standard issue with all new computers, thus creating a large original equipment manufacturer (OEM) market.

The idea of the touchpad and touchscreen

I had been serving on the board of directors of Logitech since 1983 when it was just a struggling startup company with one software product and a mechanical mouse that was not selling much. But when the mouse became established, Logitech won the competitive race with all other mouse suppliers and became the top manufacturer. Then, in the early 1990s, Logitech started producing the trackball, an inverted mechanical mouse functioning as the integrated pointing device for the early laptop computers. Trackballs were bulky and had to be periodically cleaned, and thus became a real nuisance for customers. I was CEO of Synaptics at that time and felt that something better was needed, so I challenged our most creative engineers to come up with a solid-state alternative to the trackball. I started regular brainstorming meetings with four to five people once or twice a week to come up with some original ideas.

Within a couple of months, we invented the basic concept and design of both the capacitive touchpad and touchscreen. These were wonderful group inventions that eventually changed the way we interface with our mobile devices. They were made possible by the interactive contributions of all participants in a playful climate. Instead of a single inventor, the inventor was the team.

After we proved in 1992 that the concept worked, I contacted Logitech and we agreed to develop a custom analog chip to replace the trackballs with touchpads. At that time, this Logitech project was one of several we were pursuing to find new uses for the analog neural network technology we were developing.

By 1993 we had demonstrated in all our projects that neural networks were superior to the previous top-down algorithmic methods for pattern recognition. This conclusion, however, was not shared by most practicing AI experts who still considered neural networks to be the wrong approach and instead promoted expert systems as the new direction. Expert systems were based on the idea that domain experts could articulate in detail the rules they consciously followed, which they could not.

We also proved that the emulation of neural networks with highly specialized analog chips could achieve the massive computation needed for real time cognitive applications. Unfortunately, analog chips are much more difficult and costly to develop than digital ones. Therefore, to make the business viable we needed to invent a general-purpose architecture so that the same small set of chips could be used for many different applications. Despite many efforts in that direction, no such architecture was ever found.

It is interesting to note that even today, 25 years later, there is still no known general-purpose architecture for learning systems, though neural networks have recently emerged as the correct solution for AI and robotics, vindicating our original vision. Today, with computers millions of times more powerful than those from 25 years ago, we can *simulate* a neural network by using the impressive computational power of graphical processing units (GPUs) used for video games and other graphical applications. GPUs are now being enhanced to better serve the needs of AI and robotics.

A *winning bet*

By the end of 1993, working with Logitech, we had proven the feasibility of the touchpad using an engineering chip we had developed. When it was time to negotiate the price for a production chip though, Logitech wanted such onerous conditions that it made no business sense to proceed. Therefore, I stopped the project and resigned from their board.

Gravely concerned about the lack of general-purpose neural network architecture, I started to think about whether we should go after the touchpad business ourselves. Tim Allen, who was our head of engineering, reassured me that his team could build the entire touchpad, not just the analog chip. Of all the projects we were pursuing, the touchpad was the only one with the potential to create a company. Therefore, the decision was relatively easy to make, but it meant changing directions and abandoning the original vision of developing artificial neural networks. We bet the company on the touchpad and touchscreen and gracefully terminated our other ongoing projects to focus all available resources on the new vision. Today, Synaptics is still the top producer of touchpad and touchscreens.

The story of how the touchpad took off is quite interesting and instructive because, from 1994 to 1998, Synaptics faced many challenges that could have killed the company had we taken even a single wrong turn. The big news came in May of 1994 when Apple introduced its PowerBook with a touchpad. We were stunned. At that time we were expecting to have samples of our own touchpad a few months later, and here Apple was already in production with "our" product. What happened?

A few months earlier we had heard some rumors about a company in Utah called Cirque that had been working for many years on a touchpad like ours, but we did not know for sure if that was true. It turned out it was. Cirque had licensed their technology to Apple, and Apple had then developed their own custom analog integrated circuits using Cirque's technology. We immediately bought a PowerBook at the stiff price of $5,000 to evaluate the touchpad. We found that Apple had made a very expensive unit with three custom analog chips and a microcontroller, while our design had only one analog chip and a microcontroller.

A blessing in disguise

After the initial shock, we felt much better when we realized what happened was truly a blessing in disguise because Apple was the best company in the world to promote a new idea and create a market trend. If the initial customer reactions to the touchpad would be positive, I thought, we would have a great chance of success because the IBM-compatible laptop PCs, accounting for more than 85 percent of the market, would also have to adopt the new technology.

Solid proof of this theory came many years later when we started promoting the touchscreen to mobile phone companies like Motorola, Nokia, and RIM. I had always thought it was a great idea to have a touchscreen on a phone, but for years none of our customers did, that is until Apple showed interest in our product. However, Apple wanted exclusivity, which we refused. So, they developed their own touchscreen and introduced the iPhone a couple of years later. The iPhone immediately created the market we had been unable to stimulate for many years, and we benefitted handsomely when other mobile phone companies started purchasing touchscreens from us. In retrospect, without Apple having pioneered the touchpad, we may not have succeeded on our own in convincing the industry to adopt it.

A few months after the PowerBook introduction, we also discovered that Cirque had sold a license to Alps to manufacture and sell OEM touchpads. Cirque had decided to focus only on the aftermarket for which they later introduced a PC add-on called Glidepoint, to replace the mouse. Cirque's strategy would have worked well if enough mouse users had shown a preference for the touchpad, but that did not happen. The mouse is still utilized to this day with nearly all desktop PCs because it does an adequate job, and therefore there is no reason to change. The touchpad only became compelling with the introduction of laptops. Cirque had simply been too confident that the touchpad was a better "mousetrap." The company struggled for many years to survive, supported mainly by royalties, and eventually was acquired by Alps.

Our strategy was to primarily serve the OEM market, which was almost certain, whereas we were doubtful that the touchpad could replace the entrenched and universally used mouse for desktop computers. But we also had to face Alps, a formidable and large Japanese supplier in the global OEM market, rather than just competing with Cirque, a startup like us.

In the early summer of 1994, I hired Bob Sumbs as our VP of marketing and sales. He visited potential customers in Taiwan, where most laptops were then manufactured, to showcase our Synaptics touchpad. Given the initial favorable market reaction to Apple's solution and the well-known problems with trackballs, Bob was able to stir up some customer interest. He also returned with something extremely important: a sample of the Alps touchpad. We found that our competitor's basic design was similar to ours with one custom analog chip and one microcontroller. But fortunately for us, the size of their analog chip was substantially larger than ours. The larger the chip, the higher the cost, so we knew we had a chance to win against Alps!

I asked Tim Allen to modify our design by adopting the exact physical dimensions of Alps' touchpad and changing the type and position of our connector to be the same as theirs. By doing this we transformed ourselves into a second source of Alps because our customers could interchangeably use their touchpad or ours, and any customer concerns about having to rely on us as a small startup were eliminated. One year later, we had turned the tables and Alps became the second source for our touchpads.

Synaptics started delivering production units of the touchpad in January of 1995, two months after the official announcement, and by August we had already reached profitability. Becoming profitable that soon was exceptional. I was expecting to reach that milestone not sooner than one year after our first customer would begin production, but that plan was drafted before Apple had introduced their product. Without Apple, the fate of the touchpad could have easily suffered the same five-year wait as the touchscreen did.

Alps responded by threatening to sue us and our customers, claiming that we had infringed on Cirque's patents to which they held a license. We had filed our patents, of course, and through that process had found to our surprise that there were already many patents on touchpads. Neither of us had been the first to dream of touchpads, though we had independently come up with the same idea, but with different solutions. The intellectual property landscape for the touchpad was complex and the existence of much prior art made distinguishing the differences between the various designs quite difficult. We drafted a careful analysis for our concerned customers showing them that we had used a different method than Cirque, and stated that we were prepared to hold them harmless in case we had to go to court. Once we overcame that obstacle it was clear sailing, but the honeymoon did not last long.

Our strongest suit: execution speed

Talent wins games, but teamwork and intelligence wins championships.

—Michael Jordan

The following challenges were all internal: We had to learn quickly how to make a product at a profit in a market that wanted stellar quality, perpetual price reductions, and incessant performance improvements. At the same time, we had to build our infrastructure to effectively compete with the larger, more established Alps.

Our best advantage was *execution speed*. But we had a much harder time at that than expected, primarily because many technical problems kept cropping up almost weekly, mostly due to different conditions of product use in various parts of the world. The touchpad was an incredibly difficult product to make. And the race was brutal. Our engineering team, under the outstanding leadership of Tim Allen, had no rest; and it was because of their dedication and brilliance that we even survived.

Other annoying problems were due to the failure of some suppliers to comply with the overall interface specifications of the Microsoft operating system. We also had to make continuous changes to reduce costs and improve performance. All this extra work caused a delay in the design of our new generation of products that would finally achieve the lowest possible cost by combining into a single chip the microcontroller and analog chip, what is generically called a system on a chip, or SoC.

We also knew that Logitech's management had decided to design a touchpad. This meant we would soon have another major competitor, and I feared they would introduce a product with an SoC since they were already aware of our plans. But Logitech most likely considered Alps to have been their real competitor, not us, and needed the lowest-cost solution to compete with them. Alps too would soon have an SoC touchpad. Therefore, if we had not come up urgently with our own SoC version, we would have won the battle but lost the war.

Here too, however, another gem was hidden. We were forced to learn faster than our competitors, and that crucial learning curve advantage allowed us to design the best SoC solution, whereas Logitech was faced with designing their chip without the benefit of an already consolidated learning curve. Indeed, winners in high tech business are inevitably the ones who learn the fastest, not the ones who have the most financial resources.

Logitech's fatal decision

About 18 months after we were in production, longer than I had expected, but just like I had feared, Logitech announced their touchpad with an SoC. They immediately started putting price pressure on us. This raised the bar in two ways: we had to reduce the cost of our existing design *and* we had to develop a single chip in record time, both while the engineering team was still consumed with fire-fighting on the front line. We were looking at a tough year and a half, which was the time needed to respond to Logitech since we had already decided to develop our own microcontroller to keep costs to a minimum, a direction that only a few companies would have had the stomach to undertake. But human error came to our rescue.

Logitech had made a fatal blunder. It was like a time bomb that sooner or later would explode with disastrous consequences for them. To minimize their chip cost, they had decided to use ROM (mask programmable read-only memory) to hold their firmware, rather than one-time programmable (OTP) memory. This meant that to correct any firmware problem and produce error-free parts, it would take them a couple of months instead of a couple of days. Even worse, all their inventory with the defective firmware would have to be scrapped at a great cost.

We knew about this danger for our own design from the out-set, and thus were using a microcontroller with OTP memory in our two-chip implementation. This allowed us to respond immediately to problems and avoid inventory losses through a process of efficiently loading the firmware into the microcontroller memory on prefabricated blank units just before shipment. Therefore, our single-chip design would have OTP memory as well, even though we had debugged and improved our code during the previous 18 months. Since Logitech had been successfully using ROM for their mouse and trackball, they decided to do the same for their touchpad, despite knowing we were using OTP memory. They grossly underestimated the touchpad's far greater complexity, showing once more that overconfidence is one of the greatest obstacles to business success.

Nonetheless, it was war for a while. Logitech was bombing the price, giving leverage to our customers to demand a lower price from us. We did not bend for at least another six months until we started losing some business, a sure sign that Logitech was delivering their touchpads. We figured that Logitech was selling at cost to drive us and Alps out.

Synaptics had been profitable since August of 1995, but in mid-1997 we were beginning to lose money. Not much, but it wasn't good because we couldn't respond well until we had our SoC, which was still about a year away, and risked losing the dominant market position we had worked so hard to wrestle away from Alps.

On the positive side, we knew we could beat Logitech at its game because our new chip would have a much lower manufacturing cost than theirs, even with our costlier OTP memory. This was true for two reasons. We were designing a much smaller chip than theirs, and we were a fabless semiconductor company making touchpads, rather than being like Logitech and Alps who had to buy their chips from some semiconductor vendor. Ironically, Logitech bought chips from Zilog, the company I had started 23 years earlier, that used the Zilog Z8 microcontroller, my first product idea there. Logitech had jointly designed with Zilog engineers the complex analog subsystem managed by the Z8.

Synaptics strikes back

By mid-1998, after losing some market share and suffering moderate losses, we finally had our single-chip touchpad and were positioned to fight back. Plus, we stood to make a good profit at a price even lower than the lowest one set by Logitech, which meant they could not lower their price any further without losing money. But Logitech had another clever strategy to get us. They decided to make custom touchpads, a choice we had resisted since it would have multiplied our overhead costs. This approach had the benefit of creating closer relationships with their customers and making their touchpads "stick" for the lifetime of the model utilizing the custom product, which was typically a year.

They indeed succeeded in securing a series of custom projects for the fall of 1998 that could have potentially taken a major share of the market away from us. However, their poor technological choice, the ticking bomb, was set to explode.

In the early summer of 1998, we had a visit from a frantic Taiwanese customer who had ordered a custom touchpad from Logitech. In short, the touchpad did not work. This forced the customer to hold off production of their laptop because they were sole – sourced from Logitech. It was a real disaster for them. Since it would take Logitech a couple of months to fix the problem, the customer asked us if we could design a custom touchpad in one week so that they could meet their production schedule.

Recognizing this was our chance to hit back, I overruled our marketing VP who didn't want to get involved with custom projects, and despite the extraordinary effort necessary to secure the deal, we negotiated a higher price than Logitech's and promised the customer they would have an engineering sample in two weeks. Our team came through, our touchpad worked flawlessly, we saved the day for the customer and made a formidable statement to Logitech!

That was the beginning of the end for our competitor. Words spread fast in Taiwan, and to all the other Logitech customers who had ongoing custom projects with them and who feared the same mishap could happen to them as well. Almost immediately they abandoned ship, and we got them all into our camp without having to match prices. Within a few months, Logitech exited the touchpad business with heavy losses.

A few months later we returned to profitability with quarterly sales of $15 to $20 million, and the company has been profitable ever since. The war was finally won and Synaptics had secured a commanding market position that gave it years of peace, growth, and prosperity.

The battle with Logitech, at a time when we were exhausted by confronting the many challenges necessary to make the best-performing and lowest-cost touchpad, was the closest we got to going under. That superhuman effort, however, took its toll. We lost a few key people, among them Tim Allen to whom the company owes much for creatively leading the engineering team for ten years. I hired a new marketing VP and decided to look for a CEO to take my place after 12 years of leading the company.

In January of 1999 our new CEO, Francis Lee, joined Synaptics from National Semiconductor and I became chairman of the board, a position that had been vacant for about four years since Carver Mead had left. I carried that responsibility until the middle of 2009 when I retired from business. Today, Synaptics is still the world leader in touchpads, touchscreens, and other selected human interface products.

The culture of Synaptics

The secret lies in mutual help. If you think you can arrive alone, you will remain alone and you will not arrive.

—Jorge Álvarez Camacho

One of my main reasons for leaving Intel in 1974 was because of the company culture Andy Grove created that aimed only at results. I simply felt that Andy's aggressive, hyper-competitive, and confrontational style took too high of a human toll. I felt that company objectives should be more aligned with personal objectives, and I also thought that a company should play an important educational role in the growth of its employees beyond just their immediate careers.

I remember many discussions with Ralph Ungermann trying to articulate the kind of organization I had wanted to create at Zilog. My lack of experience and maturity coupled with my reluctance to confront certain situations, however, made it impossible for me to create the culture I instinctively wanted. I also remember meeting Bill Veltrop, an outstanding organization development manager at Exxon Enterprises' headquarters. Bill introduced me to socio-technical analysis and innovative plant management. I resonated with those principles and decided to organize the new wafer fab we were then planning to build in Nampa, Idaho, near Boise, accordingly.

The factory became a jewel. Every operator was taught how each machine worked and how to operate it, adding flexibility to the workflow since the practice in the industry was to have each worker know the operation of only one type of machine. The workers were in large measure self-organizing. They solved production problems with the assistance of the technical people who played more of a consulting role than a supervising one. The production ramp-up—usually a traumatic process in a conventionally organized factory—occurred flawlessly. Turnover was minimal and the yields were better than the ones we had in our mature Cupertino fab.

That experience convinced me employees can assume much more responsibility than they are normally given, with much better results and personal satisfaction, if the company is willing to invest in proper training and support. In retrospect, I consider the Nampa manufacturing plant, the Z8, and the Z80 my three best accomplishments at Zilog. They also gave me by far the most satisfaction.

When I started Cygnet Technologies, one of the early employees I hired was Paul Gustavson, the Zilog employee development manager who had overseen the thoughtful construction of the Nampa wafer-fab culture. His job was to assist me in shaping the new company culture before bad habits could take hold. As a result, he helped me crystalize and articulate some of the principles that I had already understood but could not quite verbalize.

At Synaptics, it took several years of research with a small number of young engineers before the company took off. This slower growth fostered the creation of a coherent cultural bedrock that enabled us to deliberately select employees with similar values and assimilate them into our forming culture. Our openness in discussing the future direction of the company, the climate of mutual respect, and the practice of actively seeking input from all who could contribute, made each Synaptics employee an integral part of the company.

What I have learned is that when it comes to culture, there are no hard and fast rules. It takes good judgment and wisdom to understand the subtleties for achieving a delicate, dynamic balance in the flow of ideas and information from the top-down and from the bottom-up.

In search of meaning

I show you how deep the rabbit hole goes.
Lewis Carroll, *Alice in Wonderland*

After the awakening I described earlier, I started reading books like the *Tao Te Ching* and the *Bhagavad Gita*. These ancient texts reflected and enriched my growing awareness, revealing that since time immemorial man's inner journeys had been illuminated by experiences like mine. Before my awakening, those books would have only been of superficial interest to me, since the "soul" had little real meaning. After my awakening though, soul had come to mean the living, scintillating, loving substance of which everything is made. It had come to mean a *lived experience* rather than an intellectual idea. My awakening also opened the door to a stream of other extraordinary experiences of consciousness and further integrations that have continued to this day. They included vivid dreams, deep intuitions, and other states of consciousness that greatly expanded my previously limited conceptualizations of reality, constrained by preconceived ideas.

At that time I also had numerous dreams, some of them particularly significant. There was one, very tormented and personal, that had a powerful impact on my body, as it freed my heart from a contracted state I didn't even know was there because it had always been a part of me. Only when I experienced a feeling of great relaxation in my chest at the very moment I awoke from the dream, did I realize the difference. And afterwards, the contraction never returned.

Another dream revealed the essence of my spiritual journey: I was inside a huge house, flying face down in great concentric spirals towards the floor. My heart was open and singing and I felt excited and full of enthusiasm as I descended toward beautiful plants and colorful flowers.

As I approached such beauty, I suddenly realized that the plants and flowers were simply painted on ceramic tiles. They were not real, and I felt disappointed by that deception. I straightened up and glided without touching the floor. I moved to another part of the house that was on my left until I found myself in front of a locked, massive double door. I knew that behind the door was a large garden where the plants and flowers I had just seen painted on tiles were alive and real. To my left were two elderly women dressed in black, one standing and one sitting. They were not looking at me. They were more like icons, unaware of my presence. I knew they had the key to the door.

I woke up feeling that this dream had contained a profound message. I immediately understood that the house represented my vaster self. The painted plants and flowers that appeared so palpable and exciting, represented what I had thought was real until then. What I had thought were my real goals, were instead a world of illusions that from a distance seemed like marvelous and enticing destinations I had to reach. It was only a deception, and it had left me disappointed and empty as I got closer. The real world was beyond that locked door, which I could only enter after making friends with the mysteriously veiled figures, which I interpreted to be the unknown or rejected aspects of myself. Only by facing them would I get the key to access my authentic life.

Expansion of consciousness

Know thyself (ΓΝΩΘΙ ΣΕΑΥΤΟΝ)
—Ancient Greek aphorism carved in
the Temple of Apollo in Delphi

One day while stopped at a traffic light on my way to work, I looked to the car on my left. Behind the wheel sat a woman. I immediately felt my consciousness leap into her place and a moment later return to me. Nothing like this had ever happened before and I was stunned. The experience was too short to understand whether my consciousness had really left my body, or if it had simply expanded to include her.

When I arrived at the office, I began recording in my journal what had just happened to try to clarify the event. As I was writing, I looked up to see out the window the well-tended grounds of the Synaptics campus. It was then that my consciousness expanded everywhere, pervading everything: the soil, trees, grass, and flowers, simultaneously with feelings of bliss and peace. Just like in my awakening, I was simultaneously the trees, grass, and flowers, and I was also their observer. The same "impossible" perspective.

I then turned my attention to inside my office and saw a human figure looking at me. It was not a real person but more like a vision, and I felt that my consciousness was also inside that being. As I looked into his eyes, *I recognized myself looking at myself!* The being in front of me was simultaneously me and not-me. At that point the vision ended, and my consciousness returned to a familiar sense of myself.

I gradually began to realize that the truly important journey is the inner one. And with the same dedication I had showered into technological and scientific research, I committed to discovering the truth about myself, beyond the perceptual distortions fostered by prejudices. In my desire to deepen my understanding of the new reality I was experiencing, I sought the help of a practitioner in transpersonal psychology (a sub-field of psychology that integrates the spiritual dimension into modern psychology). She introduced me to exploration techniques that only a few months earlier I would have met with great skepticism. They were instead quite helpful in showing me just how deep my rabbit hole was because of conditioning to restrictive beliefs and ideas, and how to relive many emotions and feelings I had repressed and forgotten.

One day, during a therapeutic massage session—an exploration technique I would have previously considered bogus had I known about it—I had an important and unexpected experience: *I am 16 and I'm waiting for Dad to come and see the new model plane I have just finished building. It is my masterpiece! A glider with a wingspan of two meters, a body painted and polished in dark blue, and semitransparent yellow wings showing the elegant interlocking design of the ribs.*

I had imagined this plane and planned it in my free time during the last months of school and had built it over the summer holidays in the basement of our home where I had my workshop. *I am so proud of my creation that I take it into the living room after dinner. I assemble it and ask my father, who is in his study, to come and see it.*

My father says, "I'll be there in five minutes." After 10 to 15 minutes of waiting, I return to the study that is less than fifteen feet away, urge him to come and see the model because it is too big to take to him. He says, "I'm coming in just a bit." I wait an – other 15 minutes and then, once again, urge him to come. He says, "I'm coming right away" and after another 15 minutes he still does not show up. I realize then that he is not going to come. I slowly disassemble the model, take it downstairs to the basement and silently go to bed.

In the middle of this vivid memory, while reliving the disappointment, I burst into inconsolable tears. Here I am, fifty, crying desperately over an "insignificant" incident. I had not cried for a long time, and never before as an adult so unrestrained and disconsolately. This kind of crying was liberating, revealing, healing, and at the same time deeply sad and bitter. I understood that behind the disappointment of not being able to show my master-piece to Dad, was my deep need to feel "seen" and loved, a need that had remained hidden my whole life. This was a real opening because it disclosed for the first time, and with great surprise, the depth of my wounds caused by my father's indifference. It brought to light how much I had protected and defended my vulnerability, and my fear of not being valued in his eyes, and therefore how little I valued myself. At the time of this incident as a boy, I only felt a disappointment that I easily dismissed with a shrug of shoulders.

But now I had finally opened my heart enough to feel an unknown emotional wound. I had built an idealized image of my father, and of myself, that allowed me to hide my innermost genuine feelings. My crying was a true act of self-compassion toward the boy in me who had wanted to be seen and valued by his father. Unfortunately, Dad was too absorbed in his studies to notice my need for love and appreciation.

Other experiences

This and other similar experiences made me realize that I had almost always repressed my true feelings. To protect myself, I had denied the pain and hidden the truth about what I felt. I had worn the mask of one who is ready to joke about everything, to let hurt slide off me with a laugh. I had convinced myself that I was strong, pretended that everything was fine, when all I really did was estrange myself from my own heart. What I had done was to not recognize reality anymore. I also realized that my fictional self – image built on self-sufficiency and defiance made me vulnerable to being taken advantage of by those who intuitively understood the charade I was playing. Slowly, I began to get in touch with my true feelings and rediscovered a more authentic me, and the process continues to this day.

One night as I was about to fall asleep, I found myself floating above the bed near the bedroom ceiling while my body laid in bed.

I was stunned and disbelieving: How could such a thing be possible? How could I exist *outside* my body and still be fully awake and aware of existing? I instinctively kept my eyes closed because I felt a bit of fear. Soon the fear took over, and I was quickly sucked back into my body with a jolt. I stayed awake for a while reflecting on the meaning of what had just happened. Only much later I wondered: *What does it mean to open my eyes from a consciousness that is out of the body? Where are the real eyes?*

I had never before heard of these types of experiences called out of body experiences (OBEs or astral travels). Later I discovered that many people have had similar occurrences, and in fact have found extensive literature about OBEs. Some have traveled far away from their body to experience places and meet entities that do not appear to exist on earth as we know it.

In what kind of reality do we exist then if such journeys can happen? What kind of sensory system can consciousness possibly have when it is outside the body? It seems to have all the modalities we are familiar with and more, like telepathy and clairvoyance. How is that possible?

Finally, let me recount an interesting adventure that occurred around that time. One day Elvia and I wanted to take a long walk and so we set off for a path on the hills a few miles from our house. Along the way, a big coyote came running towards us. It came to a halt about twenty yards away, almost cutting us off from our trail, and began to observe us. We immediately stopped, unsure about what to do. We had never seen a coyote so close before. I felt reasonably safe because I had read that coyotes generally do not attack people.

Shortly thereafter, another coyote came trotting by and joined the first. At this point the situation became complicated with two large adult coyotes staring at us. With good instincts and cautious moves, Elvia began to search around for a branch, a stone, something with which we could respond in case they attacked us.

In the meantime, a third coyote arrived. At that point I began to worry. We were alone, and the situation was potentially dangerous. Fortunately, not far from us, were some branches that we could use to defend ourselves. We collected two of them and held them high.

I noticed the first coyote that arrived, which appeared to be the ringleader, kept looking at us and did not seem at all impressed by the sticks we were waving over our heads, while the other two seemed to be waiting for his decision.

A moment later I noticed a subtle change in the look of the "boss," as if he thought "maybe it's not worth attacking these two, they could be indigestible…" A few moments later, he turned his head and casually moved away and the other two trotted behind. All this lasted a few minutes, and when the coyotes were at a safe distance Elvia and I looked at each other with a sigh of relief. Never before had a lack of appreciation from a wild animal made us so happy.

Foveon and the End of My Third Life

In 1993, National Semiconductor, a company with a strong analog IC expertise, took an equity position in Synaptics. This was the last private investment in our company. Later that year, Synaptics abandoned neural networks in favor of the touchpad, which left no room for Carver Mead's interest in image sensors. Since National was already working on that technology, Carver became a consultant to them and one year later left the Synaptics board of which he had been chairman since 1987.

In the mid-1990s, the world of photography was undergoing a rapid transformation due to continuing improvements in the quality of digital cameras based on CCD technology and new digital image-processing techniques. This development had begun with the invention of the CCD at Bell Labs in 1969, followed by the first experimental digital camera developed by Kodak in 1975 using the first commercial CCDs manufactured by Fairchild with the silicon-gate technology.

The initial progress in digital photography had been quite slow, however, so that by 1995 few expected that digital cameras would rival film cameras. Companies like Polaroid and Kodak became complacent, convinced that digital cameras could not do better than film any time soon. This overconfidence led to their demise.

The exponential progress in semiconductors allowed digital cameras to achieve a picture quality close to film cameras only five years later. And from that point on, the many advantages that digital photography had been promising for years became compelling enough that the fate of film was sealed. Ten years later, photographic film essentially disappeared.

This technological change hit even the semiconductor industry because CCDs, the very sensor technology that had dominated video recorders and put digital photography on the map, was now under attack by sensors made with CMOS technology. Today CCDs have all but disappeared, except for a few specialized applications.

This was a repeat of the demise of magnetic core RAM by semiconductor dynamic RAM more than thirty years earlier, a change that in its wake also swept away the MOS shift register memories that had been the only semiconductor memory solution for a short while. In this reenactment, magnetic core played the role of film, the CCD played the role of the shift register, and the CMOS imager played the role of the dynamic RAM.

Carver Mead, heeding the advice of National's patent lawyer Mark Grant, decided to spin off a company from National and make a studio camera for professional photographers. The idea was to use three sensors attached to a special prism that would split the incoming light into the three basic colors, red, green, and blue, which when mixed in various proportions create all colors. Outputs from the three sensors would then be electronically combined into single, high-quality color images.

Carver's company was called Foveon and its initial shareholders were National Semiconductor and Synaptics, the company of which I was then the CEO. Foveon's first product, introduced in 2000, could make photographs that rivaled studio film cameras because strong artificial illumination was generally present in studio environments. The low-light sensitivity of Foveon's imagers, however, could neither match the film nor the best DSLR (digital single-lens reflex) camera sensors then available. The problem was further compounded by underestimating the progress of DSLR cameras using a single – chip CCD or CMOS sensor, and overestimating the costly benefits of using three sensors. The result was an expensive and bulky camera that became obsolete within a couple of years.

A promising technology

During that time, Dick Merrill, one of Foveon's founding engineers, came up with a highly innovative solution to replace the three sensors and the expensive and bulky prism. Merrill invented a CMOS sensor where the primary-color photodiodes were stacked one on top of the other in each pixel location instead of laid out horizontally. This method exploited the lesser-known property of silicon absorbing light of different wavelengths at different depths. Therefore, a single pixel could achieve the same color quality of a prism camera with three conventional sensors, without having to use the difficult-to-control color filters used in conventional CCD or CMOS imagers.

By arranging three photodiodes at appropriate depths, it was then possible to sense blue light with the topmost photodiode, green light with the middle one, and red light with the bottom one, so that at each pixel location the sensor could simultaneously sense all three colors. Therefore, the equivalent performance of a conventional sensor could be obtained with a smaller device that detected all of the available light without any waste.

This promising technology was called Foveon X3 and it attracted a major investment by NEA, one of the top VC firms in Silicon Valley. Foveon also landed a credible customer for its first product, the Japanese-based Sigma Corporation, a major supplier of aftermarket lenses for single-lens reflex (SLR) film cameras and for the emerging DSLR market.

Sigma had never designed a digital camera before and so they contracted with Foveon not only to supply the sensor, but also to do the design of the electronic hardware and software, concentrating their own efforts on the electro-mechanical and optical design of the camera. This project required Foveon to develop: (1) a new manufacturing process technology for the sensor; (2) a new sensor design; (3) a new and different image processing than the one used by the existing "mosaic" technology (technology that uses the repetition of a 2x2 matrix of pixels with two green, one red, and one blue sensor); and (4) a design for the electronics and software of the DSLR. It was an extraordinary undertaking, given the size of Foveon, and the competitiveness of Nikon and Canon, the companies that dominated that market.

National Semiconductor provided the necessary resources to develop the manufacturing process and produce the wafers. By 2002 the Sigma SD9 DSLR camera with the first Foveon X3 sensor was introduced to the market with much press coverage and excitement. The Sigma SD9 still had several limitations, though many of them had little to do with the X3 sensor, with the main exception being the inadequate low-light sensitivity of the sensor.

In retrospect, it was almost suicidal for Sigma-Foveon to try to compete with the highly refined technologies of Canon and Nikon and the commanding market position they fiercely defended. Nikon was using sophisticated CCD sensors built by Sony, whereas Canon had developed and produced its own CMOS sensors. Canon was the only company in the world to have mastered the CMOS image sensor technology with a "fully-depleted" photodiode process, the technology that reduces the electrical noise produced by a photodiode sensor to the minimum possible, thus matching the low-light sensitivity of CCDs.

Despite being better than the competition in many areas, Foveon's sensors' noise level was not a match for those made by Canon and Sony. This crucial limitation ended up being its Achilles' heel.

An unkept promise

The euphoria of Foveon employees and management due to the initial media fanfare around the SD9 led them to underestimating the competition and starting an ill-conceived new project for a point-and-shoot camera to further compete with sensors that had far better low-light performance. In the meantime, Sigma SD9 sales proved to be disappointing, mainly because Foveon failed to provide necessary funds to properly address the X3 sensor noise problem and develop a cost-effective image-processing solution. This was an additional requirement, since the X3 sensors could not use the commercially available chips for mosaic sensors. National was also charging a high price for the X3 wafers and was not interested in developing the necessary micro-lens process that would have further improved the SD9's performance. This last step required wafers to be shipped offshore to contract manufacturers that then added micro-lenses at substantial additional cost and time.

The disappointing sales led the Foveon board to look for a new CEO. However, given the internal difficulties, it was not easy to find the right person willing to bet his career on a company in trouble. I was a Foveon board member at that time, representing the interests of Synaptics. Discussing the situation with Francis Lee, my CEO successor at Synaptics, he asked, "Why don't you take over the job?"

At first I was taken aback, but then thought *yeah, why not?* believing that I could certainly take an interim CEO role, assess the situation, and suggest the best course of action to the board. This included, if appropriate, an option to sell the company. I took my proposal to the board, saying that I would evaluate the situation as interim CEO and report my recommendation one month later while the board continued the search for a permanent CEO.

After an in-depth technological and market review, it was clear that the choice to go after the high-end DSLR market had been ill-conceived, primarily because it underestimated the low-light sensitivity limitation of the X3 sensors. The only business where CMOS sensors had clear advantages over CCDs was in the emergent market of mobile phone cameras where top quality was less important than the size, cost, and power dissipation of the camera. Here CMOS fared much better than CCD, even though the image quality was much inferior, especially in low-light conditions.

But compared with the best commercially available CMOS sensors for mobile phones, Foveon sensors had better quality, even at low light, and had lower costs when using an offshore wafer foundry rather than National's. The only CMOS sensors better than Foveon's in low light were Canon's, a captive supplier that was neither in the sensor business nor the phone camera market.

It was clear that Foveon had to change direction and develop camera modules for mobile phones. In parallel, we also had to develop the low-noise process for future generations of cameras. To pull off this plan, we needed a new manufacturing partner willing to develop the semiconductor process for the imager and a new major customer willing to develop the image-processing chip necessary for the camera module. It was like starting over.

A new direction

One month later I presented my plan to the board saying that we had a good chance of succeeding if we changed course and executed well with a new infusion of capital. I also said that I would be happy to become a permanent CEO if the board was interested. They unanimously offered me the position, and that is how in one day I transitioned from semi-retirement to a more than full-time job.

The challenge in leading a company with a potentially disruptive technology that went against the direction of the entire industry was intoxicating and partially clouded my judgment. It was a major gamble on which I was willing to bet $3 million of my own in the new round of funding. It turned out that I also *underestimated* the competition, not by much, but enough to arrive second-best at the finish line.

The following year was exciting and transformative. First, I reorganized Foveon and reduced our staff. Then we found a suitable manufacturing partner, Dongbu Electronics, a South Korean wafer foundry with all the necessary qualifications, including its CEO's enthusiasm for our new business plan. Dongbu had to develop the complex manufacturing process for the X3 sensors, a goal almost impossible to achieve without the guarantee of a significant production volume that Foveon had yet to reach. But that large market seemed more attainable when we made a major deal with Samsung Electronics, a formidable supplier of camera modules for mobile phones, to jointly develop a top-of-the-line camera module. We would develop the imager and design the image-processing chip together. Samsung would then produce the modules. From the business side, we were set. Now we "only" had to execute.

About a year later, we received samples of the first imager along with the Samsung-built camera module prototypes after having developed the X3 manufacturing technology at Dongbu and designed the new chip. The performance was much better than all the other camera modules we had tested, but Samsung was not entirely satisfied. They wanted some improvements. They were comparing our chip with imagers built by a manufacturer unknown to us. According to Samsung, we were close, but not the best in low light.

We made changes and stayed in the race until a final bake-off between our chip and the one by our secret competitor. We scored second-best because our low-light performance was still not as good as theirs. Taking second place, despite major efforts from all involved, was a bitter pill to swallow. We later found out that the other contender was Micron, a major producer of dynamic RAM and a new entrant in the imager business. Micron had mastered the fully-depleted photodiode process that up until then only Canon possessed. We were simply too late by a few months. Had Foveon targeted this market three years earlier, rather than chasing the shining pearl of the DSLR, we could have been highly successful.

In hindsight, I should have recommended to the Foveon board that we sell or wind down the company after failing to compete with Micron. However, since I did not want to fail, I decided to chase a train that was rapidly leaving the station.

The following three years were painful. We could never catch up, even after we had developed the fully-depleted photodiode process that gave us a competitive imager in low light while also retaining the original cost advantage. The final blow was a new technology that promised to reduce the imager cost even beyond what we had achieved, while maintaining the same performance.

This approach required the photodiodes to be fabricated on the backside of the wafers, allowing for smaller chips with excellent low-light sensitivity, even when the chip size was reduced to match ours. This became the new direction that the entire industry had decided to pursue, even though it would take another two years to become available in the market. Foveon had become obsolete, leaving us no choice but to sell it or close it down.

The only company that had a stake in X3 technology was Sigma. Ironically, after having solved the low-light sensitivity problem, the X3 could now compete in the DSLR market, and Sigma ultimately bought Foveon toward the end of 2008. The original wrong direction became the only viable right one in the end, but only after having solved the difficult technical problems that should have been solved first.

Original watercolor by Giuseppe Faggin, Federico's father, who was interested in idealism. The painting was made during his visit to California in 1970. Below right is the quote by Pierre Teilhard de Chardin: *Tout ce qui monte converge* (Everything that rises converges).

The Faggin family in Kyoto, Japan, in 1997, the year Federico was awarded the prestigious Kyoto Prize (Marc was absent to prepare for exams).

Federico receives the 2009 National Medal of Technology and Innovation, the highest honor conferred by the US government, from President Obama in a White House ceremony in October 2010.

The Faggin family celebrates the awarding of the National Medal of Technology and Innovation to Federico at the White House (2010)

7

My Fourth Life

Creativity requires the courage to let go of certainties.

—Eric Fromm

A couple of years before the sale of Foveon, I had begun to take seriously the idea that consciousness could be a fundamental aspect of nature and thus already present in some fashion in the atoms and molecules of which everything is made. This idea emerged gradually due to my unsuccessful struggles to explain how consciousness may arise from the complexity of the brain—the typical explanation given by many neuroscientists.

I kept thinking *how can a physical, inert structure like a computer that possesses only outer symbolic aspects give rise to inner semantic ones? The concept of complexity seems to have nothing to do with the sensations and feelings existing in our inner world. Computers, with all of their complexity, don't have a shred of consciousness. So, the inner world of meaning must likely be a property of a richer world in which matter represents only the symbolic aspect of reality. Meaning and symbols could then be two irreducible faces of the same coin.*

But many scholars and philosophers insist that this cannot be because the implications of such an idea would contradict the interpretations of the nature of reality based on mathematical theories that have already withstood rigorous experimental tests. Others maintain that this idea smacks of religion, and that science and religion should never be mixed.

This topic fascinated me because it had the potential to explain and unify the existence of the outer and inner realities I had been exploring for almost twenty years. Science and spirituality, until now believed irreconcilable, could then find a deep union rather than be a simple juxtaposition of convenience. So immediately after Foveon was acquired, I decided to withdraw from all other activities to immerse myself in developing a model of reality based on the assumption that consciousness is irreducible. To this end, Elvia and I decided to start, in 2011, the nonprofit Federico and Elvia Faggin Foundation to support some of the best researchers in the emerging science of consciousness.

In this chapter, I will succinctly describe my current thinking on the nature of reality under the assumption that consciousness is an irreducible property of nature. The ideas I will illustrate are quite speculative at this point, and compared to the previous chapters the story becomes much more abstract and may be challenging if you are new to these subjects. Thus, I recommend reading this chapter more than once if you are interested in understanding this topic. Please do not feel discouraged if you do not immediately grasp the many concepts that would seem to contradict more common ways of thinking. Instead, try to connect the various ideas in a new vision of reality in which the engine of evolution is the desire of a conscious universe to know itself.

I do not agree with those who insist that the universe is without purpose and meaning, nor do I believe that we are machines destined to be surpassed by computers. My disagreement is not just intellectual but is also based on my own inner experiences that say otherwise. Before believing the physicalist interpretation of reality, it is wise to also know that it is based on the reductionist and materialist assumptions of classical physics which hold that only inert matter exists. These are unproven premises that cannot account for the existence of the very consciousness each of us experiences within.

Physicalism cannot explain how interiority can emerge from a reality that only has exteriority.

What is Consciousness?

Consciousness cannot be accounted for in physical terms. For consciousness is absolutely fundamental. It cannot be accounted for in terms of anything else.

—Erwin Schrödinger

As described in chapter 5 in connection with the scent of a rose and the hard problem of consciousness, consciousness is what allows us to perceive and comprehend the meaning of physical reality through a sentient experience that goes beyond a blind translation of signals into other signals devoid of meaning. In summary, I explained that the mechanical recognition of a rose by its smell can be performed by either a computer or a human brain. Both computer and brain could translate the complex electrical signals of a smell sensor into the signals corresponding to the name "rose." But a human being would go one step further by transforming its "rose" signals into the aroma or *scent* of the rose—a sensation or quale that goes much beyond electrical signals because it emotionally and cognitively connects us with the rose. This translation is performed within the consciousness of a person and cannot be explained by current science. Computers, instead, cannot feel anything.

It is only because we are conscious that we know we exist, we can enjoy life, and our life can have meaning and purpose. And it is through qualia—what something feels like—that we know our physical environment and ourselves as agents with some freedom of action to pursue our desires and goals. If we examine our inner world more closely, we can recognize four distinct classes of qualia: (1) physical sensations and feelings; (2) emotions; (3) thoughts; and (4) spiritual feelings.

The first of these, physical sensations and feelings, derive from perceiving the physical environment both inside and outside the body. For example, the taste of food, the aroma of a flower, the sensations from touching something, or the sense of the color and shape of an object. This category also includes feelings of physical well-being or pain.

The second category deals with emotions such as curiosity, friendship, compassion, joy, trust, fear, anger, sadness, pride, obstinacy, shame, envy, greed, confusion, and so on. Notice how different emotions feel compared with physical sensations. Emotions appear to come from an entirely different level of reality than the one from which our physical sensations arise.

The third category is made of thoughts, a controversial statement since most scholars do not consider thoughts to be qualia. However, if you ask yourself *how do I know I had a thought?* you will immediately recognize that you perceived some image that carried the meaning of a thought, before you translated the image into words. For most of us the translation of that fleeting, multi-dimensional image into mental or spoken words is very swift, leading us to believe we are thinking directly in verbal form, unaware of the existence of the image-quale. In other words, we are so used to the automatic reification of thoughts into symbols, that we do not notice the sentient quale that is the very essence of a thought.

Finally, the fourth category contains spiritual feelings, qualia that convey a strong *unitive* component. A spiritual feeling allows us to become one with what we experience. Examples include the feeling of intense and pure love towards our own children, the feeling of unity with the universe or with a transcendent presence greater than ourselves, and the ineffable mystical experiences that have been reported over the centuries.

We experience and know the world and ourselves through qualia. Without qualia we would be unconscious, like sleepwalkers or robots. We could still move about but would have no experience and would not even know that we exist. We are so used to being conscious that the crucial distinction between a quale—what something feels like—and the physical symbols that represent it is no longer apparent. We do not recognize that the electro-chemical signals produced by our nervous system are distinct manifestations from the sensations and feelings that allow us to "live" that symbolic information.

Qualia and knowing are produced within our consciousness, suggesting a vaster reality than unconscious physical reality. Consciousness in fact defines an *inner world*, the world of our experience, that is distinctly different from the physical world of signals I have been talking about. To avoid any misunderstanding, I would like to point out that *inner reality* does not mean the physical reality inside the body, i.e., the body's atoms, molecules, cells, and organs. That physical reality is still part of outer reality, even though it is not visible from the outside. Inner reality means instead what we feel: the qualia that constitute our conscious experience, the meaning we carry within and wish to communicate, and the capacity to communicate with free will to other conscious beings. In my understanding, outer reality only defines the *symbolic* aspect of reality, whereas inner reality defines the *semantic* aspect of reality, that which gives meaning to our lives.

The prevailing belief, however, is that unconscious physical reality is all there is, and consciousness emerges somehow from unconscious atoms and molecules. I will argue that this assumption can only explain the symbolic world of matter but cannot account for the existence of our inner conscious experience and knowing.

Perception, comprehension, and recognition

Perception is the process that translates the electromagnetic and electrochemical activities of the brain and body into qualia. We experience the world through qualia, but qualia are neither electrical signals nor bits stored in memory. Qualia constitute the sentient representation of the symbols produced by the body, and especially by the nervous system.

When we say we are conscious, we mean that we perceive qualia—that we have an inner experience based on sensations and feelings. A digital computer that has an image in its memory produced by a digital camera is not at all aware of that image as qualia, even though it has the data that inform our qualia. Qualia are the carriers of meaning. The process of obtaining meaning from qualia is called *comprehension*. It is a process even more mysterious than perception. We only know that we can understand the meaning contained in qualia. For example, if you smell something, the existence of the smell (quale) in your consciousness indicates the presence of some object in your vicinity. This is the first level of comprehension.

However, you may also recognize that the smell is coming from something burning. This identification would be enriched by the comprehension you have of things burning. You may even recognize that what is burning is a tire, and in that case your comprehension would include possible situations in which tires may be burning. Therefore, the same smell (quale) can provide varying amounts of meaning to you depending on your comprehension level. Comprehension is thus a property somewhat independent of perception.

Comprehension has a layered organization obtained by the repetition of perception-comprehension cycles through which conscious learning occurs. In the previous example, the first level of meaning is: "there is *something* nearby." Superimposed on this layer is another level with a more precise meaning: "the something is a *thing burning.*" And then a third level brings the meaning: "the burning thing is *a tire.*" This pyramidal structure is characteristic not only of comprehension, but also of the neural symbols used to represent it, even though we generally perceive their meaning as a holistic quale. For example, the concept of love is carried by a holistic quale because its meaning can only be understood as a wholeness and cannot be split into bounded, separable parts. That is also why love cannot be defined without leaving something out.

In the previous description the word "recognition" was used as a synonym for comprehension. However, there is a crucial difference between the two. Comprehension takes place the first time you know something new, whereas *re-cognition*, as the word intimates, is when an object or situation turns out to be the same as one you already know. Comprehension is when we create for the first time a new relationship, a new category, or a new concept that seems to emerge out of nowhere. It is precisely here wherein the mystery lies. Comprehension forms a new set of connections in your experience, and this track can be perfected with further experiences to eventually form real mental grooves. The intuitive jump required in the first comprehension is much greater than the one necessary in subsequent recognitions.

To comprehend you must also add the ability to discriminate, which means to discover subtle differences that allow you to leap out from your previous conceptual scheme and create two related concepts. For example, the concept of determinism was once synonymous with predictability. We now know that there are systems called Chaotic systems which are deterministic, but not predictable. This discovery required making a crucial discrimination that split predictability out of determinism.

A new comprehension corresponds to the creation of a new category to which you may assign a new name or add a new meaning to an already existing word. Comprehension is the essence of your intuitive capacity that allows the creation of ever-subtler generalizations and differentiations. That's why it is a far deeper property than qualia perception.

Recognition can also be done by computers, for example, by teaching artificial neural networks to recognize specific patterns. In this case, the patterns belonging to the same class are supplied by a human trainer together with the name of the class. For instance, we may give the computer many visual images of different apples, each with the label "apple". "Apple" is another symbol, however, not a quale, and the computer has no *comprehension* of what "apple" means. "Apple" is only the *label* for the common data correlations existing among the set of training images that a human has presented to the computer artificial neural network as exemplars of apples.

By providing a high number of examples to a properly structured neural network, the network can learn to recognize an apple even when it is later shown an image that has not been part of its training set. This is the ability to *generalize*. Artificial neural networks require many examples before being able to generalize. We humans can do it with only one or a few examples because the intuitive aspect of comprehension is always operational and guides us to generalize and discriminate so effortlessly that we seldom realize and appreciate the true and deep intellectual power we possess. I think that this power is entirely attributable to our consciousness, for we have a keen sense of "knowing that we know" and "knowing that we don't know," even though we are not infallible.

Meaning

> *People see only what they are ready to see.*
> —Ralph Waldo Emerson

Meaning is the result of comprehension. When we comprehend something for the first time, we get a meaning we did not previously know. Comprehension is akin to an invention: a creation occurring in the mind of the inventor when a flash of new meaning is first formed. This meaning must then be translated into symbolic form with either a new combination of words or with a new physical organization of matter. For example, a diagram or a physical model can be more effective to aid comprehension than a verbal description. This translation is neither automatic nor immediate and may require the intervention of another crucial human faculty: conscious reasoning, which is a logical method rooted in comprehension.

Once the new meaning has been effectively cast in symbols, it can be *intuitively* understood by people who may not have been able to invent it by themselves. Thus, the new symbols function like a mental enzyme that lowers the barrier to comprehension that may exist in other people. Imagine building, for example, a three-dimensional physical model of an invention that even a child could understand by playing with it. That kind of intuitive comprehension would be difficult to achieve only verbally. And when a new comprehension has occurred, we can then automatically recognize similar symbols without requiring conscious awareness.

At this point you could ask: "What is the difference between consciously acquired meaning and the unconscious learning acquired by a computer? If the results are the same, what difference does consciousness make?" In fact, many researchers consider consciousness as unnecessary to achieve intelligent behavior. For them, a machine can be as intelligent or even smarter than any human being, with or without consciousness.

This view is based on an inadequate definition of intelligence that does not consider the fundamental, creative aspects of comprehension, intuition, insights, and imagination. That same reductionist mindset neglects the fact that without consciousness we would be zombies and life would have no meaning or purpose.

On the other hand, when the consciousness of a human being is completely identified with the body and with the logical mind, the person's creative potential remains largely unused, and his behavior may become just as mechanical as that of a computer. This is the same difference that exists, for example, between the profound understanding of the meaning of a ritual by a person with high comprehension, compared with the mechanical imitation of the same by another person who lacks understanding. A ritual is an example of a complex symbol with almost infinite nuances of perception and comprehension. That is why there are so many variations among people's interpretations of the same situation or event.

I think that the crucial difference between man and machine is expressed by creative people with original ideas and with the capacity to turn those ideas into new symbolic forms to be communicated to everybody else. Once a novel idea has been translated into appropriate symbols, other people can comprehend it through their intuition. Intuition is what allows us to easily grasp new concepts, whereas computers can only "learn" new *mechanical* correlations without the real comprehension inherent in consciousness.

If we want to understand how consciousness and its properties may emerge from organizations of matter, we need to start from what physics is telling us about the nature of physical reality. The following section will first examine the worldview of classical physics, the physics that existed until the beginning of the twentieth century, appropriate for describing macroscopic objects. I will then illustrate quantum physics, the theory that has revolutionized our worldview and explains the behavior of elementary particles, atoms, and molecules. Most scientists believe that consciousness can be explained with classical physics, in which case a digital computer could in principle be conscious. A small number of dissenters, myself among them, believe that consciousness is entirely a quantum phenomenon and therefore classical computers may never be conscious, no matter how complex.

Revisiting the Fundamental Hypotheses

There are some realities that are not quantifiable. The universe is not my numbers: everything is pervaded by mystery. Who does not have the sense of mystery is a half-dead man.

—Albert Einstein

The scientific method has given us the best answers about the nature of reality and its functioning, helping us achieve a level of consensus never dreamed of by philosophers and theologians. Classical physics was born in the seventeenth century and, together with analytical mathematics, it slowly built a solid foundation of reasonable postulates and logical proofs of theorems, validated by experimental verifications of predictions made by its mathematical models. By the end of the nineteenth century, the conceptual framework of classical physics seemed infallible in its predictions, though there were some anomalies that were initially dismissed as inconsequential.

It took a quarter of a century to explain these anomalies, and this effort required overturning almost all the fundamental assumptions of classical physics. That creative process gave birth to quantum mechanics and general relativity: new physics with indeterminism and holism replacing the determinism and reductionism of classical physics. One century later we are still grappling with the conceptual revolution brought by these new ideas.

The final blow to the prevailing logical positivism that dominated the philosophical-scientific thought at the turn of the nineteenth century was dealt by the mathematician Kurt Gödel in 1931. Gödel demonstrated the *incompleteness* of mathematics, proving that classical logic was insufficient to determine the truth of all possible statements that followed the rules of an axiomatic system sufficiently complex to contain arithmetic. In other words, there is a fundamental difference between unprovable and false because there are *undecidable* statements that cannot be formally proven without introducing new axioms.

The indeterminism of quantum physics eliminated the possibility of knowing the whole truth about the physical world, not only in practice, but also in principle, and Gödel's theorem eliminated the completeness and absolute certainty that mathematics was thought to have.

Classical physics had proposed a deterministic and reductionist model of reality where the elementary particles were conceived as the original atoms of Democritus: extremely small, irreducible, eternal, bounded, independent, and separate from each other. In that paradigm, free will could not exist. There could only be one objective reality already laid out because reality was thought to be completely governed by the mechanical interactions of atoms obeying immutable and deterministic laws. In this view, reality is like a movie that proceeds independently from the observer because free will is an illusion, therefore our inner experience cannot have any influence on the outer world. Causality only goes from particles to systems, bottom-up, and from the outside to the inside but not vice versa. In other words, the overall system has no impact on the particles and inner experience cannot affect reality.

According to this classical model, the strict laws that specify the behavior of the elementary particles also determine how we act, regardless of what we think or feel. We are simply *mechanisms* mistakenly believing that we have real feelings and free will. In the world of classical physics, there are no free-will decisions at any level. We are a small gear made of even smaller gears, inside a giant clockwork run by immutable laws. In short, even when we are convinced that we made a free-will decision, we did not, because we are instead completely controlled by the impersonal laws governing the behavior of the atoms and molecules of which we are made, the same ones that "make us think" we made a free-will choice [21]. Despite this apparently compelling story, however, no one could explain how atoms make us think.

Quantum mechanics tells us a different story. It claims that the behavior of the elementary particles is fundamentally *probabilistic*, and it recognizes that the act of observing the world changes both the observer and the observed, even if by only a little. Quantum mechanics was soon followed by a more sophisticated theory in which each elementary particle was no longer considered as an independent and separate entity, like an object, but as an *excited state* of a quantum field—a property of a field. This theory was developed between the late 1920s and the 1950s and was called quantum field theory (QFT).

Imagine a quantum particle to be like a coin flipping in a non-physical space you cannot see. You can only know the coin's state, "heads" or "tails," when it has landed on the "table" that represents our physical reality, *without you ever seeing the coin*. When flipping in the invisible space, the coin could have been in an infinity of different orientations, but in our world it will only show up as "heads" or "tails", "up" or "down", "1" or "0". I have described the *spin* of an elementary particle, a fundamental quantum property discovered by Wolfgang Pauli in 1924.

Quantum physics describes the many different orientations of a particle spin in an *abstract space* and gives us the probability of measuring "heads" or "tails" in *our physical space.* A continuum of states in the quantum world reduces to a single bit in our classical world. The infinity of spin states can be mathematically represented by a linear combination, called *superposition,* of two pure *quantum* states "up" and "down" in an abstract space called Hilbert space. It is hard to imagine such a quantum world because it violates our intuitive sense of reality embodied in classical physics.

There are more surprises because, if two quantum particles were to interact, their spin states could become *entangled,* meaning that if we measured the spin of particle 1 and found "up," the spin of particle 2 will be found to be "down" *instantly,* independently from the distance of the two particles, as if they were joined at the hip, so to speak. This property would be impossible for two *independent* classical objects because it would violate special relativity, according to which no communication can occur faster than the speed of light.

Entanglement appears to allow superluminal communication, yet this possibility is unfeasible because, when we measure particle 1, we have the same probability of measuring "heads" as we have of finding "tails." This uncertainty does not allow us to rely on a known state to communicate superluminally to a distant friend, even though the effect of entanglement is instantaneous. The existence of entanglement has been experimentally verified in various situations starting in the 1980s. However, it is still a mystery how particle 2 can instantly "know" that particle 1 has been measured and found to be either "heads" or "tails."

With quantum superposition, entanglement, and indeterminacy, particles could no longer be considered *objects* like they were in classical physics, and thus the ontological status of particles within classical physics had to be assigned to the quantum fields of which the particles are simply excited states. Ontology moved from particles to fields.

For several reasons that will be explained later, classical physics cannot explain consciousness, whereas QFT, with some additional assumptions, may be able to accommodate the peculiar properties of consciousness and free will. However, QFT, though necessary, may not be sufficient to the task, in which case a more general theory than QFT will have to be developed. The jury is still out.

Everything is made of fields

I think that modern physics has definitely decided in favor of Plato. In fact, the smallest units of matter are not physical objects in the ordinary sense; they are forms, ideas which can be expressed unambiguously only in mathematical language.

—Werner Heisenberg

The idea of a field is one of the most fertile in physics. It was introduced by the genius of Michael Faraday in 1831 to explain the puzzling electromagnetic phenomena in which a body could move without being pushed by another body, like when a piece of iron is attracted by a magnet. Faraday conceived that the three-dimensional space around the magnet was filled with some real "field of force." Forty years later, James Clerk Maxwell generalized Faraday's magnetic field idea to electricity with the first mathematical treatment of the *electromagnetic field*. This seminal theory surprised the scientific world with the prediction of electromagnetic waves.

To imagine this field, think about the entire empty space of the universe filled with an invisible and immaterial substance in which waves can form and propagate. These waves are everywhere, they can transfer energy and information, and are also what we perceive to be *light* when their wavelengths are between .4 and .8 micrometers. They are also what we use to cook our food in a microwave oven, and what allow us to communicate wirelessly.

Another major revolution in physics occurred in 1900 with Max Planck's discovery that the transfer of electromagnetic energy is not continuous but instead occurs in discrete lumps, or quanta, whereas with classical physics such transfer could occur with arbitrarily small values of energy. This radical idea led to quantum mechanics in the 1920s. Quantum mechanics morphed in the 1950s into quantum field theory (QFT), and informed the Standard Model in the 1970s by generalizing the idea of the quantum field to additional types of matter and interactions. Based on QFT there are 17 quantum fields in superposition in space-time. These fields are not continuous like Maxwell's field, but quantized. This means that the interactions between fields occur in quanta—the minimum quantity with which the energetic transfer can occur.

In 1915, Einstein stunned the scientific community with general relativity (GR), his theory about the gravitational force. GR can be succinctly described in the words of the famous physicist John Wheeler: "Spacetime tells matter how to move; matter tells spacetime how to curve." In other words, the global distribution of matter affects the local properties of space, and the local properties of space determine how matter will move. As matter moves locally, the global distribution of matter changes, upsetting in turn the previous local properties of space. This sounds like a "snake eating its own tail," but the same analogy can also illustrate how an electromagnetic wave propagates in space since a change in the electric field causes a change in the magnetic field, and a change in the magnetic field causes a change in the electric field. These propagating changes occurring within the immaterial but real electromagnetic field cause a wave to propagate in space-time.

General relativity expresses the existence of *feedback* from the whole to the parts, and the existence of *feedforward* from the parts to the whole. Feedback is a top-down influence in which the global distribution of matter (the whole) determines the local properties of space-time that inform the local behavior of matter (the parts). Feedforward is a bottom-up influence in which the local behavior of matter determines the future global distribution of matter that constitutes the whole.

Today, quantum field theory (QFT) and general relativity (GR) form the two pillars of theoretical physics. However, GR describes a classical rather than a quantum field, inconsistent with the quantization of the other three fundamental forces: the electromagnetic force, the strong nuclear force, and the weak nuclear force. The theoretical physics community has been trying to unify QFT with GR for the last sixty to seventy years, but so far without success despite valiant efforts. This unification would describe space-time and the gravitational force as the eighteenth quantum field.

According to QFT, elementary particles, atoms, molecules, proteins, cells, organs, and living organisms constitute ever-growing hierarchical organizations of states belonging to the quantum fields. These fields have space and time in common and are the fundamental entities that create all that physically exists by interacting with each other. For example, all the electrons of your body, together with all the electrons of the rest of the universe, are quantum waves (states) of the same underlying quantum field of electrons.

The magic of quantum physics

> *Not only is the universe stranger than we think, it is even stranger than we can think.*
>
> —Werner Heisenberg

Fairy tales enchant because they transport us into a world full of magic where the strangest and most incredible things can happen. Well, quantum physics has revealed to us that physical reality is even more fantastic than any fable.

Quantum physics has brought to science topics that were previously considered outside of its domain, raising questions like "What exists before making a measurement?"; "Can something exist if it is not knowable?"; "Why is probability necessary to describe reality?"; "What does *indeterminism* really mean?"; and "Is there free will?"

These questions were previously restricted to philosophy, but now they have drifted into the domain of science.

Physics is now telling us that the ontological entities of the universe are the fields and that atoms are combinations of states of the quantum fields. Atoms do not have the same type of existence we had attributed to classical particles which make up classical objects. Classical particles are bounded, deterministic, and always existing objects. A classical wave is a property of an ensemble of classical particles. A quantum particle is almost totally different from a classical one, for it appears, disappears, and behaves like a "probability wave" with an *indeterminate* position, momentum, and magnetic spin until it is measured.

QFT postulates the perennial, probabilistic creation-annihilation of elementary particles and describes a universe that emerged somehow from the quantum vacuum, shaping the space-time and the quantum fields in its wake. This theory, known as Big Bang, can explain much about the evolution of the universe, starting from an infinitesimal region of almost infinite density and temperature that rapidly expanded to achieve a diameter of about 93 billion light-years over the span of 13.8 billion years. Yet the natures of space, time, and the quantum vacuum are still largely mysterious.

Since the mathematical framework of QFT can only predict the probability of observable events, but not which specific event will happen, many believe that this lack of determinism makes QFT compatible with free will. However, free will implies more than just free choices. It implies the existence of entities that can exercise such free will, and this is hard to fathom within the current conceptual framework of physics. I think that free will could exist if a "quantum system" had *some* freedom to determine which *classical* state will manifest out of its near-infinite quantum states. In this case, the probability of quantum physics would not express a lack of knowledge of a state already existing, but it would stand for a future state that would come into existence only after the quantum system has made its free choice. A free choice would then be a true act of creation, something impossible to know a priori, even in principle.

If we postulate that consciousness and free will are irreducible properties of nature, then it is clear they must be quantum properties of certain "quantum systems," since free will cannot be a property of deterministic classical systems. In this view, the physical body could then be controlled by a "conscious quantum system" that communicates with it, since the body is a complex quantum-classical system. If this hypothesis proves correct, the real self is the "conscious quantum system" that controls the body.

The idea that consciousness is an irreducible property of all that exists is called *panpsychism*, and it is quite old. In general, panpsychists believe that all matter, down to each single electron is conscious. But this is only because it was widely believed that electrons exist as objects, which according to QFT is no longer true. Within QFT an electron is only a *state* of the field of electrons, and electrons have no ontological status. The framework I am developing recognizes that only quantum systems with certain coherent properties have consciousness and free will. However, it is beyond the scope of this chapter to explain the highly technical distinctions between coherent and incoherent quantum systems.

The next section will provide an instructive metaphor to understand how conscious entities with free will do affect the outer physical reality, and how the physical, objective reality of symbols affects the inner reality of meaning in turn. The interplay between subjective and objective reality that I will illustrate below is seldom considered relevant in physics since all physical reality is presumed to be *objective*.

The inner and the outer worlds interact

Imagine a large town square where there are hundreds of people, animals, and objects emitting vibrations (symbols) that are perceivable as sounds (qualia). Each entity contributes a small amount of vibrations that propagate everywhere and are superimposed upon the rest of the vibrations present at each point in the space of the square. Each conscious entity can choose to pay attention only to a small fraction of these vibrations, and the ones selected constitute an *observation* that is experienced as sound and is understood to some extent. Each entity responds then to its inner experience by contributing new vibrations that are added to those of the square.

If we now consider only the conscious entities, the outer symbolic vibrational reality of the square is the sum of the vibrations produced by all those entities. The inner semantic reality of each entity is thus affected by the entity's free-will decisions about which subset of vibrations to observe and experience. In response to its observation and experience, the entity will then make a free-will decision about which vibration to contribute, thus affecting the outer reality once more. In general, each entity constantly repeats cycles of *observation or perception, comprehension or experience*, and *response or action*.

In this example, we see clearly that the outer reality affects the inner reality and that the inner reality affects the outer reality. We also see that the entity's vibrations emitted in response to the inner experience represent a top-down influence on physical reality because they affect the motion of the air molecules. Notice however that the top-down and inside-out influences upon reality are contrary to the worldview of *classical* physics but not the worldview of quantum physics.

In other words, my conscious choice of what meaning to communicate is not made by the atoms of my body, even though my conscious experience leading to that choice is affected to some extent by the physical configuration of my atoms. Once I make a choice, my conscious command will affect a subset of the atoms of my body, and these in turn will affect my physical behavior in such a way that the pattern I emit will represent the intended meaning. Said differently, that pattern has both a symbolic content (air vibrations) belonging to the outer reality, and a semantic content, the qualia and meaning that belong to my inner reality. There must be two-way communication between the semantic level of inner experience and the outer informational level, with the semantic level affecting the symbolic level and vice versa.

Let us now return to the square full of conscious entities producing vibrations. At any one time each entity observes only a small subset of the overall vibrations, neglecting the rest of them which are considered background noise. For example, my experience will be quite different from my neighbor's, who is listening to someone I am not engaged with. Similarly, in the experience of the nearby dog, who is only paying attention to the barking of other dogs, all other sounds may be considered background noise.

Notice that in the vibrational reality of the square, there are neither objective symbols nor objective noises, even though the physical vibrations could be objectively described by an equation. Since what is signal and what is noise are determined primarily by the free will choices of each observer, having a definite equation is not enough because the equation contains parameters that are unknowable until the free-will choices have been made. Furthermore, since each observer has only a single point of view, no entity can simultaneously experience the vibrational reality of the square from two or more different points of view. The point I am making here is that we often think we have solved a problem by devising a general mathematical equation but if the parameters of that equation are *impossible* to obtain, the problem has not been solved.

This example could be generalized to the electromagnetic field (EMF) created and observed by the particles, atoms, molecules, macromolecules, cells, ants, dogs, and people, each contributing its part to the same vast EMF and then *freely* observing only an infinitesimal portion of it. Had I considered electromagnetic vibrations rather than sound vibrations in the previous example, I would indeed have been closer to what is happening in our reality. However, the narrative would have been much more complicated without adding significant meaning to the basic conceptual ideas contained in the example with sound.

Symbols obey probabilistic laws but meaning is free

Within classical physics, everything is external reality because the outer properties of the elementary particles are the only determinants of the properties of any hierarchical structure made of particles. Based on this premise, no inner reality can exist in any organization of classical particles.

Within quantum physics, however, there is the possibility that each hierarchical level of quantum states might have some degree of freedom not entirely accounted for by the behaviors of the hierarchical level immediately below it. For example, the properties of a water molecule are more than the sum of the properties of the hydrogen and oxygen atoms. A water molecule has novel properties that involve some *integration* of lower-level properties into something new (not a sum), with new constraints between the parts, and new freedoms accessible to the molecule but not available to its parts.

If we imagine that consciousness and free will are inner properties of the quantum fields, then the outer state of each field could be changed by the field itself. Therefore, the outer state of the field would reflect its inner semantic reality. Those outer states would then correspond to the vibrations imposed by a conscious entity onto the air molecules in the example of the square previously described. Those vibrations would reflect the meaning that the conscious entity intends to communicate to the other fields since the outer information is correlated with the meaning.

Vibrations must be "quanta," each quantum corresponding to a discrete symbol of the language used to communicate, and each symbol is the result of a free-will choice made by the conscious entity. Therefore, the symbol that appears cannot be known a priori and can only be mathematically described by a probability. This probability, however, does not indicate a lack of knowledge, like classical, objective probability does, but refers to an act of creation. The creator knows which symbol it will emit, but no outside observer can possibly know that symbol before its creation. The probability that describes the appearance of symbols in human verbal communications is called *subjective* probability. It is the same probability used by quantum physics, even though this interpretation is not generally accepted by physicists.

An interesting reflection is that, when two people verbally communicate, the words they use do obey the probabilistic, syntactical laws of symbols of the language they use. These laws are obeyed out of *cooperation*, not out of *coercion*, because people desire to communicate and understand each other. My crucial insight here is that, while the meaning people are communicating is not predetermined, the syntactical laws of symbols in which *any* meaning will be expressed are probabilistic mathematical laws that will be *obeyed* no matter what meaning is expressed.

For example, the book I will write five years from now is guaranteed to precisely obey the syntactical laws of English—the language in which it will be written. This is true even though I have not yet decided what I am going to write about, i.e. the meaning is largely independent of the elementary symbols I am going to use to express it. For example, the probability of finding a letter "e" in my future book will be 0.12702, exactly the same probability of finding the letter "e" in this book (the probability can be found by counting the total number of letters "e" divided by the total number of letters in the book).

Most physicists believe that the universe is constructed out of the interaction of quantum fields whose states represent meaningless, abstract symbols obeying the probabilistic laws they have discovered. However, if what matters to conscious entities is the meaning expressed by those abstract symbols, I fear that physicists will never know that the universe is alive and conscious because they attribute reality only to information without meaning.

If we interpret the appearance of an elementary particle at a specific point in space and time as a communication symbol, like a letter in the alphabet of the universal language "spoken" by the conscious quantum fields, and if we take quantum entanglement as evidence that particles are part of larger organizations of symbols, then, the quantum state of a coherent quantum system that qualifies as a conscious entity may be interpreted as having a dual nature: it is a quantum symbol to the outer objective world, and a subjective meaning to the conscious entity that created that state. The only additional assumption necessary for this interpretation is to hypothesize that the quantum state of a conscious entity has a meaning to the entity itself.

A New Conceptual Framework

Consciousness is not a thing among things, it is the horizon that contains everything.

—Edmund Husserl

The universe described by QFT and general relativity (GR) is inherently dynamic and holistic, yet it represents only the outer aspect of reality and cannot account for the existence of our inner reality unless interiority is also present from the beginning. If we take seriously the evidence of our inner reality and the impossibility of explaining its existence with abstract information without meaning, all ontological entities may have an inner reality as well. This means that the quantum fields, which are the fundamental ontological entities of the known universe, must also have an inner conscious reality just as we do. To explain how a universe containing conscious beings may emerge from the quantum vacuum, we must then postulate that the quantum vacuum is inherently conscious as well.

Clearly the variety of *types* of consciousness must be unimaginably vast just by looking at the variety of species in the earth's ecosystem, as we go from a bacterium to an amoeba, to a worm, a fish, a bat, and a human. Truly, when we consider what could be the inner experience of the field of electrons, our imagination abandons us. But, just because we cannot imagine what it might feel like to be an electron field or a paramecium it does not mean that those entities are unconscious. Indeed, the conscious experience of any entity is totally private, and another entity can only know what is symbolically expressed by the free will of the communicating entity.

During the last five years I have endeavored to formulate a conceptual framework starting from the postulate that all reality is created by the free-will communications of a vast number of elementary conscious entities. It is a highly speculative model at this point, though I believe it has the potential to unify inner and outer realities and explain the coevolution of both. I will illustrate some of the basic ideas in this section and the reader interested in a deeper discussion can find additional material in Appendix 5.

We simultaneously exist in two worlds

Imagine the world of events that we can measure, emerging from a more fundamental quantum world in which much more is happening than can be measured. The first world is the *classical world* characterized by Boolean or classical information and the second world is the quantum world characterized by quantum information. These two worlds interact, meaning that quantum information can be transformed into classical information and vice versa. Because of this interaction the two worlds are not separate, yet both worlds are real, and within each world there are *entities* that can exist only in one or in the other. There are also entities that simultaneously exist in both worlds, straddling the two, so to speak. These are the living organisms.

The entities that exist only in the classical world interact with deterministic laws using classical information and thus behave mechanically like our machines and our computers. The entities existing only in the quantum world interact with quantum laws based on quantum information. Living organisms are special because they exist in both worlds and will be discussed further down. This interpretation of quantum physics assigns reality to the quantum world. It is unlike most other interpretations in which only the classical world of measurable events is considered real.

The classical world is made of Boolean information of which the binary digit or bit is its smallest unit. The bit is the simplest abstract symbol, a symbol that represents only two possible states: "yes" or "no"; "1" or "0"; "true" or "false"; "on" or "off"; "is" or "is not". The bit of a computer is represented by a *convention* that must be strictly respected in all its electronic circuits. One convention, for example, could be the following: If the voltage in a node of a circuit is between 0.6 and 1.0 volt, the state of that node corresponds to "1". If the voltage is between 0.0 and 0.3 volt, the state corresponds to "0". If the voltage is between 0.3 and 0.6 volt, the state is undetermined and could cause errors. The bit is an abstract symbol without any inherent meaning. It is a human *idea* that can physically exist only by forcing a representation of it over a man-made physical structure by a convention like the one above.

Similarly, the quantum world is made of quantum information whose elementary unit is the qubit (quantum bit). The qubit is the generalization of the bit obtained from the quantum superposition of two possible complementary *quantum* states: "1" and "0," as discussed earlier in connection with the spin of a particle. This superposition generates an infinity of states that can be represented by all the points on the surface of a sphere of radius 1, called Bloch sphere, existing in an abstract two-dimensional space of complex numbers called Hilbert space.

The qubit cannot exist in the classical world because in that world it can only exist as a Boolean bit, either the "1" or the "0" *classical* state. Qubits can also be entangled, meaning that they share some states, as discussed in the previous section. Superposition of complementary states and entanglement provide representational and information processing capabilities with no correspondence in the classical world, making the quantum world a far richer reality than the latter.

In the framework I am proposing, conscious entities can only exist in the quantum world, and these entities use quantum information to communicate with each other. To represent quantum information, I am assuming the existence of a "substance" of which everything that exists is "made," whether quantum or classical. This substance is like the energy of physics, but it has the additional property that it can experience itself. To avoid any confusion, I decided to call this universal substance, *nousym*, the portmanteau of *nous* (higher mind in Greek) and *symbol*. Nousym is a holistic and dynamic substance with extraordinary properties: it is the "stuff" that forms and connects the qubits, and it is also the one that manifests in our classical world as the matter-energy of physics.

One of the revolutionary discoveries of modern physics has been that energy only comes in discrete quanta. By induction, nousym also shares this property and its quanta can be entangled to create vast coherent structures that can exist and evolve in the quantum world. The crucial idea is to postulate that *these coherent structures are conscious entities with a unique identity and free will*. Each coherent entity has an outer aspect "made" of quantum information and an inner aspect "made" of qualia and free will. The qualia express the existence of a conscious experience and the free will expresses the capacity of the entity to affect its outer information.

If we now go back to the large town square example with people and animals producing sounds, the vibrating air carrying the sounds made by the communicating entities would be analogous to the "vibrating" nousym carrying the superposition of the information of the communicating quantum entities. Like in the case of the square, the state manifested by a conscious quantum entity A, say, would be a free-will choice made by A and therefore known by A before its manifestation. Viewed by any other entity, however, the appearance of that state would have to obey probabilistic physical laws, since it was freely chosen by A. Something similar also happens when a scientist prepares an elementary particle in a particular state. The scientist can predict with confidence the state that will be measured, whereas any other observer who does not know about the preparation can only know the probability of measuring that state.

We can now turn our attention to the systems that straddle the classical and the quantum worlds.

The amazing phenomenon of life

Many years ago, I saw a short documentary of a paramecium happily swimming inside a drop of water. A paramecium is a protozoan, a single-cell animalcule, whose body is like a miniature short cigar, about 0.1 mm long, covered by thousands of villi: microscopic whiskers that beat in unison and can propel it in water. Well, this little "thing" could swim quite fast, avoid obstacles, seek, and find food, find a mate, and generally behave intelligently with clear purpose, like a little fish.

"But the paramecium is a single cell!" I exclaimed. "It has no nervous system!", "How can just a bag of chemicals process *information* in such an exquisite manner? How can it reproduce by assembling a copy of itself *within itself?*" This is not a program that can copy itself within the computer memory. This is akin to a computer assembling another computer like itself within itself—hardware and software included—and then dividing into two complete computers! These are feats no engineer could match today. I concluded that there must be something *fundamental* going on that we do not yet understand.

Any living organism, from bacteria to man, is an *open system*, i.e. a system that exchanges matter, energy, and information with the environment in which it lives. To survive, an organism requires *food*, i.e., a continuing supply of matter and energy, and the ability to self-regulate. The capacity for self-regulation, called *homeostasis*, allows the organism to maintain internal stability by means of many interoperating dynamic processes that use negative feedback.

Stability is achieved via a dynamical equilibrium around some set points, just like what happens with a thermostat that automatically adjusts the temperature in a home. Of course, within a cell there are homeostatic cycles inside other homeostatic cycles in bewildering complexity, though the basic operating principle of each cycle is always the same, i.e. to *feed back* the value of the variable to be controlled, compare it to a set value, and drive the process until the difference between the two is negligible.

If we look closely at a eukaryotic cell, its operation is *completely* different than the way our machines work, including computers. Inside the cytoplasm of the cell there are electrons and protons (hydrogen ions); ions of simple atoms such as sodium, potassium, phosphorous, and so on; simple molecules like water, glucose, and amino acids; complex molecules like messenger RNA; proteins; organelles like ribosomes and DNA; and mitochondria that are like simple bacteria—living cells inside a larger cell.

The cell therefore contains many hierarchical organizational levels, all working seamlessly together in unbelievable complexity and with a single purpose. Each part of a cell can interact with very many other parts in both a *feedforward* and a *feedback* manner without *permanent* connections among them. This freedom is unlike any found in a computer, for in a computer the connections of its transistors are fixed once and for all by its designer, and its matter does not move in and out of its physical boundaries.

A cell is like an *irreducible whole*, a fundamental "atom" out of which complex living organisms can be constructed by using trillions of them organized in a remarkable way. In fact, when we manipulate life, we always start with a living cell, not with its component parts, and it's only because of the robustness and fault-tolerance of cells that we can make certain invasive manipulations without killing them in the process.

Everything going on in a living organism intimates that such a physical structure cannot be completely understood within the logical framework of the classical world, even though much of what is happening can. There are many properties that require quantum physics to be understood, and even many of the properties we consider classical are approximations of quantum properties good enough to classically explain what happens. What we cannot account for classically is the fact that living organisms are conscious and autonomous with probabilistic behavior.

I think it will be impossible to explain life without the concept of consciousness because the two are inextricably linked in ways we have yet to comprehend. A living organism has purpose only because it can "host" a conscious entity and can thus act as a unit endowed with free will, intention, and meaning; properties that cannot arise from a bag of unconscious *classical* atoms and molecules interacting with each other. I think that consciousness must play not only the role of the "glue" that holds together the unity of the organism, while it constantly changes, but also be the "agent" behind its free-will actions.

Life exists in a deep and abiding symbiosis with the environment with which there is a constant exchange of matter, energy, and information in a profoundly dynamic equilibrium where the organism is never the same throughout its lifetime. And so is the environment never the same from the viewpoint of the organism. In fact, the two coevolve, and what is inside the organism at one time may be outside the next, and vice versa, like two complementary aspects of a *single* dynamic and holistic structure. I will now resort again to a metaphor to more clearly explain how I envision life straddling the quantum and the classical worlds.

What is real and what is virtual?

In the framework I am developing, conscious entities exist entirely in the quantum world and each one has the qualia perception, comprehension, and free will to direct the physical body which is a quantum-classical structure. The quantum portion of the body interacts with the quantum conscious entity and the classical portion of the body interacts with the classical world of which it is part. The conscious entity is the "self" we really are, though we erroneously believe we are the body.

The classical portion of the body contains a sophisticated mechanism that controls the body as if it were an automaton, and the automaton is connected with the quantum portion of the body that is top-down controlled by the conscious entity. If we were to place the boundary of our body at the *classical-quantum information boundary*, which is what is relevant here, we may look quite different than we normally think because that boundary is not our skin and not necessarily a continuous surface in space, but is both inside and outside the body, and highly dynamic as well.

In this framework the conscious entity may control the body both directly and indirectly. Direct or explicit control is when we consciously make a choice, therefore we explicitly know the choice we make. An indirect or implicit control is when a barely conscious desire (a quale) we never consciously examined—but we could have—may direct the classical machinery of the body without us being aware of. The important point is that the "desire" is a quantum property that controls the classical information of the body.

When the conscious entity is identified with the body, meaning that it believes itself to be the body *based on the data coming from the body's classical senses,* the entity loses contact with its vaster quantum reality thinking that all that exists is the physical world with the characteristics that are registered by the senses. At this point I will resort to a virtual reality metaphor to further illustrate this situation.

Imagine controlling an avatar in a virtual reality world created by a computer. You wear sophisticated goggles, earphones, and a costume that automatically captures the movements of your body. Your voice and your motions control the actions of the avatar, and through the simulated senses of the avatar you experience a virtual world as if you were the avatar you control. In that virtual world there are virtual classical objects and other avatars, each controlled by a different person. You interact with them using the laws of the virtual world and may experience a different world than the physical one you know.

The computer program that runs the virtual world includes the avatars as subroutines and is totally classical. If you get engrossed in that virtual reality, you may almost believe for brief periods that you are the avatar and that the virtual world is real, forgetting that you exist in the physical world instead. The capacity of our consciousness to focus onto a portion of our experience about which we feel a strong interest is something we are all familiar with. In the game of life, most of us are completely identified with our body because we can only affect the world classically and therefore end up paying attention only to the classical information coming from the body. This conditioning occurs early in life, facilitated by the *seamless* interface between our consciousness and our body, contrary to the crude interface between our body and the avatar.

When you control the avatar, your body clearly exists *outside* the classical computer and the avatar is not who you are even when you are engrossed in the game. Your classical body controls top-down the avatar with classical information, but your quantum body is in turn controlled by the quantum conscious entity—the real you—that exists in the quantum world. Notice that your experience of the virtual world is also a quantum phenomenon occurring within the same "you" that controls the body that controls the avatar. Therefore, the avatar may perform actions that could not have originated digitally since they depend on your free-will decisions occurring in the quantum world.

I think that just like your body does not exist *inside* the computer that creates the virtual reality, your consciousness and free will do not exist *inside* the physical world in which your body exists. The avatar is just an *interface* allowing you to interact and have an experience in the classical virtual reality created by the computer, but your experience exists neither inside the avatar nor inside the computer. Likewise, your body is just an interface to the physical world that contains your body and the computer, but your experience of body and world is neither inside the body nor inside the physical world. It is only because you *believe* the physical world is the only reality in existence that you *attribute* your experience to the body.

The real entity is not your body but your conscious self who is "wearing the body," just like your body is "wearing the avatar." You exist solely in the quantum world and inside the quantum world there is a quantum-classical physical world in which your body exists; and inside the physical world there is classical computer in which there is a virtual world that contains an avatar that your body can control. Like Russian dolls, there are virtual realities inside virtual realities, but it is nousym that contains your conscious experiences of all those dolls and the quantum information out of which all those dolls are physically made.

The physical world as a simulation

If we go one step further in our metaphor, you can surmise that the avatar is controlled by a *portion* of the consciousness that controls your body since you simultaneously are aware of existing both as an avatar in the virtual reality and as a body in the physical world.

This is true except when you are fully identified with the avatar, in which case you "forget" you are the body. By induction we may surmise that, if we are completely identified with our physical body, the consciousness that controls our body—what we normally call *ego*—may also be a portion of a vaster consciousness controlling a vaster "body" we are currently not aware of possessing.

If this reasoning is correct, the real you may then be that vaster self you "forgot" you are, given your strong attachment and interest in physical life that wrought the belief you are just the body. That vaster self, then, may be the one who decided to wear the body you now think you are, just like you have decided to wear an avatar in a virtual reality game with which you identified for a short while. Without realizing it, we may be simply repeating the same pattern at different "levels of reality." There is indeed strong evidence for this view in the many reported near-death experiences (NDE) and in many other extraordinary conscious experiences.

A few words about the evidence of NDE [22] is appropriate to ground the inductive process just invoked. In a typical case of NDE, a person has a heart attack and arrives dead at the hospital. She is placed in cryogenic reanimation despite both heart and brain showing no electrical activity. After one hour the patient is resuscitated and, sometime later, she reports having had an extraordinary experience while clinically dead. She reports finding herself floating near the ceiling of the operating room seeing the doctors and nurses busily working on her body. She correctly describes the procedures that doctors and nurses performed, and she even catches an unspoken thought of a doctor, which he later confirms having had.

Then the person feels drawn to leave the hospital scene by moving through some sort of tunnel with a bright white light at the end, strangely attracting her. She finds herself surrounded by a pleasant non-physical light and encounters her deceased husband and friends that welcome her with much love. The feelings of joy, love, and freedom far exceed any experience she ever had in her life and she would like to stay. But now a light being tells her she must return to her body, which reluctantly she does, awakening in the recovery room of the hospital.

This type of experience with similar structure has been reported by thousands of people, especially recently, given the major medical progress made in resuscitation. As if such an experience was not remarkable enough, the mental and emotional life of the experiencer was afterward changed for the better in most reported cases. You may ask, how can a clinically dead person with a non-functioning brain and heart have any experience? And on top of it, one so powerful and coherent to irreversibly change that person's life for the better?

Going back to the simulation now, imagine yourself so engrossed in a virtual reality (VR) game that you momentarily think you are the avatar and that the VR is real. In a well-engineered system this is certainly possible in the future. Imagine now being killed in that game. When this happens, all the information coming from the VR stops reaching you. You would then immediately experience the information to which you were not previously paying attention. And you would then realize you had been captivated by the VR and remember you are really your body living in the physical world.

Truly, you do not need to wait for a better VR technology to confirm what I am saying for I have just described an experience most of us have had. It is the experience of waking up from one of those vivid and captivating dreams which you believed were real while dreaming.

Now, imagine that your body dies. Then, all the information coming from your body stops reaching your consciousness and now you become aware of a lot of other information to which you were not paying attention. You then realize you were entirely captivated by the flood of information coming from the physical world through your body. With much surprise, you discover that "you"—a different you now, but still you—are still alive, and that the body you believed was you is not "you." This is essentially what may happen to those people who have an NDE.

Said differently, when our bodies die, we lose the ability to observe the physical world from the point of view of the body, but we now can observe from the perspective of our vaster self who always existed in the quantum world and feels the same to us as before. This deeper point of view and capacity to perceive another reality, drowned during our life by the *louder* body-perspective, becomes aware again. Thus, postmortem survival is a natural consequence of this new conceptual framework.

I think that the most likely reason for being in this physical world is to learn how to voluntarily cooperate with each other at a much higher level of comprehension than we have ever known, learning to collectively build the next hierarchical level of being that requires far more coherence with each other than we now possess. I believe the time has come to wake up from the illusion that we are just our body. So far, our consciousness has been almost entirely *hypnotized* by the illusion of being the physical body, unaware that our physical reality may itself be a vaster and more sophisticated virtual reality than the one we have collectively learned to create with our computers.

Our species has developed enough that such a transformative realization can now be achieved while we are still living our "physical life." In this view, we are not the bodies we wear, and we are not "inside" the physical universe in which our body exists any more than the body that controls the avatar is "inside" the computer in which avatar and VR exist.

If my sense of the tide of human evolution is correct, mankind may be about to awaken. In the current condition of half-sleep most of us would like to continue sleeping while some of us are beginning to stir and open our eyes to a vaster and surprising reality. As we become aware of a greater world, each of us can develop our consciousness to the point that only a portion of it will be focused on the business of controlling the body, while the rest can become aware of that vaster reality in which we have our full existence.

Computers and robots cannot be conscious

The Analytical Engine has no pretensions whatever to originate anything.

—Ada Byron Lovelace

Based on the above discussion, consciousness and free will are properties of certain coherent quantum organizations existing entirely in the quantum world, which I refer to as "conscious entities." To interact within the classical world, these entities need a quantum-classical system, a "body," that can interface with the classical information of the objective classical world and with the quantum information of the quantum entity. As far as I know, the only quantum-classical systems capable of performing this remarkable feat are living organisms—known to support consciousness already.

My contention that computers cannot be conscious is based on the idea that consciousness is a quantum information phenomenon out of reach of classical information. As such, consciousness cannot interface directly with computers but can only do so *through* living organisms by using methods for the moment unknown but theoretically possible, and to my knowledge never-before investigated. Our body, being a quantum-classical system, can interface with our conscious entity on the one end and with a computer on the other. Notice also that a conscious entity can direct a computer through a body to perform actions impossible for its algorithms to specify, thanks to the comprehension and free will of the entity. This capacity may allow the human-computer combination to impact the classical *and* the quantum worlds in ways impossible to achieve with either conscious quantum systems or computers if each class were to interact only with its own kind.

A typical objection here is that the computer should be able in principle to interface with a quantum system, and therefore be conscious since the computer *hardware* is made of quantum-classical matter. I do not think this is possible because the quantum-classical

atoms and molecules of the computer hardware have been organized so that their quantum properties have been averaged out
to produce a strictly classical machine. The computer is indeed a
reductionist system in which the hardware is entirely classical and
is also separated from the software that runs on it. The computer
bits are in fact represented by statistical properties that can exist
only as averages of quantum properties of fixed atoms. Likewise,
the transistors, which are realized by an ingenious use of the quantum properties of crystals, behave as close as possible to ideal on-off
switches. In other words, the quantum-classical matter of the computer has been permanently shaped to behave only classically with
no means for it to affect the classical bits represented by it.

In a robot, the classical information of its computer brain can
indeed control its classical body parts, and the classical body parts
can send classical information to its brain. But everything is classical here, and there is no way for classical information to interface
directly with a coherent quantum system. The interaction between a
conscious entity and a living organism can instead occur because
the conscious entity can control the position or momentum of an
individual particle or an atom, for example, within a quantum-classical living cell, and these effects can be amplified, leading to classical macroscopic events within the cell itself. In other words, there
is a path from quantum to classical (and vice versa), a path that
does not exist in computers or robots so long as classical bits are
represented by statistical properties of quantum matter. Notice that
this conclusion is independent of the complexity of the classical
system. Consciousness cannot simply emerge from the algorithmic
complexity of a classical system—the current "scientific explanation" for consciousness.

On the other hand, a human being can indeed have a conscious
experience of the classical information produced by a robot and
can also control the robot's actions using his free will informed by
his conscious comprehension of the situation. This happens, for
example, when a person is remote controlling a sophisticated military drone, and is possible because the human body can interface

with both the quantum and the classical worlds. When a robot controls classically its own behavior it has no conscious experience and no comprehension of the situation. It simply reacts mechanically to the data the way it has been commanded or the way it has *mechanically* learned. This lack of comprehension could lead to a completely inappropriate behavior in response to even a slightly different situation from the one the robot had learned.

Said differently, the conscious experience and free-will control of a purely classical system cannot occur "within" a classical system, for classical systems do not have any inner reality. Inner reality exists only within coherent quantum systems. Therefore, classical robots cannot function *autonomously* in *unconstrained* and *hostile* environments for long because they lack the *real* intelligence that comes with conscious comprehension. Comprehension is not an algorithmic property. By autonomous I mean a robot that must function totally on its own, without any human supervision. By unconstrained environment I mean an open system in which it is impossible to predict all the different situations that might arise. By hostile I mean an environment in which there are intelligent entities that intend to harm the robot.

Only living organisms, as far as I know, possess the level of dynamism and the extraordinary interdependence with the environment necessary to interface with conscious entities inhabiting the quantum world and with classical entities existing in the physical world. Life exists in total symbiosis with the environment in such an intimate way that is impossible to draw a functional boundary between the organism and the environment. The organism "extends" into the environment and the environment extends into the organism in a profoundly dynamic equilibrium in which both change at every instant; and change they must just to exist.

We are not machines!

The real problem is not whether machines think but whether men do.
—B.F. Skinner

Based on the simulation metaphor discussed in the previous section, each of us observes the world with a unique perspective and in two different ways. We experience classical information produced by the body, and quantum information coming through another channel we do not yet understand. We attribute both types of information to the body since we believe that the classical world is all that exists. Through the first channel, classical information coming from the physical world is transformed by our senses and brains into symbols that give rise within our consciousness to the ordinary experience of the physical world. Through the quantum channel, instead, we get information like intuitions, imagination, original insights, vivid dreams, thoughts, and deep emotions, whose origins are currently unknown.

The more we identify with the classical body and rational mind, and thus pay attention only to the symbols produced by the body, the more we lose contact with our deeper quantum reality. In this new framework, the vaster self "wears" a body to deeply experience itself in interactions with other selves that wear similar "costumes" made of matter. In this sense, matter works like a mirror allowing the conscious self to know itself more fully. I like to think that matter is like the *ink* with which the conscious self writes the comprehension of itself and the comprehension of the world. Still, the experience—what really matters—is not *in* the ink any more than the meaning of a book is *in* the physical book. It is our consciousness that gives meaning to physical matter.

Based on this framework, computers can only have *mechanical* intelligence while humans have *real* intelligence grounded on conscious comprehension, which goes far beyond the algorithmic properties of classical information. In fact, humans controlling computers can make computers perform actions impossible for the computer to do on its own. Here is a great opportunity for creative cooperation, but only if humans understand and value the true nature of their own consciousness. I think that the idea that computers may best human beings is a dangerous fantasy based on a misinterpretation of the true nature of consciousness and the nature of physical reality.

The scientific study of inner reality

There is no greater impediment to the advancement of knowledge than the ambiguity of words.

—Thomas Reid

The traditional scientific method is based on third-person observations and experiments. Unfortunately, these experiments cannot adequately deal with the inner world of sensations, emotions, thoughts, and spiritual feelings that are exclusively first-person experiences. By making outer measurements on a person's body, it is impossible to determine the deep subjective meaning of what is measured. Only the conscious entity knows that meaning. For example, when a scientist scans a patient's brain with fMRI (functional magnetic resonance imaging) to find *correlations* between physiological measurements and subjective experience, they must rely on the patient correctly reporting on their inner state. If the patient feels angry, for example, the meaning of their anger is the crucial information. Just knowing that they are angry is not enough. And only with a careful conscious introspection is it possible to understand the hidden meaning.

This fundamental limitation of the scientific method has led many to minimize or even deny the reality of our inner world. Some even declare us as being inferior to computers and insist those machines will one day be conscious. Denying the monumental difference that consciousness makes and considering consciousness a purely classical information phenomenon is tantamount to depriving human beings of their humanity by *prejudice* rather than real science.

Quantum physics was born to explain the strange behavior of the smallest particles, and our understanding of the nature of reality had to change from the "command and control," coercive view of classical physics to the probabilistic view of quantum physics. Although quantum physics is compatible with free will, few scientists venture into free-will land because admitting the existence of free will opens a Pandora's box! If free will exists, then the "place" from which free will comes cannot look at all like the matter, energy, space, and time we are all familiar with. Free will is like the tip of an iceberg because it brings into physics everything else that belongs to the inner world: selfhood, consciousness, true agency, identity, existence, purpose, and meaning.

Physicists generally do not consider that meaning and purpose may have any physical reality. Focused only on the outer symbolic reality, they assume that consciousness spontaneously emerges only from complex organizations of classical matter—the human brain—even though there is no plausible explanation as to how this might happen. Taking a diametrically opposite position, many spiritual people believe that only the inner reality of spirit or mind exists, and they downplay or deny the reality of matter.

The approach I have taken to unite the inner and outer realities is to extend the experimentally verified ideas of quantum physics with a new interpretation of its counterintuitive aspects. The result is postulating the existence of nousym, a holistic and dynamic "substance" that forms both the quantum and the classical world in which it appears as physical energy. The quantum world has an outer aspect made of quantum information (entangled qubits in superposition) and an inner aspect made of entities with consciousness and free will. The classical world has only an outer aspect made of classical information (bits). Straddling the two worlds is the physical world that is both quantum and classical. It is made of individual quantum states that have manifested in space-time from the quantum world (probabilistic classical information), and statistical matter that behaves deterministically.

I have taken holism and dynamism to be fundamental principles and added an evolutionary principle expressed as: *All that exists seeks to know itself.* I use the name *One* for all that exists, consequently One is dynamic, holistic, and seeks to know itself. The "substance" of One is the semantic-symbolic nousym, and the coherent conscious entities I am speaking about emerge from One and are

indivisible from One. The probabilistic aspect of quantum physics is now a consequence of this new principle since the knowing
process is inner-directed—the expression of the free will choices
of the conscious entities. Therefore, quantum physical events in
spacetime correspond to free-will decisions of conscious entities
that cannot be known a priori, and the evolution of the universe
ultimately reflects the evolution of the self-knowing of One. This
subject is further explored in Appendix 5.

As time goes on, the organization of science makes it increasingly difficult to change its fundamental paradigms given the
collective investment that has been made in them. If any fundamental change becomes necessary, the "system" will forcefully
defend the status quo, delaying the acceptance of the change.
If we do not take seriously the primacy of consciousness and
free will, we run the huge risk that the entrenched materialism,
reductionism, and the information technology based on them
will become enslaving idols. Mankind may then lose the unique
and precious time window in which a gigantic and liberating leap
forward can be made.

Conclusion

You can cut all the flowers but you cannot keep spring from coming.
—Pablo Neruda

The "know thyself" principle mentioned earlier is not original
because according to ancient wisdom, the fundamental purpose of
One is self-realization in the endless pursuit of self-knowing. Within
the new framework, One knows itself through the manifestation
of what I call *consciousness units*, elementary conscious entities that
communicate and combine to create ever-expanding hierarchies
of entities that can deepen their own self-knowing, and thus One's
knowing. The inner driver of all evolution is the *urge* of One to know
itself, where "urge" contains a combination of what we experience

as desire, curiosity, impulse, satisfaction, love, determination, and will. In Appendix 5 the interested reader will find more details.

In this co-evolution of meaning and of quantum information, One comes to know its true nature reflected in the evermore complex quantum and classical information created by the conscious entities to capture and communicate the infinitely deep inner structure of their own self-knowing. Since any symbol is finite, One will never be able to capture its potentially infinite meaning. This means that One's self-realization process will never end, for no matter how much One knows itself, it will never reach the end if its infiniteness.

It may be possible that we are in this physical world to find our way back to One by remembering our true nature while believing we are alone and mortal. But in this framework, this would be the narrative from the point of view of the ego who believes to be alone and mortal. From the point of view of the vaster self, there is no need to return for we never left. We may likely be here to contribute in a special way to our own self-knowing, which is also the self-knowing of One, by combining the subjectivity of the quantum world with the objectivity of the classical world.

Arguably, the most effective way to achieve that end is to collectively create a just and loving society that teaches each person how to act for the good of all life. I believe the laws of physics cannot take us to the new order of a just society. Only the free will choices of each of us, individually, can bring such a society into being. These choices come from the semantic level of reality that hides underneath the probabilistic nature of physics and as such do not violate the syntactical laws of symbols which are the laws of physics. The real "forces" that will direct our future will then be the conscious comprehension and cooperation of all selves, not the "syntactical" laws of physics.

I predict that the strenuous efforts of those who believe that computers can become conscious, comprehend, and surpass human intelligence will find their efforts frustrated. Artificial intelligence, the spearhead of human technological prowess and a great source of pride, could paradoxically provide human beings with the necessary learning to discover and confront the mystery of our true nature. Mankind will eventually have to come to know, on a first-person basis, the true nature of consciousness—the source of true and real intelligence—and finally recognize from a deeper place within, rather than from the limited viewpoint of the rational mind, the impossibility of creating conscious machines.

I hope this happens soon for the common good because there is a real danger that human beings, seduced by the rampant culture of digital consumerism, may replace true and deep relationships with virtual and superficial ones, curtailing their own spiritual development. Technology must help us discover our true nature, not further imprison us in a virtual world without meaning. Just like the invention of the engine amplified our human muscular power, so too computers, robots, and AI can amplify our *mechanical* intellectual power and free us from monotonous, repetitive, and dangerous jobs. This great potential, however, must be placed at the service of the spiritual, mental, emotional, and physical progress of *each* human being.

Before us, the mystery of life is beginning to open with the amazing possibilities to learn how to explore the universe of light that each one of us senses in our deepest inner self. If the human journey in the information era will be illuminated by love, discipline, passion, curiosity, and courage, we will learn how to use the only remarkable tool capable of exploring the universe of living information and access the true meaning of the universe. This incredible instrument is our birthright. Its name is consciousness.

BIBLIOGRAPHY

[1]   Faggin, F., Klein, T. and Vadasz, L. *Insulated Gate Field Effect Transistor Integrated Circuits with Silicon Gates*, "International Electron Devices Meeting," Washington, D.C., October 1968, p. 22.

[2]   Bower, R. W., *Field-effect device with insulated gate*, "US Patent No. 3,472,712," to Hughes Aircraft Co., filed October 27, 1966, issued October 14, 1969.

[3]   Faggin, F. and Klein, T., *A Faster Generation of MOS Devices with Low Threshold Is Riding the Crest of the New Wave, Silicon Gate IC's*, "Electronics," Sept. 29, 1969.

[4]   Sarace, J. C., Kerwin, R. E., Klein, D. L. and Edwards, R., "Solid State Electronics" 1968, Vol. 11, p. 653

[5]   Faggin, F. and Klein, T., *Silicon Gate Technology*, "Solid-State Electronics," 1970. Vol. 13, pp. 1125-1144.

[6]   Faggin, F., *Power supply settable bi-stable circuit*, "US Patent 3,753,011," to Intel Corp., Aug. 14, 1973.

[7]   Faggin, F. and Capocaccia, F., *A New Integrated MOS Shift Register*, "Atti XV Congresso Scientifico Internazionale per l'Elettronica," Rome, April 1968, pp.143-152.

[8]   Faggin, F. et al., *The MCS-4 – An LSI Micro Computer System*, "Proc. IEEE Region Six Conference," IEEE, 1972.

[9]   Faggin, F. and Hoff, Jr. M., *Standard Parts and Custom Design Merge in Four-Chip Processor Kit*, "Electronics," April 24, 1972, pp. 112-116.

[10] Shima, M., Faggin, F., Mazor, S., *An N-channel 8-bit single-chip microprocessor*, "IEEE ISSCC," February, 1974, pp. 56-57.

[11] Faggin, F.,Shima, M., Mazor, S., *MOS computer employing a plurality of separate chips*, "US Patent 4,010,449," to Intel Corp., filed 12/31/1974, granted 3/1/77.

[12] Hoff, M., Mazor, S. and Faggin, F., *Memory System for Multi-Chip Digital Computer,* "US Patent 3,821,715," to Intel Corp., June 28, 1974.

[13] Faggin, F., *The Birth of the Microprocessor,* "Byte", March 1992, pp. 145-150.

[14] Gallippi, A., *Federico Faggin – Il padre del microprocessore,* tecniche nuove, Milan, 2011.

[15] Shima, M., Faggin, F., Ungermann, R., *Z80 Chip Set Heralds Third Microprocessor's Generation,* "Electronics," vol. 49, n. 17, 19 August, 1976, pp. 89-93.

[16] Faggin, F., *How VLSI Impacts Computer Architecture,* "IEEE Spectrum", vol. 15, n.5, May 1978, pp. 28-31.

[17] Faggin, F., Lynch, G. S., *Brain learning and recognition emulation circuitry and method for recognizing events,* "US Patent 4,802,103," to Synaptics, Inc., filed June 3, 1986, issued January 31, 1989.

[18] Platt, J. C., Faggin, F., *Networks for the separation of sources that are superimposed and delayed,* "Advances in Neural Information Processing Systems", J. E. Moody editor, volume 4, pp. 730-737, 1992.

[19] Faggin, F., Mead C., *VLSI Implementation of Neural Networks,* in "An introduction to neural and electronic networks", Steven Zornetzer editor, pp. 297-314. Academic Press, 1995.

[20] Chalmers, D., *Facing Up to the Problem of Consciousness,* "Journal of Consciousness Studies" 2(3), pp. 200-219, 1995.

[21] Faggin, F., *The Nature of Physical Reality. Proceedings of the Galileiana Academy of Arts and Science,* Padua, Italy, 2015.

[22] Parnia, S., *Death and consciousness—an overview of the mental and cognitive experience of death,* Ann. N.Y. Acad. Sci. 1330 (2014), pp. 75-93.

[23] D'Ariano, G. M., *Physics Without Physics: The Power of Information theoretical Principles,* International Journal of Theoretical Physics n. 56, pp. 97-128, 2016.

[24] D'Ariano, G.M., Perinotti, P., *Derivation of the Dirac Equation from Principles of Information Processing,* in "Physical Review A", December 2, 2014, 90, 062106.

APPENDIX 1

The MOS Silicon-Gate Technology

MOS integrated circuits

In 1967, the MOS technology allowed us to realize the same logic functions made with bipolar technology using from five to 10 times less silicon area and from five to 10 times less power dissipation. However, the speed of MOS ICs was about fifty times slower, greatly limiting their possible applications. Almost all the experts thought that MOS ICs were too slow and too unreliable to ever challenge the dominance of bipolar technology.

The MOS technology in production used P-channel transistors with aluminum gates and a threshold voltage ranging from − 4 to − 8 volts. The supply voltage was − 24 volts. Only RCA in the United States had developed an expensive CMOS (complementary MOS) manufacturing process primarily used for mobile military applications.

To avoid any interference between the various transistors of an integrated circuit, it was essential to hold the threshold voltage of the parasitic MOS transistors[1] below the supply voltage.

---

1 Note 1 – A parasitic MOS transistor is an unintentional device obtained when a metal line over the field oxide crosses two junctions. In this case, the junctions act like the source and the drain of a parasitic MOS transistor and the metal line acts as its gate. If the voltage of the metal line is higher than the threshold voltage of the parasitic MOS in which the field oxide is the "gate oxide," an inversion layer is created in the

This requirement was met by using a sufficiently thick field oxide. However, the oxide thickness could not be arbitrarily large since the aluminum lines crossing over oxide steps would thin down at the step and could break if the oxide thickness exceeded a certain value.[2] Thus, MOS technology required a delicate balance between conflicting requirements, providing only a small margin of safety.

The other major limitation was the high parasitic capacitance between the gate electrode and the source and drain of the transistor, due to the necessary alignment tolerances of the gate mask with respect to the source-and-drain mask (Fig. A2). The most damaging parasitic capacitance was Cgd, the overlap capacitance between the gate and the drain, due to the Miller effect.

The total input capacitance of a transistor in a circuit is equal to C_G + Cgs + A·Cgd, where C_G is the active capacitance of the MOS channel, Cgs is the parasitic overlap capacitance between the gate and the source, and A is the gain of the circuit of which the transistor is part (A·Cgd represents the Miller effect).

Since the gain A is generally much greater than 1 during the switching of the circuit, the impact of Cgd on the switching speed of the transistor is considerable. Moreover, the variability of Cgd due to all possible mask misalignments is very large, causing a broad wafer-to-wafer distribution of the speed of the integrated circuits (ICs).

The ideal process for MOS circuits was recognized by most insiders as early as 1966. It consisted of using wafers with [100]

---

underlying silicon leading to a weak electrical connection between the two junctions that should be isolated. A parasitic transistor is particularly damaging in the case of dynamic circuits because the information temporarily stored as an electric charge in the gate of a transistor could rapidly leak away, causing a malfunction.

2   Note 2 – The metal thinning at the oxide step, due to the vacuum evaporation of aluminum, not only causes yield problems, but it could also create serious reliability problems in the field due to electromigration. Electromigration causes the aluminum interconnections to thin down and open (over time) if the current density exceeds a certain limit.

crystal orientation instead of [111] because the threshold voltage could be lowered to be in the range of – 2 to – 4 volts, allowing the supply voltage to be reduced from – 24 to – 15 volt. This change would also reduce the power dissipation by about a factor of two. Unfortunately, using [100] wafers, the field threshold voltage would be lower than the supply voltage for the maximum permissible oxide thickness. And this problem prevented using the low-threshold-voltage technology.

In 1966, Robert Bower realized that if the gate electrode had been defined first, the boundaries of the channel between the source and the drain would be determined by a single mask, thus avoiding the excessive and variable parasitic capacitances due to the misalignment between the first two masks. Bower's method consisted of using aluminum as a mask to define the source and drain regions. However, since aluminum does not withstand the high temperature required for thermal doping, Bower proposed using ion implantation, a novel invention that allowed low-temperature doping and was under development at Hughes Aircraft where Bower worked.

Bower's idea, however, worked only in principle but not in practice, because during the ion bombardment, the silicon lattice would be altered. To restore it, it was necessary to subject the wafer to a thermal annealing process at temperatures higher than those bearable by the aluminum. A more refractory material than aluminum was needed.

The Bower process was described in U.S. Pat. 3,472,712 filed October 27, 1966 and published October 14, 1969 [2]. It was never used to produce integrated circuits as described in the patent and the details of the process were unknown before the date of publication.

In 1967, John Sarace and collaborators at Bell Labs fabricated the first *discrete* transistors with a self-aligned gate made of amorphous silicon [4]. Their experiment consisted of growing a thin oxide layer on a wafer, followed by vacuum deposition of *amorphous* silicon. The silicon was then masked in the form of a ring and therefore the drain was inside the ring and the source was in common with all the other transistors. This process allowed them to prove in the laboratory that MOS transistors with self – aligned silicon gates could be made. However, the transistors were not isolated and therefore integrated circuits could not be made.

Toward the end of 1967, Tom Klein measured the difference in working function between P+ doped amorphous silicon and monocrystalline N-doped silicon. He found that by using P+ doped silicon, the threshold voltage of a P-channel MOS transistor could be reduced by 1.1 volts compared with an identical aluminum-gate device. This was enough to make MOS transistors with low-threshold voltage using the same [111] silicon orientation employed for the high-threshold voltage process.

The overall process architecture that I *independently* invented at Fairchild was like the one described in Bower's patent, except for the use of *polycrystalline* silicon instead of aluminum and the use of thermal doping instead of ion implantation.

The invention of the ion implantation (not due to Bower) marked a major step in the history of process technology because it allowed doping in a controllable manner, especially for small doses, which was infeasible with the previous thermal methods.

Ion implantation allowed reducing the threshold voltage of MOS transistors in 1969-70, thus solving the first problem, but could not be used to create self-aligned MOS devices with the aluminum gate as Bower had taught in his patent.

The SGT allowed to simultaneously solve the two major problems of MOS technology as early as 1968 while increasing the speed, the reliability, and the circuit density of MOS ICs far beyond what ion implantation alone could achieve.

The architecture of the silicon-gate process

Figure A1 shows the essential steps of the silicon-gate process. On the right of the figure are the masks used to create the transistor.

The left shows four cross sections of a P-channel MOS transistor cut along the middle of the tub mask at various stages of the manufacturing process. The process begins with the thermal growth of the field oxide followed by the steps described below:

1. Apply the tub mask and remove the thick oxide in the areas where the source, drain, and gate of each transistor will be formed (Fig. A1-1 at left). The tub mask is the rectangle on the top right in the figure.
2. Thermally grow the thin-gate oxide (Fig. A1-2 at left).
3. Deposit a layer of silicon. Apply the silicon mask to create the silicon gates and the silicon interconnections. The silicon mask is the strip shown at right with dotted lines superimposed on the tub mask.
4. Remove the thin oxide within the tubs in the areas unprotected by the silicon, thus defining the source and the drain of each transistor. The exposed parts of the wafer are then doped with boron, including the silicon gate that acts as a mask to leave the MOS channel unaffected.
5. Thermally grow a thin layer of the best quality oxide to protect the exposed silicon areas. During this high-temperature process (1200°C) most of the source and drain diffusions occur (Fig. A1-3 at left).
6. Deposit a good-quality silicon dioxide layer by vapor deposition (called *vapox* at Fairchild).
7. Apply the contact mask and remove the silicon dioxide in the contact areas. The contact mask consists of the two small rectangles inside the tub mask shown in the third figure from the top at right.
8. Deposit a thin layer of aluminum by vacuum deposition. Apply the aluminum mask to remove the aluminum and define the metal interconnections between the transistors. The metal mask consists of the two dashed strips shown on the third figure at right. At this point, the transistor is essentially completed, as shown in Figure A1-4 at left.

9. Create an alloy between the aluminum and the silicon by subjecting the wafer to a temperature of 550°C. This process creates ohmic contacts.

10. Deposit a layer of oxide at low temperature to passivate the circuits and protect them from possible scratches during the cutting and packaging of the chips.

11. Next, the protective oxide in the aluminum areas (called "pads") located at the periphery of the circuit is removed allowing the ultrasonic welding of thin aluminum wires to connect the chip to the pins of the package.

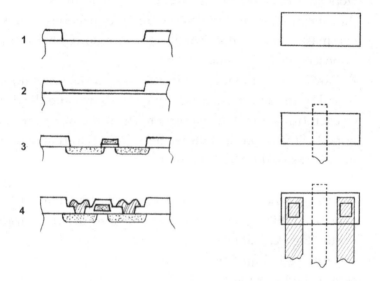

Fig. A1 – The architecture of the MOS process with the silicon gate. Illustration by F. Faggin.

Here we can see clearly why the process is called self-aligned: a misalignment between the tub and the silicon mask would slightly change the geometries of the source and the drain, leaving unchanged all the parasitic capacitances between source, drain, and the gate.

With the metal gate, the impossibility to make a perfect alignment between the first and the second mask requires a larger overlapping area between the gate mask and the source and drain mask, substantially increasing the parasitic capacitances and reducing the speed of the transistors, especially in the worst-case misalignment (Fig A2).

One might ask: How come the process I just described cannot be performed with aluminum instead of silicon? The reason is simple. After depositing the aluminum, the wafer temperature cannot rise above 570°C without damaging the circuits. The process steps that follow, however, require temperatures up to 900°C which only silicon and other possible refractory materials could withstand without problems [5].

The architecture of the MOS aluminum-gate process

To better understand the differences between metal-gate and silicon-gate technologies, figure A-2 illustrates the processing steps with aluminum gate:

1. As always, we start with a thick field-oxide layer to which the source and drain mask is applied and the oxide is etched (Fig. A2-1 at left). At the top right of figure A2, the source and drain mask is shown.
2. Boron is deposited in the exposed silicon areas (Fig. A2-2 at left).
3. An oxide layer is thermally grown. The gate mask is applied and the oxide is removed in the gate area. The gate mask is shown in the second figure at the top right of figure A2 with dotted lines.
4. The gate oxide is thermally grown at high temperature and simultaneously the junctions diffuse into the silicon. At the end of this processing step, the structure of the transistor is shown in Figure A2-3 at the left.
5. The contact mask is applied to remove the oxide in the areas where the aluminum will make ohmic contact with the junctions. The contact mask is shown in the third figure from the top at right (two small rectangles).

6. An aluminum film is vacuum-deposited and the aluminum mask is applied to define the metal lines. The metal mask is shown in the third figure from the top at right (three dashed strips).

7. The remainder of the process is identical to the one described above for the SGT and the final structure of the transistor is shown in Figure A2-4.

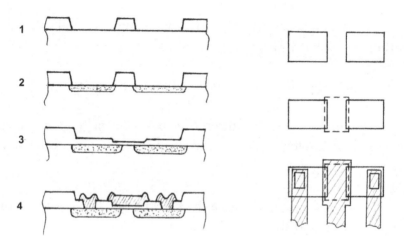

Fig. A2 – The architecture of the MOS process with an aluminum gate. Illustration by F. Faggin

In comparing figure A1-4 with figure A2-4, notice that the overlapping areas between the gate and the source and drain are much larger for the aluminum gate than for the silicon gate. In the case of perfect alignment, the parasitic capacitance of the aluminum-gate transistor is 2.5 times larger than the one with the SGT. In the worst-case misalignment, it is about four times worse. Notice also that the aluminum covers most of the area, increasing the area occupied by the transistor.

The SGT with the buried contact

The variant of the SGT process with the buried contacts requires the removal of the thin oxide in the tub areas where direct contact between the polycrystalline silicon and the single crystal silicon are desired. This requires an additional masking step. The solid line square shown in the upper part of figure A3 represents the buried contact mask.

After the etching of the gate oxide in the contact area, the process continues exactly as described in figure A1.

During the doping process, the boron atoms diffuse through the thin layer of polycrystalline silicon, continue to diffuse into the monocrystalline silicon and form a junction in the contact area. In this fashion, an isolated contact is created which is subsequently passivated with oxide, allowing aluminum lines to cross over it.

The bottom part of the figure shows a cross section of the buried contact area along the cut line AA shown on the top of the figure. Notice the layer of oxide that exists between the aluminum and the polysilicon that provides insulation.

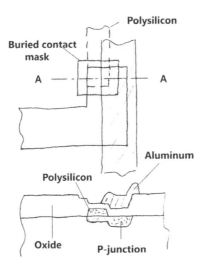

Fig. A3 – This figure shows the layout of the buried contact on the top. The bottom figure shows a cross section of the silicon along the line AA. The solid-line square surrounding the overlapping area between the tub mask (solid line) and the polysilicon mask (dashed line) is the buried-contact mask used to eliminate the thin oxide, thus allowing the polysilicon to be in direct contact with the single-crystal silicon. The boron doping that follows allows the junction to form into the single-crystal silicon as seen in the lower section. Illustration by F. Faggin.

The layout with the SGT

In figure A4 I have recreated one of the examples given to the IC designers of the MOS division to demonstrate the superiority of the SGT in making the layout of random logic circuits, especially if they had used buried contacts. The great advantage of the SGT is obvious.

In the aluminum-gate layout at left, the gates of the transistors (where the oxide is thin), are the areas enclosed by gray dotted-line rectangles. Aluminum is represented by dashed strips. P-doped diffusions, which are used for the sources, drains, and signals crossing under the aluminum, use solid lines. The contact areas between the diffusions and the aluminum are gray rectangles where metal strips and junctions overlap.

In the silicon-gate layout at right, I used the same conventions except for the polysilicon mask that uses gray dotted lines. In this case, the gates of the transistors are the areas of overlap between the tub mask (solid line) and the polysilicon mask.

It is important to note that the parasitic capacitances of the silicon lines used for interconnections were many times lower than those of the diffusions. This further contributed to the greater speed and the layout flexibility of the SGT circuits. With the metal-gate technology, diffusions were the only alternative interconnection layer that could cross the aluminum lines.

In figure A4 on the right, under the aluminum line called S1, there is a buried contact connecting the diffusion corresponding to the output O with a silicon line that becomes the gate of another transistor (not shown in the figure). Naturally, the output O could also cross under the aluminum as a diffusion, exactly like in the case of the metal gate.

I used a buried contact to show the speed advantage offered by the SGT because the silicon output makes the circuit faster than the diffusion output even though the circuit size is unaffected in this case. In most other cases, the buried contact is essential to obtaining a denser layout.

The fundamental advantage of the buried contact is to enable going from diffusion to polysilicon directly, without using aluminum. Aluminum signals can then cross the buried contacts, thus increasing the circuit density and speed.

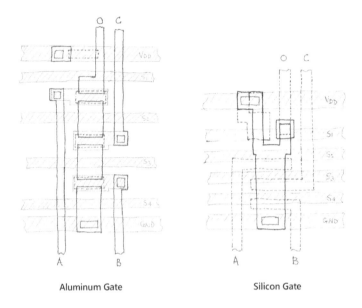

Aluminum Gate   Silicon Gate

Fig. A4 – On the left is the layout of a NAND logic gate with three inputs: A, B, and C and with output, O, made with aluminum gate. There are also four signals: S_1, S_2, S_3, and S_4 that must traverse the circuit, a typical situation for a random-logic integrated circuit. On the right is the layout of the same circuit made with the SGT. The area used in the metal-gate version is almost twice the one used with SGT. The speed of the SGT circuit is five times higher than that with the aluminum gate. Since the production cost is proportional to the area, the advantage of SGT is not only in performance but also in cost. Illustration by F. Faggin.

The bootstrap load

The bootstrap load allowed obtaining an output voltage equal to the supply voltage in a dynamic logic gate, enhancing an efficient and widely used design technique called two – phase dynamic logic. This technique was also called quasi-static logic because one could mix static with dynamic logic circuits.

Let's consider the case of an inverter with a normal load and with a supply voltage of – 15 volts as shown on the left of figure A5. When the transistor T1 is turned off, the output Out is typically about – 10 volts (from – 8 to – 11.5 volts, with process variations). When T1 is on, Out is typically at – 0.5 volts.

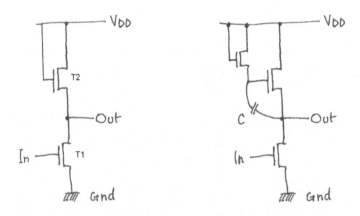

Fig. A5 – Circuit diagram of an inverter with the normal load (figure on the left) and with boot – strap load (figure on the right). Illustration by F. Faggin.

Now consider an inverter with a bootstrap load shown on the right of figure A5. When the input voltage (In) goes from – 10 volts to 0.5 volts, the output voltage (Out) goes from – 0.5 volts to – 10 volts. The capacitor C causes the voltage at node B, which is normally at about – 10 volts, to become more negative, completely turning off transistor T3.

A negative change in the output voltage of one volt leads to about a change of – 0.8 volts at node B (the value depends on the ratio between the parasitic capacitance of node B and the capacitance C of the bootstrap). Therefore, the voltage at node B continues to decrease in line with the output voltage, keeping the transistor T2 on, even when the output voltage reaches – 10 volts at which time the voltage at node B will be – 10.8 volts. When the output voltage reaches the supply voltage, node B will be at about – 22 volts.

To make a bootstrap load physically, an isolated capacitor was needed. This was trivial to do with metal-gate technology, but impossible with silicon gate since the polysilicon prevents a junction to form under the thin oxide.

No one thought it was possible to make a bootstrap load with silicon gate, myself included. But I did not surrender to the evidence of reasoning that turned out to be only partly correct. I kept thinking about how I could circumvent the problem.

One day I noticed that the metal electrode of the capacitor in the metal-gate bootstrap load was always polarized to keep an inversion layer in the silicon below *if I assumed that the diffusion under the thin oxide had been removed* (counterfactual thinking). In other words, the operating conditions of the bootstrap load were such that there would always be a "virtual diffusion" under the polysilicon. Therefore, I could have an equally effective capacitor even without a real diffusion! All that was needed was to create a large polysilicon area inside a large tub without obstructing the passage from the drain of transistor T1 to the source of transistor T2, as shown in figure A6.

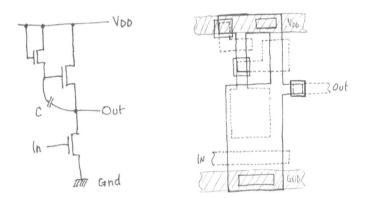

Fig. A6 – The circuit diagram of the bootstrap load is shown on the left. On the right is the layout of the same circuit using the SGT. The capacitor is the large polysilicon rectangle inside the tub which also acts as a drain of the transistor T1. Note the three buried contacts that allow this circuit to be completely "crossable" by other metal lines, a huge advantage since with the metal-gate technology the same circuit would be completely uncrossable by other aluminum lines. Illustration by F. Faggin.

The pass transistor

To make a quasi-static circuit we used a pass transistor, the gate of which was typically driven by a logic gate as shown by the node A in figure A7. The drain of the pass transistor was connected to the output B of a logic gate and the source was connected to the gate of another transistor (node C).

The great advantage of a MOS transistor was the ability to temporarily store a charge (information) in the capacitance of the gate of a transistor, like the node C, after the pass transistor had been deactivated.

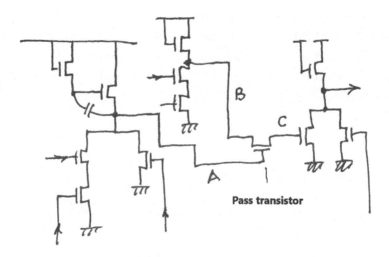

Fig. A7 – Example of a random-logic circuit where the gate of a pass transistor must be driven by a logic port with a bootstrap load to work. Illustration by F. Faggin.

The worst-case output signal produced by a logic gate with a normal load was – 8 volts. If this signal had been applied to the gate of a pass transistor, the output voltage of the latter would have been about – 4 volts, slightly higher than the worst-case threshold voltage of a transistor (-3.5 volts). This condition would render unusable the precious function of a pass transistor.

To take advantage of the information storage allowed by the pass transistors it was necessary to use a bootstrap load in the logic gate that controlled the transistor as shown in figure A7.

This "trick" allowed for drastically reducing the number of transistors needed to make a dynamic MOS logic circuit, compared to a static circuit. It was also the main reason why MOS technology required far fewer transistors than bipolar to make the same logical function. For example, with a pass transistor, it was possible to realize a dynamic flip-flop with only three transistors, while a static MOS flip-flop would require a minimum of six and a bipolar flip-flop more than 15. Without the bootstrap load, the only alternative was to use static logic circuits that required many more transistors and far greater power dissipation for the same speed.

Push-pull buffers

Another essential circuit that required bootstrap loads was the push-pull buffer. Buffers were needed whenever a logic gate had to drive a large capacitive load without dissipating excessive power. For example, these buffers were indispensable in complex logic circuits to drive internal buses.

A push-pull buffer is shown in figure A8. When IN has a logic value "0," the transistors T1 and T2 are off, node A is at logic value "1" and therefore T3 is on.

When IN has a logic value "1" the transistors T1 and T2 are on and node A is at logic value "0." In this case, T3 is off.

Therefore, when T2 is on, T3 is off and vice versa. This allows both T2 and T3 to be large transistors capable of driving large capacitive loads, impossible to do if T2 and T3 were both on as it occurs in a normal inverter.

The bootstrap load is necessary to drive T3, otherwise, the output voltage (OUT) would be − 4 volts, in the worst-case, instead of − 8 volts, the minimum voltage required for the logical value "1."

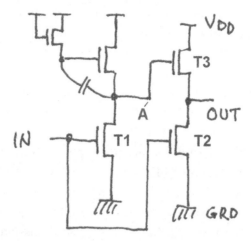

Fig. A8 – Push-pull buffer. The bootstrap load is necessary for the same reason discussed in the case of the pass transistor. Without the bootstrap load, the output voltage (OUT) would be – 4 volts (in the worst-case) instead of – 8 volts, the minimum voltage required for the logical value "1." Illustration by F. Faggin.

The depletion load

Consider an N-channel transistor in which the starting material is a P-type wafer and the source and drain junctions are N-doped. This device has a positive threshold voltage and the supply voltage V_{DD} is also positive. In the following description, we assume that V_{DD} is 5 volts. For conduction to occur, a voltage more positive than the threshold voltage must be applied to the gate of the transistor. When the gate is at zero volts, the transistor is off (does not conduct). A transistor that is off when its gate voltage is at the same potential as its source is called *enhancement mode.*

Surprisingly, it is also possible to fabricate N-channel transistors which are normally on when its gate is at the same potential as its source. This type of transistor is called *depletion mode.*

To fabricate a depletion-mode transistor it is necessary to create a weak N-channel at the interface between the silicon and the gate oxide using arsenic ion implantation (type N). The result is a transistor with a *negative* threshold voltage instead of a positive one, making it always conducting for the normal positive voltages available in an N-channel integrated circuit.

To turn the transistor off, a negative voltage larger than its threshold voltage would be required — a voltage unavailable in a chip with only a +5-volt supply voltage. This property would make a depletion-mode transistor useless for normal applications. However, if it were used as a load device to replace a normal enhancement-mode transistor, this property would be priceless. Let's see why.

Figure A9 shows how the load current (I) varies with the variation of the output voltage (V) for a normal enhancement load and a depletion load when the two loads are sized to have the same maximum current (I_M) and therefore the same power dissipation.

With normal load, the output voltage is $V_{DD} - V_T$, which in the worst-case is about 2.5 volts, a value about 1 volt higher than the maximum threshold voltage of an enhancement transistor. With the depletion load, the output voltage is 5 volts, equal to the supply voltage. The speed of the load when driving the gate of another transistor is proportional to the area marked with a double line in the case of the normal load and the area marked with a single line in the case of the depletion load. The clear superiority of the depletion load can be immediately appreciated by the figure.

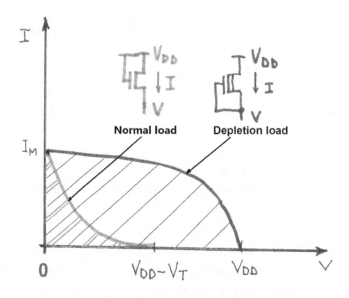

Fig. A9 – The characteristics of normal load and depletion load. Illustration by F. Faggin.

A depletion load behaves like a bootstrap load to obtain an output voltage equal to the supply voltage, with the additional advantage of being static rather than a dynamic circuit.

N-channel technology with depletion load made it possible in 1973-1974 to design fast integrated circuits with a supply voltage of only 5 volts, the standard supply voltage used by all bipolar logic circuits. This technology was universally used for 10 to 15 years before being superseded by CMOS technology, the dominant technology today.

Appendix 2

The Mask-Making Process

Today an engineer sits in front of the display of his workstation and assembles a hierarchy of logic circuits, assisted by a powerful design software that goes by the name of EDA (electronic design automation). When the engineer is finished with the logic design described by using a high-level language, the software takes over, and, employing a rich library of predesigned and pre-characterized circuit layouts, *compiles* the rest of the chip design and then proceeds to design the masks automatically.

In 1970, each step of the way was essentially done manually. The composite layout was the key document that translated the logical-circuit description of the electronic system into the silicon topology obtained by overlaying several layers of different materials, the pattern of which was determined by the masks.

Unlike today, the composite was hand-drawn on a reclining drawing table with a ruler and colored pencils at 400 to 500 times the actual scale, using a mylar sheet instead of paper to maintain greater dimensional control, especially with changes of humidity and temperature. The name *composite* indicated that all the mask layers were drawn in the same document, allowing for the visualization of their alignment.

To create the masks, it was necessary to generate a separate document—called *rubylith* or ruby—for each mask. The ruby was a sheet of transparent mylar coated with a thin red semitransparent mylar film that could be cut on a cutting table and peeled away.

Under the ruby was placed the composite that served as a guide for the process of cutting and peeling, showing the areas to be removed.

The ruby cutting was a long and error-prone process that required careful checking before sending the ruby to the mask-making service that produced the working plates. Since each ruby represented only one mask of the chip, it was necessary to super-impose two or more rubies in various sequences over a light table to check the alignment and integrity of the patterns. With this method, we could create as many shades of red as there were super-imposed layers, facilitating the recognition of possible mistakes.

When the rubies were ready, many people were recruited from the lab to help uncover all the mistakes and imperfections.

The ruby was then hung on a wall and photographed by a giant camera to be reduced to a 10x image called a "reticle." The reticle was then mounted on a step-and-repeat machine to produce the master plate. The master was a 2.5 x 2.5-inch photographic plate containing as many rows of chip patterns at actual scale as would fit in 2.5 inches. The repeated pattern was obtained by photo-reduction of the reticle to 1x (actual scale) and successive exposures of the chip pattern on the master plate to complete a row of patterns. Then a new row would be done the same way until the entire surface of the plate would be filled with as many copies of the same pattern as would fit.

The master plate was then used to create sub-masters by contact photography and each sub-master originated several working plates that represented the actual tooling to be used for wafer production. The working plates were then mounted in the mask-aligner, a machine that was in the cleanroom where the wafers were processed. The working plates could only be used a small number of times because they were invariably damaged by microscopic scratches due to the contact between the wafer and the mask.

The masking process consisted of covering the wafer with a thin layer of photoresist that behaved like a photographic emulsion sensitive to ultraviolet (UV) light. The transparent areas of the mask let the light through causing the exposed photoresist to harden. Underneath the opaque areas of the mask, the photoresist would remain unaffected. The photoresist would then be "developed" like a photographic film by chemically removing it from the areas that were not exposed to UV light, whereas the hardened photoresist protected the wafer from the chemical attack, of the now exposed areas, that would follow.

After the chemical attack, the hardened photoresist was stripped completely off and then the wafer was subjected to a variety of thermal and/or chemical processes depending on the process specified in the run sheet.

The entire cycle from the photoresist to masking and thermo-chemical processing was then repeated as many times as there were masks.

APPENDIX 3

A Brief History of Computers

The Abacus, the Pascaline, and the Arithmomètre

The roots of modern computers are much deeper than those of microelectronics and go back 4,600 years to the *abacus*, the first known arithmetic calculation tool. The next innovation was the *Pascaline*, invented by Blaise Pascal in 1642. It was a mechanical calculator that could only perform additions and subtractions and therefore its utility was rather limited.

In 1673, Gottfried Wilhelm von Leibniz devised a conceptual method to mechanically make multiplications and divisions, but the technology of his time was not precise enough to manufacture such a device. It took another 178 years before Leibniz's method could be realized, giving birth to the first four-function mechanical calculator. This calculator was invented by the Frenchman Thomas de Colmar and was first commercialized in 1851 with the name Arithmomètre, exactly 100 years before Univac I, the first commercial electronic computer, was sold.

The Arithmomètre was a robust and practical solution to be used routinely. It launched an industry that lasted until the 1970s when electronic calculators based on microchips quickly replaced electromechanical calculators.

The Jacquard loom and the electromechanical tabulator

The first known *programmable* machine was the Jacquard loom, invented in 1801 by Frenchman Joseph Marie Jacquard to automatically weave fabrics with complex designs. The loom was controlled by punched cards that memorized the program by directing the step-by-step operation of the loom.

This was not only a successful invention, it was also *the first example of an automatic system controlled by a program*, i.e., by a procedure that could be changed without changing the machine itself. The programmable loom was indeed the real precursor of modern computers, even though at first blush it appears to have little in common with computers.

The idea of using punched cards was later used by Herman Hollerith to produce an electromechanical tabulator able to quickly format data. This device was used for the 1890 census data in the United States, demonstrating major improvements over manual tabulation. The company founded by Hollerith was called the Tabulating Machine Company and later became IBM.

The relay

Another important thread intertwined in the history of modern computers is associated with automatic telephone exchanges based on relay switches. The relay was invented in 1835 by Joseph Henry and was used as an electrically operated switch. In the period between 1935 and 1937, Victor Shestakov in Russia and Claude Shannon at Bell Labs in the United States, independently discovered that Boolean logic, a binary logic invented in 1840 by George Boole, was the perfect mathematical formalism to describe switching systems and relay-based machines.

The Turing machine

In an unrelated development, Alan Turing in England invented the Turing machine in 1936. It was part of a mental experiment that allowed to falsify Hilbert's *decision problem*, a problem famously posed by the mathematician David Hilbert in 1928. The universal Turing machine provided an abstract model describing a class of universal machines capable of executing any general algorithm, thus giving rise to *information science*, another fundamental branch of the information revolution.

The first electromechanical programmable computer: Zuse's Z3

All these strands were combined in 1941 with the design and construction of the first fully functioning Turing-complete electromechanical computer: the Z3, designed and built by Konrad Zuse in Germany. This machine used a binary floating-point architecture based on 22-bit words and a CPU made with about 2,300 relays—as many relays as there were transistors in the 4004!

The memory for the data and the program was ingeniously implemented using a 35 mm punched film, the same film then used in film cameras, naturally without the emulsion. The clock frequency was about five Hz. To put that in perspective, today microchips can have clock frequencies exceeding five GHz, one billion times faster.

The Z3 led us to the threshold of the electronic computer era, in 1943, with a secret project funded by the US Army to develop a computer that could quickly calculate ballistic trajectories. The key idea was to replace the relay with a vacuum tube that, acting as a switch, could turn electric current on and off from 10,000 to 100,000 times faster than a relay. This was not obvious in 1943 because vacuum tubes were generally used as signal amplifiers and not as switches.

ENIAC, the first electronic computer

The result was ENIAC, the first fully functioning electronic computer, designed and built by John Mauchly and J. Presper Eckert and completed in 1946. ENIAC had a 200-microsecond instruction cycle with the program provided by mechanical plugs and switches, a rudimentary and laborious method. It employed 17,468 vacuum tubes, occupied an area of 167 m², dissipated 150 kW of power, and weighed 30 tons. The average time between failures was a few hours, due to the poor reliability of the vacuum tubes. However, ENIAC was much faster than the Z3, although conceptually inferior, because it could not yet memorize a program.

The first electronic computer to have all the essential characteristics of modern computers was the EDSAC, the first computer with a stored program. It was developed at the University of Cambridge by Maurice Wilkes, with the collaboration of the famous mathematician John von Neumann, to whom credit is given for using the same memory to store both data and programs. The EDSAC was completed in 1949 and it had a serial memory with 1,024 words of 17 bits each, made by using a mercury delay line. Random-access memory (RAM) based on magnetic cores had not yet been invented.

UNIVAC 1, the first commercial electronic computer

All the first computers were research machines of which only one exemplar was ever built. It took a few more years before the introduction of the first commercial electronic computer, the UNIVAC I. The UNIVAC I was a stored-program computer with a 12-bit serial main memory of 1,024 words (1.5 KB). It used for the first time a magnetic tape as a secondary memory to increase the overall storage.

The UNIVAC I used 5,200 vacuum tubes that dissipated 125 kW. It could perform 500 multiplications per second. At a cost of more than one million dollars per unit, 46 units were sold, demonstrating for the first time the existence of a market for computers. Twenty years later, a computer made with the Intel 4004 microprocessor had similar performance as the UNIVAC I in a single 25 x 25 cm^2 printed circuit board, dissipating 10 W and costing a few hundred dollars. Ten years later, that single-board computer could be integrated into a single silicon chip with less than 1 W of power dissipation, cost less than $10, and run more than ten times faster than the Univac I.

All early computers used vacuum tubes until 1957, when the Philco Transac S-2000, the first commercial transistorized computer was introduced. Two years later, the transistorized IBM 7090 and the Olivetti Elea 9003 were also introduced. From that point on, all new computer models used transistors. With transistors, the physical dimensions of computers, their power dissipation, speed, and especially their reliability, were drastically improved.

The minicomputer

In the 1960s, thanks to the progress of microelectronics—the move from germanium to faster silicon transistors and the commercialization of the integrated circuits—computers evolved rapidly with powerful supercomputers at the high-end and minicomputers at the low-end. For example, in 1963 the SAGE system began operation. Designed by IBM in collaboration with the US Air Force to coordinate the tasks of 24 radar stations in North America, SAGE became the largest computer ever built (floor area: 2000 m^2, weight: 275 tons, energy consumption: 3 MW). It was also the world's first real-time computer network.

In 1964 IBM introduced System/360, a large family of compatible and scalable computers, capable of covering a wide range of applications. It was equipped with the first sophisticated operating system and enjoyed great market success. In the same year, Control Data Corporation introduced the CDC 6600, the world's first supercomputer. The CDC 6600 was designed by Seymour Cray who later founded Cray Computers, the leading supercomputer company for many years. The CDC 6600 cost more than $8 million and was 10 times faster than its nearest rival.

In 1965, the use of integrated circuits allowed for reducing the dimensions of computers to those of a small piece of furniture, giving life to the minicomputer. The minicomputer was a smaller version of a mainframe computer, intended for applications where mainframes could not be used on account of their bulk and cost.

Introduced by Digital Equipment Corporation (DEC) with the PDP-8 model, minicomputers opened new application areas for computers, especially in control and telecommunications systems, further expanding the reach and impact of computers.

FEDERICO FAGGIN

The versatility of computers

The computer is a *universal symbol manipulator* and its versatility is due to its programmability. Therefore, the hardware is necessary but not sufficient to solve any specific problem. The other essential ingredient is the software, the program that makes the hardware-software combination capable of performing the desired function. With the availability of increasingly powerful computers, i.e., computers with more memory and more execution speed, new application areas became possible. And as computers became smaller, faster, less power-hungry, and less expensive, the number of applications increased exponentially. In parallel with the hardware development, the creation of the software led to the rise of an independent software industry.

Among the early computer applications, some appeared incongruous with what was expected from a computer, with reactions like: "But what does voice recognition have to do with computers? Computers should only calculate." Computers can indeed solve many problems that at first sight may appear outside their domain. The art of programming is based on the ability to conceptualize how to break down a problem or a process into a series of algorithms, i.e., a sequence of automatic procedures that a computer can perform efficiently.

The importance of programming has increased over time and, where the cost of the hardware has steadily decreased, the cost of software has steadily increased to the point of becoming the dominant cost of information processing today. The software is like the mind and the hardware is like the body. Both are needed, and must work in perfect collaboration to solve any problem.

In recent years it has finally become possible to create computers that *learn* almost by themselves—instead of being programmed by explicit algorithms—with the help of artificial neural networks, structures that imitate the essential information processing performed by the biological neural networks we have in our nervous system. Neural networks find the implicit rules (statistical correlations) contained in the training data through a bottom-up learning process, achieving far better results for pattern recognition than had been possible with traditional top-down programming.

The information revolution that is transforming society has brought to the fore the profound and completely unsuspected relationship between the nature of information and the nature of reality. This is a particularly fascinating topic that was unknown to physicists and philosophers until the 1950s, a subject that will profoundly change our understanding of the nature of reality, the nature of life, and the nature of consciousness.

The mother of the computer

While there are many fathers of the computer, there is only one sure mother: Ada Byron Lovelace (1815-1852). Long before the computer was invented, she was the first to envision the modern computer. In her interesting notes to the text of Luigi Federico Menabrea *"Notions sur la machine analytique de Charles Babbage,"* which she translated into English, Lovelace explains her idea of a "mechanism capable of combining general symbols, in unlimited sequences for variety and extension." In the notes, she presented an *algorithm* for the Babbage analytic machine to generate Bernoulli numbers. This is the first example of software programming in history.

Lovelace also anticipated the ability of machines to learn and develop increasingly complex solutions, but she decidedly declined the possibility of creating conscious machines. It was quite clear to her that "the analytical machine has no pretension to *conceive* anything."

Appendix 4

The Fundamental Differences Between Human and Artificial Intelligence

Paper presented by Federico Faggin at the V Congress of the Future Santiago, Chile, January 21, 2016

There is much speculation today about a possible future where mankind will be surpassed, perhaps even destroyed by machines. We hear of self-driving cars, Big Data, the resurgence of artificial intelligence, and even of transhumanism, the idea that it may be possible to download our experience and consciousness in a computer and live forever. We also hear major warnings by public figures, such as Stephen Hawking, Bill Gates, and Elon Musk, about the dangers of robotics and AI. So, what is true and what is fiction in this picture?

In all these projections, it is assumed that it will be possible to make truly intelligent and autonomous machines in the not too distant future; machines that are at least as good, if not better than we are. But is this assumption correct? I will argue that *real* intelligence requires consciousness and consciousness is something our machines do not have and will never have.

Today most scientists believe that we are just machines; sophisticated information processing systems based on wetware. That's why they believe it will be possible to make machines that will surpass human beings. They believe that consciousness is an *epiphenomenon* of the operation of the brain produced by something like the software that runs in our computers. Therefore, with more sophisticated software our robots will eventually be conscious. But is this future really possible?

Well, let's start by defining what I mean by consciousness: I know within myself that I exist. But how do I know? I am sure I exist because I *feel* so. So, it is the *feeling* that carries the knowing; and the capacity to feel is the essential property here. When I smell a rose, I *feel* the smell. But careful! The feeling is not the set of electrical signals produced by the olfactory receptors inside my nose. Those signals carry objective information, but that information is translated within my consciousness into a *subjective* feeling: what the smell of that rose *feels like* to me.

We can build a robot capable of detecting the specific molecules that carry the smell of a rose and correctly identify a rose by its smell, for example. However, the robot would have no feeling whatsoever. It would not be *aware* of the smell as a *sensation*. To be aware one must feel. But the robot stops at the electrical signals and from those signals, it can generate other signals to cause some response, some action. We do much more than that because we do *feel* the smell of the rose and through that feeling, we *connect* with that rose in a special way and we can also make a free-will decision that is *informed* by that feeling.

Consciousness could be defined simply as the capacity to feel. But feeling implies the existence of a subject that feels: a *self.* Therefore, consciousness is inextricably linked to a self and is the inherent capacity of a self to perceive and know through feelings, through a sentient experience; it is a defining property of a self.

Now, feelings are a different category of phenomena than electrical signals, incommensurable with them. Philosophers have coined the word *quale* to indicate what something feels like and explaining qualia is called the *hard problem of consciousness* because nobody has been able to solve it. In the rest of my talk, I will use the word qualia to refer to four different classes of feelings: physical sensations, emotions, thoughts, and spiritual feelings.

Electrical signals, be they in a computer or in a brain, do not produce qualia. Indeed, there is nothing in the laws of physics that tells us how to translate electrical signals into qualia. How is it possible then to have qualia-perceptions?

Having studied the problem for nearly thirty years, I have concluded that consciousness may be an *irreducible* aspect of nature, an inherent property of the energy out of which space, time, and matter emerged in the Big Bang.

From my perspective, far from being an epiphenomenon, consciousness is *real*. In other words, the stuff out of which everything is made is *cognitive* stuff and the highest material expression of consciousness is what we call *life*. In this view, consciousness is not an emergent property of a complex system, but it's the other way around: a complex system is an emergent property of the conscious energy out of which everything physical is made.

Thus, consciousness cannot magically emerge from algorithms, but its seeds are already present in the stuff of creation. In this view, consciousness and complex physical systems co-evolve.

There is no time to explore this subject in-depth because I want to make a convincing case that to make truly intelligent, autonomous machines, consciousness is indispensable and that consciousness is not a property that will emerge from computers. Some people may then insist that computers may be able to perform better than humans without consciousness. And that's what I would like to discuss next. I want to show that *comprehension* is a fundamental property of consciousness, even more important than qualia-perception and that comprehension is a defining property of *intelligence*. Therefore, if there is no consciousness there is no comprehension, without comprehension there is no intelligence and without intelligence, a system cannot be autonomous for long.

Let's consider how human beings make decisions. Our sensory system converts various forms of energy in our environment into electrical signals which are then sent to the brain for processing. The result of the processing is another set of electrical signals representing multi-sensory information: visual, auditory, tactile, and so on. At the end of this process, we have a certain amount of *objective* information about the world. Computers can arrive up to this point. This information is then converted somehow within our consciousness into *semantic* information: An *integrated* multisensory qualia-display of the state of the world that includes both the *inner* world and the *outer* world. It may be even more accurate to say that the outer world has been brought *inside of us* into a representation that integrates both worlds.

This is what I call qualia-perception. But this is only the raw *semantic* data out of which comprehension is achieved through an additional process even more mysterious than the one that produced qualia-perception. Comprehension is what allows us to *understand* the current situation within the context of our overall experience and the set of our desires, aspirations, and intentions.

Understanding then is the next necessary step before an intelligent choice can be made. It is understanding that allows us to decide if an action is needed and if so, what action is the optimal one. And the degree to which consciousness is involved in deciding what action to take has a huge range, going from no involvement whatsoever, all the way to a protracted conscious reflection and pondering that may take days or weeks.

When a situation is judged to be like other situations where a certain action produced good results, the same action can be subconsciously chosen, causing something akin to a conditioned response. On the other extreme, there are situations unlike anything encountered before in which case the various choices based on our prior experience are likely to be inadequate. Here is where our consciousness gets deeply involved, allowing us to come up with a *creative* solution. Here we find the cutting edge of human consciousness, where consciousness is indispensable, not in solving trivial problems. Therefore, real intelligence is the ability to correctly judge a situation and find an innovative approach. Real intelligence requires comprehension.

Now, to have true autonomy, a robot needs to be able to operate in unconstrained environments, successfully handling the huge variability of real-life situations. But even more, it must also handle situations in hostile environments where there are deception and aggression. It is the near-infinite variability of these situations that make comprehension necessary. Only comprehension can reduce or remove the *ambiguity* present in the objective data. A trivial example of this problem is handwriting recognition or language translation where the *syntactical* information is ambiguous. Therefore, there is not enough information at that level to be able to solve the problem.

Autonomous robots are only possible in situations where the environment is either artificially controlled or its expected variability is relatively small. If qualia-perception is the hard problem of consciousness, comprehension is the *hardest* problem of consciousness. Here is where the difference between a machine and a human being cannot be bridged.

All the machines we build, computers included, are made by assembling many *separate* parts. Therefore, we can, at least in principle, disassemble a machine in all its separate components and reassemble it and the machine will work again. However, we cannot disassemble a *living* cell into its atomic and molecular components and then reassemble the parts hoping that the cell will work again. The living cell is a dynamic system of a different kind than our machines: it uses *quantum components* that have no definable boundaries.

We study cells reductively as if they were machines, but cells are *holistic* systems. A cell is also an *open* system because it constantly exchanges energy and matter with the environment in which it exists. Thus, the physical structure of the cell is *dynamic*; it is recreated from moment to moment with parts constantly flowing in and out of it, even if it seems to us that the cell stays the same. Therefore, a cell cannot be separated from the environment with which it is in symbiosis without *losing* something. A computer instead, for as long as it works, has the same atoms and molecules that it had when it was first constructed. Nothing changes in its hardware and in that sense, it is a *static* system.

The kind of information processing done in a cell is completely different than what goes on in our computers. In a computer, the transistors are interconnected in a fixed pattern; in a cell, the parts interact freely with each other, processing information in ways we do not yet understand. For as long as we study cells as *reductive* biochemical systems rather than quantum information-processing systems, we will not be able to understand the difference between them and our computers.

When we study a cell reductively and separate from its environment, we are reducing a holistic system into the sum of its parts, throwing away what is more than the sum of the parts. *That's where consciousness is.* Consciousness exists only in the *open dynamism* of life and life is inextricably linked to the dynamism we see in the cells, which are the indivisible atoms out of which all living organisms are built. The bottom line is that life and consciousness are not reducible to *classical* physics, while computers are.

Without consciousness there can be no self and no interiority, just mechanisms going through their mindless paces, *imitating* a living thing. But what would our life be if we didn't feel anything? If we didn't feel love, joy, enthusiasm, a sense of beauty, and why not, even pain? A machine is a zombie, going through the motions. There is no inner life in a mechanism; it is all exteriority. In a living organism, even the outer world is brought inside, so to speak, to give it meaning. And it is consciousness that gives *meaning* to life.

The idea that classical computers can become smarter than human beings is a dangerous fantasy. Dangerous because, if we accept it, we will limit ourselves to express only a very small fraction of who we are. This idea takes away our power, freedom, and humanity: qualities that pertain to our consciousness and not to the machine we are told we are.

In my opinion, the real danger of the progress in robotics and AI will not be to create machines that will take over humanity because they will be more perfect than us. The real danger is that men of ill will may cause serious damage to mankind, by using ever-more powerful computers and robots to evil ends. But then it will be man, not the machine, to cause the trouble. And this is a major challenge that society will have to face as soon as possible.

Used properly, computers and AI will allow us to discover the magnificence of life as we critically compare ourselves to them; and this new knowledge can accelerate our spiritual evolution. Used poorly, AI may enslave us to hateful men. The choice is ours and ours alone.

APPENDIX 5

One and the Consciousness Units

The following appendix is about the nature of reality and the nature of consciousness, the subject of chapter 7, under the assumption that consciousness is a fundamental and irreducible aspect of all that is. These ideas are clearly speculative and most likely non-falsifiable based on the current axioms of physics. On the other hand, the widely accepted assumptions about the nature of reality cannot explain the existence and the properties of consciousness. I believe that to explain both objective and subjective reality we need to start from a different set of concepts than the current ones in which consciousness may only emerge with *classical* living organisms.

Many of the ideas described below originate from the "perennial philosophy" expressed throughout recorded history, starting as early as 3500 years ago in the Vedas, the philosophical-spiritual foundations of Hinduism. I recommend suspending the quick rejection of ideas that may superficially appear to contradict commonly held beliefs. Let the entire new framework emerge and then you can carefully reflect about the potential of this different "beginning" to explain the existence of both inner and outer realities with the crucial aspects you recognize deep within yourself.

Quantum physics is about information

The theoretical physicist Giacomo Mauro D'Ariano and his collaborators recently showed that quantum mechanics and field theory are entirely derivable from six purely informational postulates [23], [24]. Quantum physics, therefore, could be interpreted to say that matter is simply "made" of organizations of quantum bits, or qubits, the quantum mechanical generalization of the Boolean bits used in classical computers. The qubit is obtained by the quantum superposition of two complementary *quantum* states: "1" and "0" as discussed on chapter 7.

Within quantum physics, then, physical matter—whether an atom, a stone, a computer, or a living organism—derives from purely abstract quantum information, information without any intuitive or obvious meaning. If we wish to introduce meaning and free will, we need to postulate the existence of an inner reality where consciousness and free will reside. This is not what physics currently proposes or accepts, though physics never intended to describe inner reality.

A few centuries ago, physicists had embraced Cartesian dualism where a clear division had been drawn between mind and matter. The recent progress of physics, however, has shown that reality is holistic and therefore there can be no real separation between mind and matter. Thus, mind-body dualism should be abandoned in favor of a *monistic* theory, despite the good service done by dualism in mitigating the age-old dispute between science and religions.

This also means that the nature of consciousness might be accepted into the domain of physics as a legitimate subject of research since it can no longer be considered somebody else's problem. If we deny the existence of free will and consciousness, as many positivists do, then neither we nor our computers should be conscious. If instead we accept their existence, they will likely be irreducible properties of nature and therefore must have had a fundamental impact on our universe from its very beginning. I think that physics as we know it is *incomplete* because it can only describe that portion of reality that can be expressed with abstract symbols devoid of meaning.

As discussed in chapter 7, to explain the nature of consciousness, physics needs to take seriously the possibility that the quantum fields of elementary particles are somehow conscious fields. The concept of field must then be extended beyond its current definition within quantum field theory (QFT) because the quantum information that currently describes quantum physics can also be felt as qualia by the fields, or by some organization of states of the fields.

I should point out that the measurable matter of our physical world can only represent abstract Boolean information describable with bits. It cannot represent the quantum information that requires entangled qubits currently represented with vectors in a complex multi-dimensional space called Hilbert space. Quantum computers, for example, cannot exist entirely in our physical world in the sense that only the setting up of the program and the recording of the result of the computation can be done in our classical world, but the quantum information processing itself cannot be performed in our space-time.

However, quantum computers, as currently conceived, are deterministic and therefore they cannot support the free-will decisions of conscious entities because those decisions could not be known *a priori* by a deterministic quantum (or classical) algorithm. In other words, no algorithm can possibly compute the actual state that will manifest in our physical reality if that state is determined by a free-will choice. To have both free will and consciousness requires a more general quantum system than a deterministic quantum computer. It takes a system capable of freely choosing a specific quantum or classical state to manifest, and perhaps even choosing, or creating, which operator to use.

The universe is dynamic and holistic

As above so below, as within so without, as the universe so the soul.
—Hermes Trismegistus

The quantum universe is not only a highly dynamic world but is also an indivisible *whole*—a holistic system. Imagine an infinite ocean in which waves keep emerging, changing, and disappearing without leaving a trace—forms that never repeat themselves and have no permanence. This type of universe could not have any identifiable parts because there would be nothing with any permanence. It would simply be an indivisible wholeness. The universe described by quantum physics, however, appears to be less general than the one just portrayed, because it contains many *identifiable* quantum fields, "parts" that have something that persists, something that makes their identification possible, while they are also indivisible and inseparable from the whole.

For example, the quantum field of electrons produces "forms" that all behave the same way. That field can then be identified by the indistinguishability of the electrons (quanta) it manifests. This field should then be called *part-whole* because it is not the only field and yet it has no boundaries, for it extends throughout the whole, it is inseparable from the whole, and yet it can be identified because its signature "waves" have something repeatable that "reveal" its identity, otherwise it could not be identified.

Parts-whole can be influenced by the whole, top-down, in addition to combining from the bottom-up into hierarchies of states. This whole-to-part feedback is represented by quantum entanglement, a remarkable property in which interacting fields create states with joint nonlocal properties that are independent of space and time.

Interestingly, top-down and bottom-up influences are also present in general relativity. Before special and general relativity, space, time, mass, and energy were considered completely *independent* variables. With the experimental verification of general relativity, we now know that they are not. Space and time are not absolute, as Newton assumed, but the structure of space depends in part on time, mass, and energy in ways unknown to classical physics. And the same is true for the other three variables, though in many cases the influences between them are so small as to be negligible for everyday practical situations.

It is only because these dependencies are either small enough to be ignored, or can be accounted for, that we can mathematically solve certain classes of problems. Otherwise, we would encounter insurmountable difficulties. Just the fact that these influences exist, though, makes a fundamental difference because even small effects can be amplified and become relevant due to the nonlinearities existing in nature. In our holistic and dynamic universe, there are already clear examples that the whole influences the parts-whole. For instance, in general relativity the global mass distribution determines the local geometry of space-time, as previously discussed, and in quantum physics the feedback from the whole to the parts-whole manifests in the existence of entanglement.

Another general feature of our holistic physical universe is that the quantum fields self-organize hierarchically to create complex systems like molecules, living organisms, and the overall ecosystem of our planet. Out of this process, nucleons, atoms, molecules, cells, organs, animals, and so on emerge. These are ever more complex hierarchies of connections between groups of states among the quantum fields.

Notice that since ontology resides only in the quantum fields, the "stuff" of which all hierarchical levels are composed is ultimately the stuff that makes such fields, what I called nousym in chapter 7. What we conceive as "atoms" and "molecules" only exist as particular combinations of connections among the dynamical states within the fields. These are ultimately "states of nousym," the substance with the capacity to represent quantum information and qualia as complementary aspects of itself.

One and the Consciousness Units

Why do you insist the universe is not a conscious intelligence, when it gives birth to conscious intelligences?

—Cicero

One is defined as All that exists. To manifest a universe like the one we know, One must be dynamic, holistic, and have both interiority and exteriority. Exteriority is what is currently described by physics. Interiority is what is needed to explain the existence of consciousness and free-will actions, the crucial properties that are missing in the current physical theories. Consciousness and free-will action express the *capacity* and the *urge* of One to *experience* and *know* itself. These human words are clearly inadequate to describe what moves One to know itself, and yet we share in our depth the same *urge to know*, variously felt as a combination of desire, curiosity, impulse, satisfaction, love, determination, and will.

Dynamism means that One can never be the same, instant after instant. Holism means that One has no separable parts, i.e., within One everything is connected. And finally, the urge of One to know itself is the cause of all manifestation and evolution, implying also that the self-knowing of One must continuously grow. Dynamism, holism, and self-knowing must then be intertwined aspects of One, facets of an indivisible whole rather than "independent variables." This also means that existence and self-knowing may well be two sides of the same coin in the sense that coming into existence may be equivalent to being known for the first time. I think that *to exist is to be known*, and vice versa, and once known, that self-knowing can never be annihilated. Therefore, the *memory* of the self-knowing must somehow exist within the "substance" of One, what I called nousym. All these are assumptions, of course.

Where is One's self-knowing coming from? It must come from *within* itself since One is all that is. Therefore, One must contain *potential* existence and *actual* existence, where actual existence is what One knows and potential existence is the self-knowing that is not yet known. In other words, potential existence is the "unconscious" of One, what has yet to reveal itself—the "unknown" of One that can eventually be known by it. For the remainder of the chapter I will use *existence* to mean actual existence and the expression "potential existence" to indicate what is still unknown, but knowable, by One.

I will call each "unit of self-knowing" a *consciousness unit* or CU. Thus, each CU is a *part-whole* of One; a whole because it cannot be separated from One and from the other CUs, yet a part because there are many CUs, and each CU has a unique identity that allows it to be distinguished and recognized from the other CUs. Like

One, each CU cannot be the same from instant to instant (dynamism), it can never be separated from One and from the other CUs (holism), and it has the same urge of One to deepen its own self-knowing. The holistic substance that is shaped by the self-knowing of One and that can know itself and the other CUs through qualia is nousym. It is what appears as energy within physics.

Notice that One's creation of multiple CUs, all connected from the inside, has also created an "outside" world—from the perspective of each CU. Here I assume that each CU can perceive the other CUs as "units" like itself and yet knows itself as "distinct" from the others. Thus, the urge of each CU to know itself will also extend to knowing the other CUs, since the inner realities of all CUs are deeply interconnected. I should point out here that in this framework, the CUs exist before matter, energy, space, and time. Thus, they can be thought of as collectively constituting the quantum vacuum out of which our universe emerged.

We have seen that each new self-knowing of One creates a CU. Each CU is then an entity endowed with three fundamental properties: consciousness, identity, and agency. Consciousness is the capacity of the CU to know itself and to perceive and know the other CUs. *Identity* is the capacity of the CU to *know* itself within itself and to be identifiable (knowable) as a CU by the other CUs. Agency is a property connected with the existence of an "outer reality" populated by many CUs. It is the capacity of each CU to *communicate with free will* with the other CUs for the purpose of deepening its own self-knowing and the knowing of the others. Communication requires that each CU be capable of *shaping symbols* out of its own "substance" (nousym) to communicate. It requires the transformation of inner meaning, which is private, into outer symbols (forms, states) that appear in its outer reality. This transformation defines *action*. It is worth noting that the CUs are conceptually related to the *Monads* described by Gottfried Wilhelm von Leibniz in his famous book entitled *Lehrsätze über die Monadologie* and published in 1720.

I mentioned earlier that each CU is a part-whole of One, therefore, as a whole, each CU perceives the other CUs as itself. As a part, it knows itself as distinct from the other CUs and can distinguish the other identities from its own. This would be a contradiction only in a reductionist reality in which each entity is separable from the others. This property can be understood in a *unitive* experience, like the awakening experience described in chapter 5, in which I experienced myself as both the world and the observer of the world. These experiences, though infrequent, have been reported by many people over the centuries.

Properties of the consciousness units

> *A single force, Love, links and gives life to infinite worlds.*
> —Giordano Bruno

A crucial feature of this framework is that *experience*—the inner semantic reality—is about subjective and private meaning, whereas *information*, the outer symbolic reality, is a public, objective representation of meaning. The outer reality of each CU represents its recognizable identity field with the superposed voluntary symbols that convey the specific meaning the CU wishes to communicate. When a CU observes another CU, it can only perceive as qualia the outer symbolic reality existing within the identity field of the observed CU. The inner reality of any given CU can only be known directly by that CU and by One, and no one else. The qualia perceived by a CU by the transformation of outer symbols can only be comprehended to the extent that the meanings of those symbols are known. Notice that this requirement also exists for us, since to understand the meaning of a new word, a person must already know a similar meaning.

Essential to this framework is also the idea that the symbolic aspect of each CU stands in some correspondence with its meaning, and that this correspondence is the same for all the CUs, given the unity of the inner reality of One. Therefore, it becomes possible to bootstrap a *universal* communication language between the CUs, thus creating an indispensable tool for the CUs to know one another and for deepening their self-knowing. This essential communication is also what leads the CUs to *combine* into a hierarchy of conscious entities, just like the quantum fields "combine" to create atoms, molecules, macro-molecules, and so on.

The CUs are the *ontological* entities out of which all possible worlds are "constructed," and therefore the quantum fields of our physical world are organizations of CUs. However, what physicists call a quantum field is only the outer aspect of the corresponding organization of CUs. In this framework, a combination entity is conscious, has a unique identity, and has free-will agency just like the CUs. Therefore, the quantum fields of physics and the corresponding conscious fields I am proposing are quite different entities. By adding "selfhood" to the quantum fields, the nature of reality changes in a fundamental way.

In this framework, the urge of One to know itself gives birth to many CUs that can greatly expand One's self-knowing. Notice that only One knows the interiority of every CU and every combination of CUs. In fact, One knows all manifestations from the inside and is also *what connects all from the inside*. One is the creative interiority of all that exists, partaking in the experience of every entity. What matters to One is the self-knowing gained by the hierarchy of communicating CUs. Therefore, One may even be disinterested about the outer symbolic reality of the CUs and organizations of CUs. This is a strong statement to make, but I considered it realistic since the outer reality is only a means for the self-knowing of the conscious entities, guaranteed to converge to the inner meaning of One. The self-knowing of One is the sum of the self-knowing of all the CUs and their combinations. One is thus *within* each conscious entity and each conscious entity is within One.

The CIP Framework

The set of symbols created by the CUs, like the words of our languages, form the ever-growing vocabulary of a universal language. The symbols of the next higher level in the hierarchy are combinations of these basic symbols, and so on. The selves belonging to a specific hierarchical level may comprehend all the symbols of lower hierarchical levels but may only partially comprehend the symbols of higher levels than theirs. The ever-growing number of public symbols of all CUs and their combinations form an *informational* space, or what I call I-space.

The totality of the inner semantic knowing of all CUs and their combinations forms a *semantic space* called consciousness space, or C-space. C-space and I-space form a holistic structure that describes the irreducible, semantic-symbolic nature of nousym, the substance of One. C-space and I-space are not physical spaces like the space of our universe. They are realities existing before the birth of any physical world. Physical worlds are called P-spaces, and P-spaces are essentially virtual worlds, as we will discuss next.

I call this overall conceptual structure the *CIP Framework,* where C stands for consciousness space, I stands for informational space, and P stands for physical spaces. Notice that our concepts of space, time, and quantum fields represent how we currently *imagine* physical reality to be constructed, though we do not really understand *what* these concepts mean. Scientists have postulated that certain mathematical relationships exist among them, allowing for predicting much of what can be measured. However, these concepts, as currently defined in physics, can neither predict nor explain the existence of consciousness, meaning, and purpose, which in this framework cannot be separated from the symbolic reality described by physics.

The creation of physical realities

The combination of communicating conscious entities, each with its own free will, gives birth to hierarchies of: (1) selves; (2) meaning; (3) symbols; (4) syntactical rules; and (5) languages. In so doing, the conscious selves create various organizational structures, layer after layer, in which to experience themselves and increase their self-knowing.

Since each organization must be held in place by the free-will cooperation of the selves, rather than through the coercion of top-down laws, the more complex the structure, the more improbable its construction becomes. This statement brings up a fundamental difference between the CIP framework and the framework of physics in which mathematics is supposed to determine top-down how a system behaves. Let me explain.

Within CIP, reality manifests through the co-evolution of the semantic and symbolic aspects of the CUs through which One knows itself. The "order of nature" expresses the order inherent in the meaning of One, which is also expressed in the correlated order found in the symbolic expressions of that meaning. In other words, the structure of the universal language of the CUs reflects the "order" within One—order coming from the coherent wholeness of One. Mathematics can then express only the order found in the symbolic aspects of reality. This order was not imposed by mathematics on these symbols, however, for it was discovered in the meaning arising in the dialectic relationships of the CUs. Therefore, mathematics is an *effect*, not the *cause* of the order found in nature.

Given that symbols and syntactical rules carry the essential order of One and given that physical reality is an expression of this language, there must be some correspondence between this universal language and the concepts and laws of physics. For example, certain combinations of symbols may have the abstract properties attributed to the elementary fermions, the *matter* of the universe, and the syntactical rules that determine how the symbols "lawfully" combine with each other may have the properties attributed to the elementary bosons, the *forces* that connect the fermions or keep them apart.

Ergo, the mathematics that models our physical world may express some of the order inherent in the universal language of the CUs. As such, it must be probabilistic since no algorithm can prescribe the choice of symbols to describe a freely chosen meaning. Such mathematics is therefore *descriptive, not prescriptive* the way it is used in physics. Moreover, a language requires syntactical rules agreed by all users and *obeyed out of the users' desire to communicate, not out of coercion.* Within CIP, the laws of quantum physics express the syntactical laws of the universal language used by the CUs.

To learn how to cooperatively create a higher-level organization, it may become necessary to create special environments in which the entities that desire to cooperate acquire the necessary comprehension to be able to do it. We do the same in our world as demonstrated by the various educational institutions we have created for that purpose. I am guided in my hypotheses by Hermes Trismegistus's principle quoted earlier, and this is the only sensible way in which I can explain the existence of entities temporarily "embodied" in physical bodies and interacting in a physical world.

In this interpretation, a physical world is an artfully constructed "constrained environment" that can give each conscious entity the feedback necessary to learn what keeps it from fully cooperating. The thinking here is that the unconstrained environment of C-space and I-space may be insufficient to achieve that goal. It would be much like kids left on their own rather than attending school, unable to learn what they need without a certain amount of discipline and guidance. Hence, I imagine a physical world being like an interactive "educational system" in which each entity can safely discover what lack of comprehension, or miscomprehension, keeps it from voluntarily collaborating with other entities in the construction of complex organizations.

If so, our physical world would behave like a virtual reality (VR) created in a computer in which sophisticated avatars controlled by conscious human beings interact with each other in a virtual world. In this case, the body that controls the avatar exists outside the computer and is not part of the program. Likewise, the conscious entity that controls the body exists outside the physical world in which the body exists. This idea has already been explored in chapter 7.

We are conscious beings existing in C-space and I-space, the irreducible and fundamental semantic-symbolic reality of One.

And just like the Boolean symbols that make up the VR are constructed out of the quantum-classical symbols of the physical world, our physical world is made of the special I-space symbols that make up I-space, all organized by a large number of cooperating CUs and organizations of CUs. In chapter 7 these symbols have been described by quantum information, which is necessary, but may not be sufficient to fully describe I-space symbols.

The physical universe behaves then like a giant quantum-classical virtual machine created by a hierarchy of cooperating conscious entities. These conscious entities seek learning experiences by controlling "bodies" which are more sophisticated avatars made of the quantum-classical information of which the physical universe is made. In this hypothesis there is no central computer made by aliens. The computations are inherent in the symbolic interactions arising from the simultaneous "conversations" that a vast hierarchy of conscious entities are having to explore their own inner and outer realities. Within CIP, the consciousness that controls the body and experiences human life, what is generally called *ego*, may only be a portion of a vaster consciousness, the consciousness of the real entity we are.

If we start from the hypothesis that CUs exist before physical reality, the present concepts of space, time, matter, and energy, which are considered primitive in physics, need to be reconceptualized as deriving directly from the nature of the CUs' interactions. This new vision requires a complete rethinking of what we have up to now accepted as fundamental axioms. Only after a robust and self-consistent conceptual framework has been developed, together with the beginning of an appropriate mathematical structure, can we evaluate its consequences and refine the model. The payoff will be a science in which inner and outer realities can be joined in a meaningful and purposeful universe.

ACKNOWLEDGMENTS

Writing my autobiography has led me to relive the most significant experiences of my life and reflect on the many people
who have played a significant role in my journey. In so doing, I
realized that I learned not only from the people who cared about
me, but also from those who opposed me. Therefore, I thank the
individuals I mentioned in this book because in one way or another
they made me grow by helping me understand both my strengths
and weaknesses.

Special thanks go to the people who assisted me with this book.
Originally written in English, the text was translated into Italian by
Elvia, my wife, with excellent suggestions and edits by my sisters-in-
law Viviana and Irene Sardei. Viviana also provided most citations.

Our grateful thoughts will always go to Viviana and her husband Franco Bertotti because they have also been parents to Marc
and Eric, our youngest children, during times when it was important to give them an educational experience in Italy.

I also wish to thank the many people who have shared my path
of exploration of consciousness. There are too many to name them
all. I, therefore, limit myself to those with whom I have interacted in
recent years and have contributed to my work with their construc-
tive observations: Andrea Di Blas, who has read and commented on
the first version of this book; Don Hoffman and his team: Chetan
Prakash, Chris Fields, Manish Singh, and Robert Prentner. Don is a
cognitive scientist at the University of California, Irvine, who shares
the idea that consciousness is an irreducible property of nature;
Giacomo Mauro D'Ariano, the head of the theoretical physics

group at the University of Pavia, Italy, who developed with his collaborators a purely informational theory of quantum physics; Jeff Tollaksen of Chapman University, California; Nicola Galvanetto, Mark Grant, Mike Malone, Guido Meardi, Raffaello Colasante, and Rufo Munari for their useful advice and observations. Special thanks go to Angelo Gallippi, who wrote my biography almost twenty years ago, to my book agent, Enrica Bortolazzi, and finally to Sabrina Parisi and Matteo Stroppa for their final editing of the manuscript.

Made in the USA
Las Vegas, NV
15 September 2023

77588492R00167